COMMUNITY POWER STRUCTURE

COMMUNITY POWER STRUCTURE

A STUDY OF
DECISION MAKERS

By
FLOYD HUNTER

CHAPEL HILL

THE UNIVERSITY OF NORTH CAROLINA PRESS

© 1953 by The University of North Carolina Press
All rights reserved
Manufactured in the United States of America
ISBN 0-8078-0639-0 (alk. paper)
ISBN 0-8078-4033-5 (pbk: alk. paper)
Library of Congress Catalog Card Number 53-10042

94   93   92   91   90   10   9   8   7   6

To
MY FAMILY

PREFACE

ON occasion I have considered the possibility of re-studying the power structure of Regional City. Primarily because certain bits of information have indicated that the power structure in question has not very fundamentally changed its basic form or course in recent years, I have decided against such re-study.

Some of the evidence of the stability of Regional City's power structure has come to me directly through observation and inquiry during brief visits there, through reading subsequent studies by others, and through releases in national publications and newscasts which have indicated that at least five of the ten top leaders I came to know around 1950 are still operating at their same locations. Mr. Homer, at the apex of power then, is still there. One of the top businessmen has become mayor, replacing another businessman mayor. A prominent banker is espousing a token paint-up, clean-up campaign in the slums. These men are working with the same police chief. Several expendable personnel in the civic machine, professionals like Joe Cratchett and Denny North, have come and gone. All continue to grapple ineffectively with problems of poverty and inequality of Afro-Americans, whom I earlier called Negroes. The Afro-Americans, in turn, are continuing to organize politically. Some have rioted. Others have enriched themselves just a little more, but not in anything like the amounts accumulated by their counterparts in the larger power scheme. The little fellows in the black community, like those in the white community, in lesser proportion and with lesser awareness of what is happening to them through credit and inflationary bondage and political hocus pocus, continue to come out on the short end of things. Thus, the structure would seem to have remained tight-knit, quite durable.

Further, in the context of recent history, I must say that some of my conjectures related to the desirabiity of integrating Afro-Americans into the power structure for more fruitful community development now seem naive. It would seem in 1968 that Regional City may experience wider black and white power separations and ensuing negotiations stemming from greater power equality before any meaningful integrations of power processes may come into being.

Like any published work that is subjected to extensive scholarly criticism, positive and negative, this one has taken on a life of its own. Certainly, it has put the term "power structure" into the language, on the streets as well as in the media. Its relatively simple methods of study have been widely used by others. It has become a classical text in social science classes. It has enjoyed, without publicity, a steadily expanding group of readers (to whom it has been useful) outside the universities.

While some of the conclusions drawn from it by scholars and the uses to which the book has been put by active politicians often surprise me, it has never seemed to be correct that I should attempt to answer the critics or users of the book. It must speak for itself. I am grateful that it has spoken to so many.

Of the many who have found the book politically useful, I like to quote Charles R. Sims, President of the Deacons for Defense and Justice, Bogalusa, Louisiana. Mr. Sims had been asked by a reporter what difference his defense organization may have made in local power relations. He replied: "Well, when the white power structure found out that [the Deacons] had mens, Negro mens that had made up their minds to stand up for their people and give no ground, would not tolerate no more police brutality, it had a tendency to keep the night-riders out of the neighborhood."

Recognizing the correctness of Mr. Sims's understanding of power relationships, one may know that the message of *Community Power Structure* has arrived at an important destination.

FLOYD HUNTER

El Cerrito, California
June, 1968

ix

CONTENTS

TABLES

FIGURES

COMMUNITY POWER STRUCTURE

1 INTRODUCTION

IT has been evident to the writer for some years that policies on vital matters affecting community life seem to appear suddenly. They are acted upon, but with no precise knowledge on the part of the majority of citizens as to how these policies originated or by whom they are really sponsored. Much is done, but much is left undone. Some of the things done appear to be manipulated to the advantage of relatively few.

There appears to be a tenuous line of communication between the governors of our society and the governed. This situation does not square with the concepts of democracy we have been taught to revere. The line of communication between the leaders and the people needs to be broadened and strengthened—and by more than a series of public-relations and propaganda campaigns—else our concept of democracy is in danger of losing vitality in dealing with problems that affect all in common.

With these thoughts in mind, I have studied power leadership patterns in a city of half a million population, which I choose to call Regional City. If this study of leadership and power relations can help to clarify the fact that one may find out who our real leaders are and something of how they operate in relation to each other, the present task will have been accomplished. Only by such understanding can we hope to solve the many and complex problems that confront every American community today.

Power will be defined, as the study proceeds, in relatively simple terms. Moralizing on the subject of power will be avoided. The primary interest here is in discussing the nature of the exercise of power in a selected community and as this community relates to the larger society. One hypothesis taken is that power is a necessary function in a society. Power is also a necessary function in the community, for it involves decision-making and it also involves the function of executing determined policies—or seeing to it that things get done which have been deemed necessary to be done. The social rights and prerogatives implied in power functions must be delegated to specific men to achieve social goals in any society.

In our society, men of authority are called power and influence leaders. Such leaders will be discussed here, with full recognition that they are men and women very like other men and women in many respects. The difference between the leaders and other men lies in the fact that social groupings have apparently given definite social functions over to certain persons and not to others. The functions suggested are those related to power.

Throughout this discussion I shall be using the concept of community as a frame of reference for an analysis of power relations. This is done because of a strong conviction that the community is a primary power center and because it is a place in which power relations can be most easily observed. Within the community frame of reference, an attempt will be made to keep the definition of power "operational," that is, power will be defined in terms of men and their actions in relation to one another.

The term "power" is no reified concept, but an abstract term denoting a structural description of social processes. Or, in simpler terms, *Power is a word that will be used to describe the acts of men going about the business of moving other men to act in relation to themselves or in relation to organic or inorganic things.* This concept can be talked about with some sureness, but there are elements of power about which one cannot speak so surely. These latter elements will be called, after the manner of the social scientist, "residual categories," by which is meant those ideas and conceptualizations which are related to power but fall outside the scope of the present study.

Three residual categories of power may be cited of which one should be aware in the discussion of community power structure. The first might be called historical reference; the second, motivation and other psychological concepts; and the third, values, moral and ethical considerations. Each of these categories may perhaps appear in later analyses, but they will be incidental to the problem under consideration, namely, that of analyzing the structure of power. Each will here be briefly summarized.

As to historical reference, it would be possible to become bogged down in a survey of theories of power relations, if one attempted to consider everything that has ever been said about it. The history of philosophy and of social thought is full of power topics. They may be found in the writings of Plato, Aristotle, Cicero, Machiavelli, Hobbes, Locke, Mill, Marx, Laski, and a host of others. There has also been much discussion of the "contractual" relations of men and power, and of "constitutional" types of power formulation and delegation, with which political scientists are often concerned, and which seem to stem from a preoccupation with contractual ideas having their roots in the thinking and writing of the past. Quite possibly any of these sources might have some bearing on community power relations, as might also the generalizations of many writers on the historical aspects of power—shifting power relations in social organization under autocracies, feudal systems, democracies, and socialist states of various sorts. Any such materials will be used most sparingly, for although they might clarify some points in the present study, the main emphasis here is on current history, rather than on the past. Thus, for all practical purposes, historical reference becomes a residual category.

Psychological motivation in power relations is another residual category—an area of thought which is intriguing in its possibilities, but one in which the materials of the study are inadequate for more than a superficial analysis. Economic "interests" will be discussed. Aggression on the part of individuals and groups toward one another will come in for consideration. Curiosity will be expressed as to what holds the power structure together and an assumption will be made that an explanation of the "cement" of the relations described must lie in the realm of social psychology. Other related topics will be touched upon as the discussion of power proceeds, but no attempt will be made to interpret the psychological motives behind individual or group behavior. There is an open field for study in this area, but materials have not been exploited fully enough in power-relations studies to make them more than illustratively useful. The concepts of fear, pessimism, and silence will be used at a later stage, but suggestively, not analytically.

In the third residual category mentioned, that of values, morals, and ethical considerations, the literature on power relations is shot through with these concepts. Once power is defined as the ability of men to command the services of other men, it is tempting to speculate on what commands should be, or should not be, given at any particular time. Sages abound who know the answers to "proper" statecraft which power implies. I have my own ideas, too, of what ought to be done in many social situations, but such values might stand in the way of an adequate description of the power structure in Regional City. Newspapers, radio, and other channels of communication in American society are constantly telling the citizenry what is right, just, and good. I propose not to follow their example at this time. Power, as it is presently discussed, will have a neutral content in an ideological sense, in so far as this feat can be achieved in a description of its structure in Regional City.

The men in this city who influence others in power relationships are cognizant of values. They, as well as the men of lesser power, recognize that power-wielding is functional in the society of which they are a part. Most men in Regional City apparently believe that goods and services must be moved toward definite objectives. The observable "busy-ness" of the city would indicate that this activity is deemed valuable. The real question of conflicting values in the situation arises over who is to derive the most benefit from the composite of activity.

In passing, it might be said that this study assumes the existence of two great ideological considerations which help men to shape policy in industrial communities in the world today, namely, capitalism and socialism. The author is not unaware of these forces. Both ideologies are packaged for local consumption in various ways in different nations. In discussing power, one might take either of these major ideological clusterings as a frame of reference. Both have many moral and ethical aspects, according to their adherents. No conscious choice of either is made in this writing, which will be concerned with power structure operating in a capitalistic community. The descriptions of the workings of the power structure may not always look "good," but suggesting alternatives is not a primary concern here, and ideological considerations are, thus, a residual category.

One other set of abstractions must be given before arriving at more concrete descriptions of Regional City and its system of power relations. These abstractions relate to the postulates and hypotheses of the study, and they are comprehensive of the several aspects of power already suggested. Drawn from readings relating to power relationships and from observations of power personnel extending over several years, the postulates and hypotheses to follow are put forward to guide the study of community power structure. The postulates are these:

POSTULATES ON POWER STRUCTURE

1. Power involves relationships between individuals and groups, both controlled and controlling.

>   Corollary 1. Because power involves such relationships, it can be described structurally.

2. Power is structured socially, in the United States, into a dual relationship between governmental and economic authorities on national, state, and local levels.

>   Corollary 1. Both types of authorities may have functional, social, and institutional power units subsidiary to them.

3. Power is a relatively constant factor in social relationships with policies as variables.

>   Corollary 1. Wealth, social status, and prestige are factors in the "power constant."

>   Corollary 2. Variation in the strength between power units, or a shift in policy within one of these units, affects the whole power structure.

4. Power of the individual must be structured into associational, clique, or institutional patterns to be effective.

>   Corollary 1. The community provides a microcosm of organized power relations in which individuals exercise the maximum effective influence.

>   Corollary 2. Representative democracy offers the greatest possibility of assuring the individual a voice in policy determination and extension.

The postulates seem to the author to be self-evident propositions. During the field investigation they formed a mental backdrop, an abstract frame of reference. The second portion of this frame of reference is contained in the following hypotheses:

HYPOTHESES ON POWER STRUCTURE

1. Power is exercised as a necessary function in social relationships.

2. The exercise of power is limited and directed by the formulation and extension of social policy within a framework of socially sanctioned authority.

3. In a given power unit (organization) a smaller number of individuals will be found formulating and extending policy than those exercising power.

> Corollary 1. All policy makers are "men of power."
>
> Corollary 2. All "men of power" are not, *per se*, policy makers.

If these abstract hypotheses seem obscure at this point, they may become less so as the discussion proceeds. The postulates and hypotheses will be referred to in concrete illustrations in subsequent portions of the book.

As stated earlier, the community is the easiest place to locate and study the relations between men of power. I believe this statement is true. It is now possible to be specific and to analyze the relations of power as existent in Regional City.

2 LOCATION OF POWER IN REGIONAL CITY

IN order to keep the discussion of power in operational terms, it is necessary to locate power as resident in a community, and—more important still— as resident in the men who wield power in the community. Thus, in describing the physical setting in which Regional City leaders operate, it should be stressed that the physical community is dominated by the men in it, rather than that the men are dominated by topography, climate, or any other physical element.

Regional City's geographical location makes it a focal point for transportation operations and financial transactions both within and beyond its region. Commercial transactions supply goods to an extensive hinterland through storage, assembly, and distribution activities. Raw materials supplied by the hinterland make possible many branches of both light and heavy industry. The position of Regional City makes it a center devoted to finance, commerce, and industry, in about that order of importance. The activities centered in these areas of activity engross most men of Regional City from Monday through Saturday of each week. To paraphrase a president of the United States, "The business of Regional City is business," and if the word business is put in its original form, "busy-ness," the community is well described.

By day there is a constant roar of traffic over the congested streets carrying goods and people to their destinations. By night the great diesel trucks and busses blast the air with their exhausts, telling those who may hear that Regional City never sleeps. The all-night restaurants thrive in the commercial and warehouse areas, catering to men and women who ply their trades through the night shift. The whistles of trains and the "revving up" of airline motors add to the sounds made when men move goods and people. Regional City is always moving. It never stops. And it is filled with activity, more, perhaps, than many other cities, because of its strategic geographical location.

Twelve major highway trunks converge on the city. Ten air routes and eight major rail lines radiate from it. The volume of traffic over these routes is heavy. More than 500 passenger cars a day go over the rail lines. Nearly 400 busses run daily along the highways leading to and from the city. More than 150 scheduled planes operate daily from the municipal airport. The motor truck lines and private passenger cars traveling the highways and streets add an unestimated volume of traffic to the city's transportation load.

Because of all this physical activity involved in moving goods and services in the complex system designated as Regional City, it is obvious that a social order, or system, must be maintained there. Broadly speaking, the maintenance of this order falls to the lot of almost every man in the community, but the *establishment of changes* in the old order falls to the lot of relatively few. In a city as old and as large as Regional City, the existing order has been a cumulative process. It has been handed down to the present generation by the past. Consequently, the men in power in Regional City may be said to have inherited its present order. But new times bring new problems, and decisions have to be made concerning changed conditions. Policies have to be formulated and made effective.

The physical community plays a vital part in maintaining the existing order by helping to differentiate men from one another. The men of power and policy decision in Regional City have definite places in which they are active. There are certain places in which they make decisions and formulate policies to meet the many changing conditions that confront them. In locating these men of power in a community one finds them, when not at home or at work, dividing their time between their clubs, the hotel luncheon and committee rooms, and other public and semi-public meeting places. And the appearance of a man's surroundings is very considerably determined by the kind of work he does, the money he is paid for it, and the status his occupation has in the community.

A description, therefore, of the physical features which surround the men of power, such as their offices, industrial plants, or commercial establishments, as well as their clubs, homes, and other personal living quarters, seems more pertinent to the present discussion than do facts about most other parts of the physical community. Men are ranked and classified by other men, in some degree, by the physical elements around them. An office with soft carpeting, wood-panelled walls, and rich draperies immediately suggests that the man occupying it is more influential than the man who walks on composition concrete floors and looks at plaster-board walls each day, and whose only window decoration is a fifty-cent pull-down shade. Such physical characteristics may not give a completely accurate picture of power and influence, but they are indicative of power, position, and status in our culture. They are a part of the power structure in any community, in its physical aspects. As will be developed later, where men locate their homes is another measure of status on a class basis.[1]

Within the physical setting of the community, power itself is resident in the men who inhabit it. To locate power in Regional City, it is therefore necessary to identify some of the men who wield power, as well as to describe the physical

1. Raymond W. Mack, Housing as an Index of Social Class (unpublished Master's Thesis, University of North Carolina, 1951), pp. 40-45.

setting in which they operate. In Regional City the men of power were located by finding persons in prominent positions in four groups that may be assumed to have power connections.[2] These groups were identified with business, government, civic associations, and "society" activities. From the recognized, or nominal, leaders of the groups mentioned, lists of persons presumed to have power in community affairs were obtained. Through a process of selection, utilizing a cross section of "judges" in determining leadership rank, and finally by a further process of self-selection, a rather long list of possible power leadership candidates was cut down to manageable size for the specific purpose of this study. Forty persons in the top levels of power in Regional City were selected from more than 175 names. Many more persons were interviewed than the basic forty, but they were interviewed in relation to the forty. The whole method will unfold as the analysis proceeds. All individuals and all organizations dealt with in this study are given fictitious names.

The forty persons with whom this study is chiefly concerned are the following:

Percy Latham, Adam Graves, Fargo Dunham, Elsworth Mines, Grover Smith, Hetty Farley, John Webster, Truman Worth, Cary Stokes, Gary Stone, Epworth Simpson, Harvey Aiken, Brenda Howe, George Delbert, Samuel Farris, Gloria Stevens, Norman Trable, Herman Schmidt, Edna Moore, Harold Farmer, Peter Barner, Mark Parks, Philip Gould, Edward Stokes, Mabel Gordon, Avery Spear, Joseph Hardy, Claudia Mills, Ralph Spade, Russell Gregory, Harry Parker, John (Jack) Williams, Horace Black, Bert Tidwell, Arthur Tarbell, Ray Moster, James Treat, Luke Street, Howard Rake and Charles Homer.

If the reader has had the patience to plow through this list, he will have recognized none of them. Some of the real names of leaders were familiar to the writer before the present study

2. For a fuller discussion of method, see Appendix.

was made, and they were recognized as influential persons, but on the whole they were just names, with little more meaning for the writer than for the reader at this moment. It was only by getting at the relationships between persons that real significance became attached to any individual name. The process of listing, however, was a first step in getting a structural picture of power in Regional City. The names will later be brought to life through extending the structural concepts concerning them. We now know who some of Regional City's leaders are by name. We shall know more about Regional City when we know where these persons are in relation to each other, and what they do in relation to each other so far as policy-making and policy-execution are concerned.

What men do for a living, as already suggested, locates them in a community setting. The occupations of the men studied in Regional City tended to fall into groupings commensurate with the physical location of the city and its functions as a regional center of activities. In an occupational array of the kinds of activities in which the forty men named were engaged, one finds certain clusterings.

Of the forty persons studied, the largest number are to be found directing or administering major portions of the activities of large commercial enterprises. There are eleven such men in the list. Since Regional City has been described as a commercial center, this fact is not surprising. Financial direction and supervision of banking and investment operations are represented by the next largest number, namely, seven persons. Again, the occupations of the leaders turned up in the study follow one of the major functions of the community activities concerned with finance. Regional City is a "service" city also, and its service functions are represented on the list by six professional persons, five lawyers and one dentist. Five persons have major industrial responsibilities. Governmental personnel are represented on the list by four persons, which also fits into the functional scheme of the community, since it is both a regional and a state center for many important governmental activities. Two labor leaders are on the list, representing large unions. The five remaining persons in the list of forty leaders may be classified as leisure personnel. They are persons who have social or civic organization leadership capacities and yet do not have business offices or similar places in which they conduct their day-by-day affairs. One of these persons is a woman who actually spends very little time in Regional City, but who contributes approximately $100,000 annually to charitable purposes in the community and is looked upon by many as a leader.

These occupational groupings are mentioned at this time merely to indicate that the leaders are a differentiated group as a whole, and their differences in work or leisure activities set them apart physically from other members of the community. The places in which the different groups work vary in appearance, luxury, and comfort of appointments. Even the meeting places of the different groups may vary. These facts seem to be of structural significance.

Working space "allotted" to these persons differs according to their occupation. The most luxurious offices are occupied by the men of finance. Typically their offices are equipped with heavily upholstered furnishings, either in classical design or in modified-modern-functional patterns. The color schemes are subdued, and the lighting is indirect. Air conditioning is a universal phenomenon with this group. Sound-proofed ceilings and heavy draperies eliminate outside and inner office noises. Typically there is a waiting room with comfortable chairs and other furnishings in keeping with the leader's inner office. Hardwood panelling is standard wall construction. Wall pictures are absent in most offices. Some may have an oil painting of the founder of the particular business or a portrait of the present occupant of the office. In gaining admittance to the man who occupies the office, one has contact with anywhere from one to six outer secretaries.

For example, Charles Homer, perhaps the most powerful man in Regional City, who will be discussed in detail later, has a receptionist at the elevator entrance, who directs one to the general offices. There a receptionist guides the visitor, whose business may be in some question, to the secretary of the director of general office operations. She introduces the visitor to the general secretary, who in turn may summon the secretary of Mr. Homer's personal secretary, the latter being a man who goes further into the business at hand and makes the final decision as to whether the visitor may see Mr. Homer. It becomes apparent, in the process of getting into the inner chambers, that Mr. Homer is quite isolated and protected from most of his community contemporaries. Access by persons close to him might conceivably short-circuit several of the secretarial entourage.

Two men in the finance group have private elevators which carry them to their offices, making a trip through the general outer offices unnecessary. With the very top leaders, the pattern of having male secretaries in the outer offices is apparently a badge of prestige. The public-relations attitude among all outer office personnel is generally genteel and sympathetically responsive.

The offices of the top professional men, the lawyers to the larger interests in Regional City, follow much the same pattern of furnishings and design as the offices of the interests they represent. Their secretarial staffs may not be as numerous as those of the financiers and industrialists.

The offices of the industrialists may be of the same general pattern as the financiers' and lawyers', but they may tend toward more heavy design, and in some instances the wood panelling may be of pine or oak rather than the darker woods. Their offices stand in real contrast to the offices in other parts of the enterprise; for example, the office of the engineer in charge of production may be well furnished, but the style is rougher, more severe, and the office is considerably more accessible than that of the director. A foreman's office may be of raw boards built in shanty style with panel windows looking out over the shop. The foreman's desk is ordinarily light oak. Commercial calendars may be his wall decorations.

The commercial employer's office may be described typically as somewhere between the financier's and the industrialist's. His office may be a reserved area walled away from a part of the general activities of his enterprise. For example, Jack Williams' offices are located on the men's furnishing floor of his large mercantile establishment. The interior design is tastefully arranged, but it does not have the mellowed and hushed atmosphere of Joseph Hardy's, a man who directs the operations of the Investment Company of Old State.

Some of the professional personnel who made our list of top leaders, do not have the resources at their command that we have just implied, and consequently their offices reflect this fact. A dentist's office, Perry Latham's, for example, stands in stark but neat contrast to the other men mentioned. The offices of the under-professional men, whose earnings are in the neighborhood of $5000 a year, are in sharper contrast to the top power personnel than is the office of the dentist, who has a certain professional right to sterile and unadorned furnishings. Wallboard panelling is common in the under-professional's offices. The buildings in which they conduct their work are often third rate, considering them in a rough-and-ready scale of values. One professional office visited during the course of the study can be entered only by a freight elevator which formerly served a warehouse, now converted into an office building for some of the community's leading social service agencies. Secretaries in the latter establishments often have a peevish tendency, or are not too responsive or helpful. The differentiation between the professionals in civic and social work and the top power leaders is physically apparent. The physical surroundings reflect social values and a social structuring of community life.

Meetings in Regional City are generally held in the hotels, in several civic centers, in private clubs, or in fraternal halls. The "top flight" meetings—those of a high policy nature—are held in the private clubs or in private homes. The club meetings are famous in Regional City, and the leaders of the community are often referred to as "that Grandview Club crowd," this organization being the most exclusive athletic club in the community and a place where many decisions affecting the future course of events in the community take root. Only select community leaders may enter the Club for luncheons upon invitation by members. It does not cater to the general public in any sense. Private homes also serve as places where decisions of considerable consequence are reached. One leader, when asked about his social contacts, stated, "I have no purely social contacts. All my contacts relate to business. Generally I have people with whom I want to do business visit my home, whether that business concerns only me or the community at large." Homes were mentioned by others as being important places of contact for informal decisions.

The hotels cater to the Chamber of Commerce type of meeting. Many leaders may be involved in the endless luncheons that go on in the hotels. One leader described the men who attend the hotel meetings regularly, whether they be the like of Rotary, Kiwanis, or privately sponsored gatherings, as men who belong to the "luncheon circuit." It is common knowledge that the same men are seen over and over again in the same places. This frequency of contact makes for community solidarity among the leaders, a solidarity which springs partially out of carefully selected meeting locations. Places tend to center activities. Luncheons and meetings differ in their fundamental purposes, and those devoted to policy matters are usually held in the places already described.

Professional and other associational groups tend to hold their meetings in establishments less pretentious in appearance and serving relatively inexpensive meals. The Y. M. C. A. and the

Y. W. C. A. are favorite meeting places for these groups. The service is laggard and the food not too good, but it is not too expensive, either. It must be added parenthetically that the food served in the more exclusive establishments is also not too good, subjectively speaking, but it is expensive. Lodge halls, often second-story lofts, and church basements are also utilized by the understructure of the power groupings. The drab surroundings of these places need not be dwelt upon. Overhanging heating pipes and water conduits are commonplace sights, rather than the ornate and heavy ceiling decorations which cover such honest utility conveyances in the more luxurious meeting places. The point, now obvious in its repetition, that the meeting places of men of power and of men without overt power differ physically, need not be further elaborated.

Some of the showcase homes of Regional City are occupied by the top leaders. Two of these men live in apartments, however, in an old residential section of the city. I visited the homes of some of the leaders on the list but not all. I have driven through the neighborhoods of most of them. They are in most instances isolated retreats with wooded acres and with gardened areas surrounding them. Their interiors run to French, colonial, or ultra-modern, depending upon the taste of the owner. They tend to polished ornate extremes of a genuine nature, rather than to the reproductions of the ornate found in the homes of the professional group, with whom we contrast the upper echelons of power. More need not be said of the leaders' homes. Pictures of them are commonplace in the movies and in the Sunday news supplements. The interest here lies rather in the place of residence. Living quarters set the men of power apart in Regional City, as persons of status are set apart in all communities, from primitive island societies to Park Avenue. Regional City is no exception to this commonplace phenomenon.

There tends to be a clustering of residential quarters of the leaders, and a rough evaluation of the "desirable" areas of

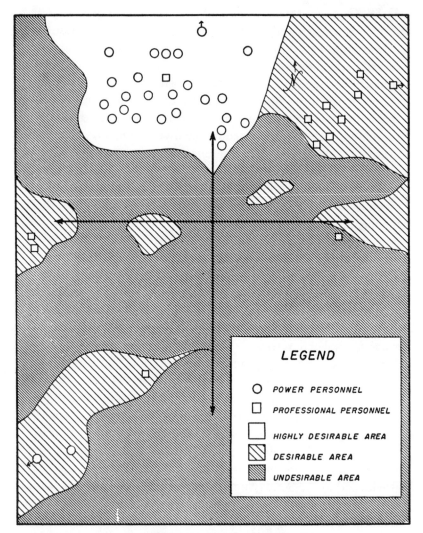

Fig. 1. Residential Areas Occupied by
Policy-Makers and Professional Personnel.

Regional City was made to see where the men of power live
in relation to these neighborhoods. The "A-1" areas of the
community zoning maps, and so on down the scale, were used

as an estimate of desirability. The map in Figure 1 indicates approximately where the leaders reside. Obviously there is a clustering of professional personnel in one section of the city and of power leaders in another.

It has been taken as a criterion that large homes with an absence of heavy traffic, slum housing, industry, or commercial enterprises in the immediate vicinity would be more desirable than those which are at the opposite pole. The smaller home, typically F.H.A.-inspired and Cape-Cod shingled, on narrower lots than the larger homes, has been considered desirable. The obvious slum and rooming house areas have been considered undesirable, and Regional City abounds in such. No extensive survey need be made of any community to determine the most desirable and the least desirable areas in which to live. Any person new to a community is quickly apprised of the phenomenon of desirability. Surveys for slum clearance projects may give one a "scientific" appraisal of desirability for all practical purposes in any community, if more than hearsay is needed to come to some value judgment on desirability.

Only one professional person lived in the area which has been described as highly desirable. This man was an educator who has been looked upon favorably by the community leaders but who cannot be described as a powerful person. He, like many other persons of lesser power, have their homes in the general area inhabited by the leaders considered here. The labor organizers included in this analysis are not found in the exclusive area but near each other at the opposite end of the community. They represent competing unions but live in close range of each other in an area occupied pretty largely by production managers and other highly skilled employees. They do not live in the districts inhabited by the rank and file in their unions.

Office space occupied by the union leaders, particularly by one of the newer union groups, has undergone an interesting transformation in Regional City within the last decade. In the late 1930's the writer visited the union headquarters of one of the newer unions. The building was a ramshackle structure, poorly lighted, and badly ventilated. The stairs were wooden, creaky conveyances leading from the building entrance into a large open hall which was used as an informal and formal meeting place. There was a constant stream of traffic up and down the stairs, and groups of labor representatives would gather in buzzing knots to discuss their organization plans. Doors to the small offices flanked the open hall, and there was a steady shuffling of men in and out of these offices. Most visitors and union officials were in their shirt sleeves.

On a recent field trip to Regional City it was found that the newer union had moved its headquarters to a better building and one more centrally located. An elevator carried visitors to the main offices. The walls were painted in light colors. Fluorescent lighting was utilized. The office interiors were furnished with new furniture, rugs, and draperies. The leader of one of the largest unions had a large hardwood "conference type" desk. Leather-upholstered chairs flanked the desk. Visits from sub-officials of the union were held in scheduled conferences. There was no shuffling and milling of men in the outer office. The leaders interviewed were conservatively dressed. In short, the atmosphere was one of subdued orderliness. Labor in Regional City is in the process of arriving, and the physical surroundings of the leaders reflect this fact.

The older union group in the community has long occupied space in a building that is on a par with the surroundings of the present quarters of the newer union. The furnishings are not new, but they are substantial. Scheduled conferences in adequate meeting rooms have been the general rule with the older union. The leaders have been noted for their correct dress and for their public-relations programs, which take into account physical factors.

The Negro population of Regional City is largely segregated and concentrated in the center of the metropolitan area.

A belt of Negro population extends eastward and westward from the center of the city with the westward area tending toward better living facilities for its inhabitants. The leaders in the Negro community, in locating their homes, have followed the westward trend of population movement. Thus, the pattern of residential differentiation between leaders and followers among Negroes themselves parallels that of the larger community. This pattern will be described and illustrated more fully when Negro community leadership is analyzed in a later chapter.

The office buildings and the offices of the Negro leaders are of relatively inferior construction and design. With three exceptions the buildings are apparently twenty-five to thirty years old. They are drab in appearance and poorly maintained. Space in all of the offices seems to be at a premium, and even in the newer buildings the private offices of the power leaders appear as cubicles compared with the offices of some of the leaders in the larger community. Meeting places for Negroes, with the possible exception of places in local Negro colleges, tend to be as colorless as the meeting places of the professional, civic, and social personnel in the larger community.

It may be said, then, that the leaders selected for study in the larger community meet in common places and live in close proximity to each other. This is structurally significant.

The location of the men of power in Regional City tends to isolate them from the mass of people in that community. Consequently they are isolated from many of the problems which affect the average citizen. They daily shuttle by automobile between their homes, their work, and their meeting places. The streets over which they travel pass through many "blighted areas," but the sights of poverty are hidden from view, along most of the routes, by relatively new store fronts, neon signs, and the gleaming chromium of the new cars on display along "automobile row." This is not to say that the men of power in Regional City are unaware of the many social problems behind the façade of their daily route, Commercial Avenue. These problems are a constant causal background of many of the meetings attended by the leaders brought to them secondhand, in many instances, by the professional men who are less isolated from the problems. It can only be said that location *tends* to isolate the men of power from the mass of citizens less powerful than themselves and from community problems.

The professional men, used as a contrasting group in this study, take different routes from home to work. Their way runs through an industrial and warehouse area. The store fronts are painted in sombre colors which are smoke-faded, giving the impression of dominant browns and grays. There are loan shops, feed stores, tool shops, small neighborhood grocery stores, and many other struggling small business establishments crowded into blocks of unpainted, rotting, wooden dwellings off Independence Boulevard. It is true that the professional men turn into pleasanter suburban streets at the end of their homeward journey, but most of the route is depressing to anyone sensitive to social disorder. The smoke pall, grassless yards, unwashed children rolling abandoned automobile tires as hoops, gray dogs, and the bargain clothing emporiums are constant reminders of decisions which press for attention on the leaders and their executors of power in the community.

Only two men among our power leaders travel a route comparable to the one described for the professionals. They are Gary Stone and Russell Gregory, the labor leaders. The other power leaders travel at high speeds along Pine Grove expressway to their homes and to their work. The image held by groups residing in different parts of the physical community may consequently vary. Physical structure may thus affect social structure and its functioning.

One other spatial feature of Regional City must be mentioned. The city spreads over a large area. It is a metropolitan community. Its growth has pushed its natural bounds into large portions of the County of Hilldale and two outlying counties in which, and near which, the original city was located. The city boundaries have never caught up with the ever-widening population distribution of the metropolis. As population moved into the outlying areas, city services such as water supply, gas supply, fire and police protection, and road construction and maintenance were demanded of the local units of government. The city charter did not allow the city government to go beyond its corporate limits in providing such services, and consequently the county government was called upon to take on functions which are normally considered within the jurisdiction of a city.

Differing tax rates in the three counties making up the metropolitan area of Regional City, overlapping jurisdictions of governmental units of city and county administrations, and other related matters have brought a cumulative set of problems to the attention of the general community within recent years and to the leaders of Regional City specifically. The nature of these problems will be pursued further under a discussion of projects and issues, but the spatial arrangements of the community are prominent in the discussions on this topic in organized groups and between individuals in the city and in the outlying areas. Decisions of grave import, revolving around these space problems, are being demanded of the men of decision.

The concern here has been with the physical structure of the community studied. It is obviously impossible to talk about structure without becoming concerned with action. In describing the physical structure of Regional City in some of its aspects related to power personnel, one notes movement. Men move over highways to and from their homes. They attend meetings. They talk about one another. The community is a locus of action—a structured, organized entity that can be measured, charted, plotted. It has "reality" in a stronger sense than many other materials with which social scientists must work. Men create the structure of Regional City's physical plants, its streets, and its dormitory areas, and in the creation they bring into being social structures. The physical structures are a part of the social structure in that they help to regularize and routinize the behavior patterns of the men around which physical features are built. There is, therefore, an interaction between the physical characteristics of the community and the patterned actions of men. The physical structures, once created, act as passive barriers or channels for the dynamic actions of men.

In the description of individual leaders to follow, it should be borne in mind that most of the leaders are persons of power status. In some cases they have the machinery of government at their bidding. In many cases they control large industries in which they reign supreme in matters of decision affecting large numbers of the citizenry. They are persons of dominance, prestige, and influence. They are, in part, the decision-makers for the total community. They are able to enforce their decisions by persuasion, intimidation, coercion, and, if necessary, force. Because of these elements of compulsion, power-wielding is often a hidden process. The men involved do not wish to become identified with the negative aspects which the process implies, and their anonymity will be respected.

It should be repeated here that all the leaders described bear pseudonyms. Their business connections are disguised. A professional occupation may be changed to one that corresponds. But every effort has been made to maintain situational dynamics intact. It must be admitted that the problem has been difficult, but not uncommon, perhaps, for the social scientist. The analytical task would undoubtedly be easier if names and places could be given without regard for personal privacy, but one would by no means advocate the loss of so valuable a human right. Yet, in spite of admitted restrictions and limitations, it is believed that in a technical sense "reality" will be presented. The reality is, of course, as the author sees it and in relation to the objective measures of study employed.

3 WHAT SOME LEADERS ARE LIKE

THE descriptions of selected leaders now to be given cannot avoid entirely a discussion of the dynamics of relationships, but no attempt is made at this point to describe a leadership "system." Such a complete description actually comprises this whole study. The present phase of analysis defines in some detail the characteristics of the community leaders involved, leaving until later the placing of them in their structural relationships. It has been indicated already, by fictional names, who the men are, and these names will here be given substance as personalities, so that their actions will convey a sense of reality. Since the structured actions of an actual group of men is the primary concern of this study, such actions as occur in the following descriptions will be those that bear a relationship to the hypotheses already stated.

What kind of men, then, are the men in power in Regional City? The question may be answered partially. Not all of the leaders will be described. The descriptions here presented will merely set the stage for the analysis of pertinent activities and relationships. These descriptions must be partial because admittedly one cannot know so many men in intimate detail, but it is possible to know some of their traits and interests. One might guess at their motivations, but to carry the analysis far would take one into the realm of psychology, which, as suggested earlier, is regarded as a residual category in this study. The materials here presented are drawn from personal observations, from news accounts of the men, from data given by them in interviews, and from things said about them by other people. The leaders highlighted may be considered fairly typical of the top leaders in Regional City. Individually, of course, all men in Regional City are different, and no attempt is made to formulate a typology of the total group of leaders, but there are enough common characteristics among the men here described in grouped relations to make it seem that some typology may be implied.

Let us begin with one man, an older leader in Regional City, Mark Parks. Mr. Parks is sixty-seven years old and a vigorous, spry little man for his age. His business is a commercial enterprise connected with the distribution of paper boxes. It was left to him by his father, who had inherited it from his father before him. The business is a leading one in Regional City and has branches in several other cities within the region. It has been an extremely profitable enterprise. By utilizing the services of one of the large banks in the community, the enormous assets of his business have given Mr. Parks a leading role in this bank through membership on its board. He is very proud of his banking connections, which he mentioned several times during my interview with him, and he hurried from the interview to a meeting of the First State Bank board.

Because of his long residence in the community and because of an apparently genuine interest in community life, Mr. Parks is considered both a community leader and a social leader. He belongs to an exclusive club. He is interested in the symphony subscription drive. He has been elected to the national board of his paper-dealers' association. He is an honored member of his church and a liberal contributor to its mission fund. His wife is considered a gracious hostess to selected friends.

Mr. Parks has one son, Mark, Jr., who is now the more active member of the team he and his father represent. He is an alert

and capable man, as active in a variety of civic affairs as his
father is said to have been some years ago. His rise in the company was from the bottom up. Several of the leaders in Regional City who have inherited businesses have followed the
pattern of beginning at the bottom of the ladder in the company. The rise of these men has been meteoric, in many
instances, but the newspapers in biographical accounts of the
lives of such persons solemnly report that they have "worked
their way to the top." The occupational ascent of Mark Parks,
Jr., illustrates the rapidity of such a rise up the ladder of
success. The pattern is in the American tradition, but most men
find the ascent a longer process than did Mark, Jr.

Young Mark, upon graduation from college, came into his
father's business as a shipping clerk. He became successively
a stock-room clerk, a stock foreman, and an office manager for
one of the branch warehouses. Two years after he started as
shipping clerk, he was elected a director of the corporation
and placed in charge of one of the major subsidiaries of the
company. Three years later he was named treasurer of the
company, and in three years more he became operations vice-
president. After two years in this position he was made president. His father then became chairman of the board and has
since gradually relinquished active control of the business in
favor of his son. He still retains a firm control in matters of
general policy, however. Mark, Jr., is the authority on administrative matters. So we see that within ten years this young man
rose from stock clerk to company president. It is claimed, and
rightly so perhaps, that by dint of hard work he made good.
Certainly it cannot be denied that so young a person as he was
in the earlier years of his service in the business shouldered
considerable responsibility and has continued to do so increasingly. It may be surmised, nevertheless, that his father's position in the company was extremely helpful in his business
success.

Out of forty top policy leaders, fifteen inherited their

father's business. Three others also fell heir to an inheritance of another sort. They inherited position in the leadership scale. Illustrious and industrious fathers helped to place their sons in responsible positions. Some of the leaders inherited wealth from their fathers and have found their way to the top of businesses founded by them or have become influential in other ways. Fifteen of the leaders may be said to have gained positions of prominence on their own. In other words, theirs is achieved position rather than ascribed.

Mark Parks, Jr.'s, position, to get back to the Parks family, may be said to be ascribed in the sense that he inherited his status. He has, of course, also achieved position on his own merits. He has taken on both business and social responsibilities as his father has relinquished them. The line of achieved status and ascribed status is difficult to draw in this case, but we feel that "ascribed" is a better descriptive term than the ones employed by the newspapers in designating a man in Parks's position as "self-made" in the American tradition. The newspaper evaluation does not coincide with a strict interpretation of the term "achieved."

As Mark Parks, Sr., gradually retired from active participation in the management of his business, a part of his civic duties fell to his son. Mr. Parks became more and more selective in his civic interests. His devotion to the arts became more pronounced. His board participation became more exclusive. He is still active in the merchants' association, but he holds no elective position in it. He is an honorary member of the board of the national association of his trade. His Chamber of Commerce activities have ceased. He belongs to only one civic welfare board, whereas he had previously belonged to several. And, as was suggested, he finds himself more and more absorbed with his membership on the board of his bank and in cultural activities.

Mr. Parks belongs to the "older crowd," as the long-recognized leaders are called in Regional City. Decisions made by the older crowd are generally respected by the younger leaders. However, the power wielded by the older group is sometimes resented by some of the younger men, such as Percy Latham, Adam Graves, Elsworth Mines, and Joseph Hardy who, among others, represent the latter group. Joseph Hardy, a younger man, put it this way in an interview with him:

"When something big is on the fire, eventually it gets to such men as Charles Homer, James Treat, Harry Parker, or Mark Parks. Too many things go that way, I think. What Regional City needs is more leaders. That is one of our biggest problems, developing leaders."

It was evident that Joseph Hardy resented the fact that clearances had to be made with the older group. He told of an experience in which he was out to change policies in the Community Chest and had been thwarted by the older crowd. In the interview Hardy displayed considerable feeling concerning the older group. The members of the older group, in turn, think of Hardy as a pushing young man, and Parks said of him, "In the next ten years he will either be one of the biggest leaders Regional City has ever known, or he will be its biggest damn fool!" Hardy is difficult for the older leaders to put down, because he inherited his father's investment company and evidently has managed it with considerable skill. Adam Graves, another younger man, was quite outspoken on the controls exercised by the older men, but he, unlike his contemporary Hardy, is not bucking the system. He goes along, biding his time. He is more acceptable to the older men.

Mark Parks, Sr., has reached an age in life where he is rather mellowed in his homespun philosophy. He is given, periodically, to releasing mildly moral nostrums to the press, and when an issue comes up which concerns most of the citizens, Mr. Parks can be depended upon for a statement. This pattern holds true for other leaders of his status and age—as well as for some of the younger men.

Mr. Parks is a leading savant in Regional City. His age and status in the community as a business leader allow him to pronounce on the problems of youth, on business conditions, whether they concern his own business or not, population problems, the issues of war and peace, and many other matters which he discusses with assured learnedness. The newspapers carry his words as being authoritative. If there are rebuttals to them they usually are not printed. Some of Mr. Parks's pronouncements run in this vein: "A young man starting out in business must be alert to false values in his career. By holding true to the values which have made America great, those willing to sacrifice and work hard will pull themselves up the ladder of success."

Mr. Parks at another time was out of patience with the wasteful policies of the federal government in its spending operations and was so quoted in an exclusive interview. Another time he predicted a million population for Regional City within a decade. The prediction did not come true, but there was a tremendous growth in the city, and in the American tradition for liking bigness in population the statement had "a good healthy ring."

Several times Mr. Parks has spoken out on opportunity for young men within the region, and he is aided and abetted by many other men in giving this friendly advice. Almost every Sunday edition of the *Regional City Star* carries an item on the subject of opportunity for young men who are willing to stick to their jobs in the region.

Two or three years ago the papers carried statements concerning juvenile delinquency, and the older men came out against it, along with some of the ministers in the understructure of the social hierarchy of the city. News commentators and columnists were drawn into the discussion, but within a few months the topic lost interest. Usually one or two organizations are behind such news releases, which draw one or more of the potent leaders into the discussion. We do not wish, at this point, to carry this phase of our analysis so far that it involves too much emphasis on the dynamics within the power structure, but it may be stated that such issues as are indicated here do bring into play activities of the upper-structure, particularly the older men.

Mr. Parks's mild manner, general kindly appearance, and gentle concern with the careening direction of the world around him often lead to his being described as "our beloved" leader, when he is introduced at public gatherings. He may be described as a man with a matured view of happenings, and people seem interested in what he has to say on many subjects. He apparently takes as a matter of course the approbation accorded him in the press and in public meeting places. That is the kind of leader he is.

Such terms as hardheaded, tough-minded, battle-hardened, hard-nosed, cold-eyed, or heavy-handed, do not aptly describe Mr. Parks, although some of the writings on businessmen and speakers at luncheons of the National Association of Manufacturers and Chambers of Commerce may be prone to use such terms. As a matter of fact, such terms do not apply altogether to any of the men interviewed in Regional City. "Tough-minded" might apply to some, but in general the men of power in the community are better described by other adjectives. Some of the men of greatest power might even be described as soft, in their general appearance. Certainly, the terms gracious and polite could be applied for the most part to their behavior in the interviewing process. The harsher terms might possibly be used concerning some of the men in administrative and executive positions below the men in the policy realm such as Mr. Parks. "Good public relations" would seem to be a keynote to behavior among the upper group of leaders.

Of all the men interviewed, only Gary Stone and Russell Gregory, the labor leaders, and Grover Smith, a merchant, were not college graduates. Sixteen out of twenty-seven men interviewed, and considered policy-makers, claim Old State as their place of birth. Twelve of these sixteen men born in Old State are natives of Regional City. This fact is significant, because there is a general belief that very few leaders are born in this city. Time after time the interviewer received the statement, "I am one of the few men in Regional City who were born here." Four of the sixteen leaders born in Regional City might be classified as men who had achieved status. The remaining twelve inherited property in eleven cases, and in the other case the leader's father was a prominent professional man.

Since Regional City has a large influx of population from outlying areas of the region, the myth has become prevalent that such population constitutes a majority in the city. A majority of the policy leaders, however, are locally born, at least that portion of them upon whom we have such supporting data. It would appear that the home-town boy can make good in Regional City. Of those leaders born outside the state, three have achieved status by long residence and devotion to local activities, two brought inherited wealth with them to the community from other states, and one came as a labor organizer to his position. The last has been in the community several years.

Among the self-made men Avery Spear is a good example. Mr. Spear was born in a neighboring state and came to Regional City as a young attorney. After several years of increasingly effective law practice, he was taken into the Homer Chemical Company in one of the executive positions of the firm's several divisions. He had no wealth or family behind him but was a favored employee of Charles Homer, owner and later to become chairman of the board of the enterprise. Gradually Spear accumulated considerable wealth through stock purchases from his high earnings. For several years he acted as a public-relations man for the company, serving as a "front man," as such men are called in Regional City, substituting for Mr. Homer on innumerable civic boards and committees locally and in the state. Now a man past middle age, he cannot be described as belonging to the older crowd in the community even though his years might make him eligible. His immediate superior, Charles Homer, occupies a place within this older select membership. To have him function in this group would, perhaps, represent a duplication of effort in matters of decision. There are clearances, of course, between Mr. Homer and Mr. Spear on matters of civic importance, but most final decisions ultimately must be made by Mr. Homer. The latter attends no formal community board or committee meetings. Mr. Spear does, but within recent years he has limited his efforts to working with organizations concerned with major policy matters in welfare and education.

During the middle 1930's Mr. Spear was one of three men in the company who became involved in an inner corporation struggle for its presidency. Mr. Homer favored Spear, and he eventually won out in the battle for power within the corporation. The other two men left the company, one to retirement and the other as head of another allied company in the region. Mr. Spear's accession to the second position in the company was reflected in his community activities. He, like Mark Parks, Sr., became more selective in his community work and delegated many of his civic duties to a subordinate. His aggressiveness in the company power struggle is reflected in his community actions. He is a firm believer in holding down costs of civic improvement and will fight to get his way. His philosophy concerning charitable organizations may be summed up in his statement, "Charity should tread no primrose path!" Expenditures for charitable purposes should be held down to a bare minimum for survival, in Mr. Spear's opinion, and no "fancy coddling" and handouts to charity cases should be tolerated. His opinions are quoted by others in the community, and when a project is up for discussion among professional workers in the charitable agencies, someone is liable to ask whether or not Mr. Spear has been consulted in the matter, or whether there is likelihood of his approval or disapproval if the project is to require the expenditure of tax or privately subscribed dollars. Mr. Spear also has a steady hand on expenditures for educational purposes in Regional City and is accorded the same deference in relation to school expenditures by the teaching profession as that given him by the social workers. Other policy leaders also look to Mr. Spear for advice in these matters and will make no commitments related to either until they have consulted with him.

Mr. Spear cannot be considered a social leader in the community in a "society" sense. He scoffed at the idea when it was presented to him in an interview. He said, "I have never gone in for that stuff [social club activities, elaborate entertaining]. I have never had time, and I would not have wasted time on it if I could have!" He scornfully mentioned Edward Stokes, of the Stokes Gear Company, as an example of a society leader. He said, "Stokes is one of your society leaders. He is, in my opinion, a sellout, and I'll tell you why. There is a man who had a fourth-generation business behind him—a business that was founded long before the Civil War. He had everything to make him a real leader around this town. I see you have got him on your list, but he is no leader in my opinion. He has sold that fine business to an out-of-state firm. I guess he got enough for it, and maybe it's because of his money that some people think he is a leader. But he'd rather sit around the Grandview Club all day and drink whiskey and play cards than tend to that fine business. If that is leadership, then you can have it!"

Spear mentioned with evident disapproval some of the entertaining that Stokes does in his home. "A leader, in my opinion," he continued, "is a man that has the gumption to shake the lead out of his pants. Stokes has not got that kind of gumption!"

Spear went on to talk about some of the higher-paid executives who are sent to Regional City from New York, Chicago, and other cities by their companies: "A lot of them," he said, "come in with big salaries and with entertainment accounts. They make a big splash. They take in all the clubs and make all the parties. A lot of them burn themselves out. They make the society pages, but they are not leaders. Anybody with any money to spend could do the things I'm talking about, but that would not make them leaders. When people talk about society leaders I do not know what they are talking about!"

Mr. Spear was talking the language of many of the self-made men of Regional City. Some were not as vehement in their statements about society leaders, and recognized their existence. "Business first" is the keynote to the actions of most of the Regional City leaders.

Among the society leaders in Regional City is Gloria Stevens. Her father and mother were social leaders before her. Her father inherited wealth from his father's interests in the Homer Chemical Company. Her father was a brother of Charles Homer, chairman of the company. He never took an active part in the business. Though he nominally held some post in the company, he spent most of his time traveling in many parts of the world. He married a Philadelphia girl of means, who brought Gloria up in the grand manner. In her father's later years his funds were put into a trust, which passed to Gloria's mother and to her at the time of his death. Gloria married a young man, Jeffrey Stevens, who entered the business operated by her uncle, Charles Homer. He has never risen very high in the business and has had little interest in doing so. The Stevenses have three residences to which they devote a portion of each year. One is on the Gulf of Mexico, another in New England, and the third just outside Regional City. They spend a part of the social season in Regional City and entertain people from other parts of the country as well as selected members of local society groups. Hunting and horsemanship are two of the activities which engross the Stevenses during their stay in Old State. Gloria contributes very generously to local educational and charitable enterprises, but the actual management of the funds from the trust made available for these purposes is in the hands of her lawyer and confidant, Ray Moster. He makes all contributions in her name but with explicit instructions that no publicity be given the matter. Many professional persons try to get to Mrs. Stevens with various schemes and projects for her approval. Some of them are successful, and she may give them passing attention, but, generally speaking, all matters of expenditure must be originated with Mr. Moster, who meets with Mrs. Stevens once or twice a year to discuss in a general way proposals for her charitable contributions. Her community leadership consists mainly in making resources available. She is on no civic boards and does not participate actively on any committees. According to the society editor of the *Regional City Star*, she rarely receives publicity in the papers, either on her social activities or in regard to her charitable contributions. This is in accordance with her own wishes and this pattern of non-publicity seems to be general among the group which Mrs. Stevens represents. To be invited to her home, according to an informant, is considered a rare privilege.

The social life of Regional City that most consistently makes the newspapers is not the upper-crust group, as the top layer of Regional City is unimaginatively called. "People who get their names in the paper are often on the make," I was told. It was explained that many of the persons whose names appear in the news actually represent the fast crowd or the smart set, as the country club groups are sometimes called. This group differs from the old-line families, such as the one represented by Mrs. Stevens, who may belong to the Grandview Club. Among these old families are those represented by Ralph Spade, a retired banker's son, Hetty Fairly, a wealthy spinster, Bert Tidwell, a lawyer of prominence, Claudia Mills, the wife of a society physician, Harold Farmer, a man who draws his income from investments in sugar importation, and Mark

Parks, already described. Such families have little contact, beyond passing acquaintance, with those in the smart set. Men in the smart set are often employed in the under-echelons of business in Regional City, or they may be dissolute members of older families who have lost favor with their family groups.

The society editor of one of the local papers stated, "It is often difficult to keep many of these people [the smart set] out of the old family homes. They try all kinds of ways to get in. Recently Mrs. Stevens had a large group of wives of newspaper owners and editors to an informal tea, while their husbands were at a meeting in the city. Mrs. Stevens complained later that several of these women had brought local and undesirable people with them as uninvited guests. They [the smart set women] had wangled invitations from the wives of some of the editors just to see what Mrs. Stevens' home was like." Some of Mrs. Stevens' flowers had been trampled "as if by a herd of wild cows," she said later.

Among many of the leaders interviewed in Regional City there was a flat denial that the community has much of a society set. They say, "Regional City is about as free of society sets as any town in the country." Or, "There may be some groups that play around at some of the clubs, but Regional City is a community that is too busy for much high life." Partial findings did not indicate this to be true, but the author was not interested primarily in "society" structure with its processes of inclusion and exclusion, except as it impinged upon power structure. Mrs. Stevens represents a link between the two areas of structure because of her wealth. This fact was of interest, and it was deemed desirable to see whether other persons in her social position are functionally affiliated with the processes of policy formulation and execution. It was found that society leaders are not particularly active in these areas, but this will be discussed later.

Some of the socially prominent persons in Regional City are said to engage in "active work," while others do not.

Those engaged in active work are more likely to be picked as leaders by both workers and non-workers, as will be seen when an examination of their choices of leadership within the top structure is made.

Herman Schmidt represents a banking enterprise, the First State Bank of Regional City. He is a man whose influence has waned. For many years his bank was one of the fastest-growing financial concerns in the community. Herman Schmidt "was on every committee in town." During the depression he was prominent in a back-to-the-farm movement, which to his mind would have solved many of the problems which confronted Regional City during those trying times. He devoted much time and energy to convincing people of his point of view. He bitterly opposed many of the New Deal programs which sought to relocate people and which he felt were not as sound or as fundamental as his own scheme. He had many adherents to his idea both locally and throughout the country. He had put forward his plan as a panacea in many respectable journals. No one had ever tried fully to exploit Mr. Schmidt's plan, and there was skepticism concerning it in many quarters. But he was determined to make an experiment.

Mr. Schmidt consequently decided to act. He announced through the newspapers that on a certain day he would have fifty trucks lined up in front of his bank prepared to take back to the farm all who were "interested in starting anew." He had arranged that these people would be taken to plantations over the state, where they might attach themselves to farms as tenant laborers with small cash allowances to be provided by the owners, who were willing to "cooperate" with Mr. Schmidt. It is rumored that he held debtors' papers in many instances on the properties he had chosen. It has been suggested that others were interested in the plan, especially during the crop season, because it seemed like a way of getting a relatively inexpensive supply of labor.

Through the local relief administrator, pressure was put upon the social case workers to urge all their able-bodied clients to accept this offer of "real work" and stop accepting handouts. The difficulty in executing the whole scheme was revealed when only about a dozen men showed up to go back to the farms. The trucks, which had been pressed into service from the local utility companies and the city government, were all in front of the bank and ready to go on the appointed day, but the passengers did not appear in as large numbers as Mr. Schmidt had anticipated. This was a real disappointment to him. The news editorials lamented the fact that able-bodied men would not work when honest labor was offered to them, which may have consoled him somewhat, but it is said that, after this failure to achieve what appeared to him a possible and logical goal, Schmidt began to withdraw from activities designed to help the underprivileged. The very large sums of money at his disposal for charitable purposes were turned to the development of "year-'round pasture grasses" for cattle grazing in the region.

For several years Schmidt acted in the role of elder consultant to many of the younger leaders, but he was not a person of overt action in the community. As he grew older he was not as aggressive in expanding his banking operations as he had been previously. Today he is an old man, and his advice is sought frequently enough for him to have made our list of top policy-makers. One informant said of him, "Schmidt is a powerful man even yet, but he has grown satisfied. The bank is not aggressive or progressive, and Schmidt won't let go in favor of the younger men. Schmidt could do a lot, but you can't get him to work on anything. The First State Bank represents a lot of dead wood, in my opinion." It will be recalled that Mark Parks, an older man, is influential on the board of this same bank.

It is not age alone that determines a man's influence in Regional City affairs, and there is no wish to imply this in the case of Herman Schmidt. As long as a man is actively engaged in decision-making, he may be looked to with great deference by others below him in age. All of our very top leaders are about fifty years of age. Several of them are well past sixty. Beyond sixty, a man either becomes a member of the influential older crowd and relatively less active, or he may actually decline in influence.

The next figure on our list to be highlighted is Percy Latham, a dentist. He has been devoted to civic associational life. He belongs to a couple of lodges and has been a member of almost every civic committee of any importance in Regional City for the past several years. He is not a man of means, for he has, in some measure, neglected his practice of dentistry in order to be active in the community. His name appears in the paper very regularly as a participant in one civic enterprise or another. His contacts in the community are widespread. He can get the ear of the top leaders easily, and he can talk readily with many of the under-structure personnel. The under-structure people look upon Dr. Latham with a mixed feeling of contempt and awe. He is a person, they say, who "has no will of his own." He is called by many a cat's-paw for the "big boys." He is used as a source of information by both the over-structure and the under-structure. He will always take the side of the men of larger decision, but in a straddling way. He wants to keep his friends, and some of his contortions in behalf of the larger interests in times of crisis bring down upon him private contempt—a contempt which, however, is concealed from him. He is a useful tool for all concerned. He apparently enjoys the role he plays, and, because of his relative security with some of the biggest men in Regional City, he is looked upon as a person to be deferred to by many who know him but slightly. He has ingratiated himself particularly with the Parkses, father and son, and he draws considerably on them for support in the many things he is called upon to do for the community. He also has the confidence of George Delbert, a utilities man in Regional City who is very powerful. Latham's tie-in with Delbert adds to his prestige in the community. He is described by many of the leaders as "a man with his feet on the ground." One of the under-personnel revived the old quip, "Yes, Latham's feet are on the ground up to his hips!"

The hostility of the under-structure toward the upper leaders is expressed in various ways in the community. Over a period of time such terms as might be used in characterizing the upper-structure were collected. Power, in its coercive aspects, brings reaction to it, and the reaction is expressed in derogatory terms toward leaders above one in the power hierarchy. Some of the terms suggest respect as well as disrespect, and they sometimes reflect envy of the position of others. Among these terms are the following: bigwig, big wheel, high mogul, high-muckedy-muck, big cheese, pooh-bah, fat cat, big shot, fat boy, big boy, big operator, reactionary, and the like. Persons acting on a plane comparatively equal with that of personnel in the under-structure may use certain derogatory terms toward others who are trying to curry favor with the leaders by doing their bidding with too much alacrity. The terms fire-ball, hot-shot, stoolie, punk, fall guy, or hatchet man may be applied to such persons. This vernacular may be followed by more colorful and expressive expletives in certain situations where the person named is held in rigid contempt. Percy Latham is variously called a hot-shot, a stoolie, a punk, and a fat boy by those who know him well. Some persons call him a civic leader, however, and that is what he will be called here. It is of no interest, at the moment, to know in what esteem he is held by his contemporaries. The concern here is related to his function within a social structure, and it is apparent that he serves a rather specific function.

Two other men who should be described are the labor leaders, Gary Stone and Russell Gregory. One represents a conservative union, the other a newer, more aggressive union that has struggled for recognition for several years in the region, and in Regional City particularly. Within recent years both unions have grown, but neither represents great power as yet. Their influence has increased, however, with observable gains in their membership.

Gary Stone was born in Regional City. After a high school education he began his career as a day laborer in the Regional Gas Heat Company, where he actively participated in the organizational strife of the late 1920's and early 1930's which resulted in the recognition of the Consolidated Fuel Workers Union. He thus became the spokesman for more than 6,000 workers in the local industry. Mr. Stone served as secretary-treasurer of the union for several years. He has been very active in state politics.

In many ways Stone's activities paralleled those of the Regional Gas Heat Company president, Robert (Bob) Vines. Vines was a rough-and-tumble executive who fought the unions throughout his working career. When extra-legal force became inoperative in his fight to keep labor within the bounds of traditional management practices current in the 1920's, he went to the state legislature to legalize the company's position. It is common knowledge that Vines and his company retained lawyers in many key counties throughout Old State and were instrumental in getting many of them elected to the legislature. It is rumored that those representatives to the legislature whom he could not elect he "reasoned with" in order to maintain a balance of power through the manipulation of a tight unit minority. At any rate, Vines was for many years the most influential man in Old State politics so far as the legislature was concerned.

The Consolidated Union was active in matters of legislation, but its effort centered around lobbying activities in the halls of the State Capitol. Gary Stone became a leading and familiar figure in Old State politics. He was frequently quoted in the press as "giving labor's views" on any matter before the state Assembly; and by popular appeals and by threatened or actual strikes he was able to exert considerable pressure on the Gas Heat Company and indirectly on the legislature.

Within the community of Regional City Stone could not be considered a popular community leader. For many years he received a bad press. He was blamed for labor strife. He was not asked to belong to any of the civic associations, community committees, or charitable agency boards. In recent years this situation has changed somewhat, particularly since the recognition of the right of labor to bargain collectively with employers. Gary Stone is now asked to serve on many committees where it is felt desirable to have labor represented, but Stone has not been active on any of the purely civic enterprises. As a labor representative, his name is used on organizational letterheads, and his advice is sought informally on many issues; but his own interest has remained openly and almost exclusively political. For the better part of the past two decades he has served as president of his union and has continued his interest in lobbying activities. He faithfully attends meetings on political matters and shuns other kinds of organizational gatherings. He is prominent in several fraternal organizations, since he looks upon these groupings as potential political allies.

Stone has become a skilled hand at compromise. He can make concessions in the political arena which he believes advance the cause of labor, but which often appear to the liberals in the state as sellouts. There is much gossip in Regional City concerning how "sold out," in principle, Gary Stone is.

In my interview with him, he constantly referred to "our Company" and the "man we work for [Fargo Dunham]," indicating a close working relationship with the company, and he stated that he would "rather compromise than strike" in disputed situations. But we must take his word for it that he "has the welfare of the union workers in mind at all times." Strikes are, in his opinion, a last resort in a dispute and place a heavy burden on the working man.

Stone gives the impression of a cautious man, but a fairly frank one in his discussion of Old State politics. He would name no names, cite no dates, indicate no places in his description of legislative events; but he was perfectly willing to describe in detail the workings of what he termed the "third house" in the General Assembly. The third house in Old State politics seems to be a "council" of lobbyists which serves informally to coordinate opinion among its members. Mr. Stone is quite influential in the third house, and indicated that it is there that many concessions and compromises are made on legislative matters before they reach legislative committees or the floor of the Capitol chambers. His activities in connection with the third house lead to the description of him as a smooth operator by those who know him well. Those who basically disagree with him call him a controversial figure. Perhaps this term best describes him.

Stone's counterpart leader in the labor movement is Russell Gregory. The latter has been as rough as the former has been smooth in his operations. Within the last decade Russell Gregory has successfully organized the steel wire industry of Regional City. The organization has been accompanied by bitter and violent action between the owners of the industry and the workers. Gregory has been in the front ranks of each battle and has remained a leader throughout. His union has been consistently victorious in their struggles for control of the rank and file membership, and a disciplined hierarchy within the union swears allegiance to Gregory.

When he speaks for his union, he speaks with great author-ity. His manners are considered crude, and he is given to strong language on any occasion. At one fund-raising luncheon to which he was invited he was asked to say a few words, following a series of "good-fellow-and-harmony" remarks by the presiding officer. He arose and said, "As I look around this room, I see a bunch of fat cats. Most of you are interested in getting your pusses in the papers to tell the town what good guys you are. I ain't sure you really mean what you say about wanting to help people. You ask labor to give their dough to this fund drive, and then a few of you decide how to spend it. Labor ain't in on that part of the deal. You invite me to be here, but you never put anything in the papers about the locals who help raise a big chunk of this money. If we're going to help on this thing we want a say in how the money spent, and we want the town to know that we helped to raise the money through our locals, just like the Old State Bank is supposed to be helping or any other bunch in this town."

Gregory sat down. The chairman of the meeting was hard put to get the meeting back on a good-fellowship basis. Gregory's motives were perhaps not entirely unselfish. He was appealing for recognition of his union's power, and to get the "pusses" of some of his local leaders into the papers to show "what good guys" they were. The press the next day merely commented on Gregory's presence at the meeting and mentioned his local union affiliation.

One of Regional City's leaders commented on Gregory as being "an ignorant fellow," and "one of whom you would never be quite sure what he might say in a meeting." In spite of Gregory's so-called crudeness he is being increasingly asked to sit on Regional City civic committees. At the time of the study, he indicated that he was on "about seventeen local boards or committees." He believes in being active in local affairs and encourages participation in organized civic and community life by shop stewards and others of the union membership. He states that most of the union members are not much interested in such affairs. They either do not have the time to participate, since many meetings are held in the afternoons when the men are on their jobs and taking time off costs them money, or they go to some of the night meetings, become bored with the proceedings, and do not return. "They don't understand what a lot of these things are all about," said Mr. Gregory.

Gregory stated that after he had "told off" a lot of the townspeople about "labor's not being represented on things," he noticed that some of the "bigwigs" would see him on the street and stop to ask him how labor felt on this or that. Continuing, he said, "For a while I did not catch on to what was going on, and I'd give them answers off the cuff. But finally I said to some of them, 'I can't give you an opinion here on the street. If I did, it might not really be the opinion of labor. If you really want to know what labor thinks, write me a letter. I'll take it up with the membership and give you an answer, or I'll come to a meeting on the subject and have my say.' Pretty soon I began to be invited to meetings, and some of these guys now call me on the phone about things."

In this interview Gregory seemed interested in finding out what the townspeople thought of him as compared with Gary Stone, his senior in point of tenure in Regional City. On this point he said, "I still can't figure some of these birds. I'll be in a meeting with one of them. Maybe thirty minutes later I'll see him on the street and he'll act like he doesn't see me, especially if he is with another of those big knockers. Now Luke Street is not that way. [Street is a successful Republican corporation attorney.] Street is a real man. He'll come down the street with a couple of others and see me. He is just as like as not to wave them on and stop and talk for a few minutes. I've told my boys to vote Republican if they want to 'protest vote,' and I think Street has a lot to do with my ideas on the matter. Mostly we vote Democratic, but if we don't like a Democrat, we can protest by voting Republican. That scares the pants off some of these Democrats. It's a protest that counts."

Politically, Gregory has flirted with left-wing activities, but his swing to what he terms hard-boiled politics is summed up .

in the statement above. He is active in lobbying in the state legislature, but he is not as effective, according to his own admission, as Gary Stone, with whom he teams up on occasion. He describes his political activities as "behind the scenes."

Logically, perhaps, the next person to be described is a politician, per se. He is Truman Worth, a man who is the boss of a large suburban development, Websterville, lying in the metropolitan area of the community but outside of the legal jurisdiction of either the city or Hilldale County, in which Regional City is located. The county in which Websterville is located is a part of the congressional district in which Regional City has grown up. Because of the size of Websterville's population it can swing any closely contested congressional election one way or the other. Truman Worth is county treasurer of Websterville, a position in which he has gradually assumed many prerogatives of patronage such as job distribution and the letting of all governmental contracts for the county. He has several businesses of medium proportion on the side. He has been undisputed boss of Websterville for many years. He is a power in the state legislature, and because of his strategic position in proximity to Regional City, he actually has much to say concerning what will pass in the legislature which may be of interest to the city. No move is made on a metropolitan basis until Truman Worth has been consulted.

Regional City proper has no single boss so far as could be ascertained. No one man in the political field can dictate total policy. The larger economic interests may get together on things and by united action put across almost any project, but rarely, if ever, would any one of the "crowds" act alone.[1] Politically, Truman Worth comes about as near being a boss as anyone else in the community, but he does not exercise the kind of control over the whole metropolitan area that he does within his own bailiwick, Websterville. Worth is not very im-

1. The "crowds" are discussed in the next chapter.

aginative, to judge from the impression received of him and from what others say about him. He does hold a good deal of power in the community and for years has opposed any attempt to coordinate metropolitan services. He is thus of special interest, for this situation is what is called "controversial" in Regional City today.

Another sub-community leader is Calvert Smith. Mr. Smith is not a native-born citizen of Regional City, but he has lived in the community for more than fifty of his sixty-seven years of life. He is a Negro who has by his own efforts gained the confidence of his community, and he has secured a grudging respect from the white community leaders. He is a weekly news publisher and the leading Negro politician in Old State. He belongs to so many organizations that he "cannot conveniently remember them all." No meeting of any consequence in the Negro community is quite complete without a few words from Calvert Smith. He is a mild-mannered man with an immense capacity for concentrating on the words of any person who may be talking to him. He listens more than he talks, but when he does speak, he sums up the gist of a conversation with a penetrating question or an apt and helpful remark. He is a man of ample means, gradually accumulated over the years.

His enemies call him a radical leader. His friends characterize him as "militant but steady." He is prone to listen to both the radical and the conservative side of any question, and then come to an independent decision. If the question concerns racial matters, his decisions are liable to appear radical to the white community and conservative to some of his own people. He firmly believes that "segregation in all its forms must go," and he believes that the reform implied can be brought about by organizing the Negro people of Old State into a cohesive political unit. To achieve his ends, he has spent many years in travel, speechmaking, and committee work in Old State. He has contributed time and money to court battles waged in behalf of civil rights for Old State's largest minority group.

Both factions of Old State's one political party, called the Old Guard and the New Guard respectively, court Smith's favor. The Old Guard seeks his advice covertly, the New Guard more openly. It has been estimated that Smith "can swing fifty thousand votes in any state election," and when elections are closely contested or when several candidates in the primary elections split the vote badly, Smith's pocket voters, as they are called, may determine a winner. His balance of power in the state parallels that of Truman Worth in Regional City congressional elections. Smith and his Organized Voters, the state Negro political organization, are factors thoughtfully considered by "wise" politicians. This does not say that the "Negro question" is solved in Old State by any means, but there is growing recognition of its urgency.

Within the city limits of Regional City almost a third of the population are Negroes. Thousands of them are registered voters, and on issues which affect them directly they are prone to follow the Organized Voters' lead in their choice of candidates. Cries of "pocket voting" are always raised by the unfavored candidate, but this only tends to weld the Negro vote into a more solid expression of political strength. Everyone politically inclined is aware of the power of the Negro vote to swing elections within the city, and Smith gets unfeigned deference from the city's elected officials, as well as from many of the state politicians.

Calvert Smith is a Regional City leader. He is a man of influence. His power lies in his persuasion of his own group and his appeals to their group interests, rather than in the kind of coercive power that may be wielded by many of the white leaders. His publications help him to mould public opinion, and it is possible that he can displace any dissident factions which threaten his leadership; but still, relatively speaking, his power cannot be called coercive. The machinery of government is not at his command.

Two leaders of the larger community need to be mentioned in terms of popularity. Epworth Simpson is a popular leader. Samuel Farris is an unpopular leader. In Mr. Simpson's case his popularity stems from the fact that he was elected international president of one of the most esteemed luncheon clubs. Much fanfare was carried in the papers over his election to the international post. He was a comparatively young man, and his rise to national civic prominence was quite rapid. After World War II, Epworth Simpson's father began a backstage campaign for his veteran son's election to the presidency of International Goodfellows. Simpson's father has always been ambitious for his son, and one of the top leaders remarked, "Simpson has been running that boy of his for something since he was twelve years old!" Several informants were in doubt as to whether Epworth Simpson, Junior, or Senior, should be named as a leader. Most agreed that it should be the younger man, but they recognized that his father was behind him in his upward climb. The notion is prevalent that the younger man is being groomed for the governorship of Old State, but people have not quite made up their minds about him yet. "He needs a little more than he's got," say some. Others say, "Epworth Simpson may be a flash in the pan. He's got a lot to learn!" He evidently does not represent stable leadership, but his father holds a fairly high position in the Investment Company of Old State, and people of Regional City respect that. They are willing to "wait and see how young Simpson takes his honors."

Samuel Farris, the unpopular leader, is a man of enormous resources. He has made his money in buying and selling small businesses and has managed within the last two decades to move in on some of the most desirable business properties in

Regional City. His ways of doing business have not endeared him to the hearts of other Regional City leaders, but they have respect for his shrewdness and for his ruthless ways of getting what he goes after. Mr. Farris is a man somewhat uncouth in appearance, and "seems to care very little what others think of him." His ambition has been to make money by fair means or foul, as the townspeople put it. He has made money, and he occupies a position of leadership. He has helped others make money, as he has made it, with the exception of a few unpaid creditors, and he has been fairly generous with his "tax deductible monies" so far as local charitable contributions are concerned. He takes no active part in civic organizations but can be depended upon for substantial support in money terms "when the chips are down on any civic enterprise." His contributions do not, however, make him popular. In a certain sense they are "conscience monies that do not hurt Sam Farris," as one man put it. "He hates to see money part from him, whether to his creditors or to the government. If he is forced to part with it, he would rather see it stay in some local scheme than go all the way to Washington!" Neither the popular leader nor the unpopular leader represents stable leadership in the sense that the Parks family does.

Two more men will be described before turning to a brief summary statement on what Regional City leaders are like and before placing them in a structural pattern.

Cary Stokes is a young man who is getting ahead. His father could not help him to position in Regional City, as we have seen some other fathers do in this group of case profiles. Stokes's father was a small-town hardware merchant, who still operates his store a few miles from Regional City. The father is a religious fundamentalist who reared Cary to be an "upstanding young man." Cary took his training well and appears to be a conservative, capable, and trustworthy young fellow. He was trained in business administration at

Old State College and, after graduation, made a rather good business connection with an oil pipe line firm. He was popular both in and out of college and was quite a joiner. In the war years he was elected president of Old State Jolly Luncheon Clubs. During World War II he was given extra responsibilities by his company in war work with the government on a dollar-a-year basis. After the war he was made president of a firm which is a competitor of his original employer. Each thing he has done has won approbation, and he has been "taken in" to the over-all structure of power in the city. He is not a top man yet, but he is on the way. He is well liked. He may be called a stable, popular leader in contrast to Epworth Simpson. In 1947 Stokes ran for public office and rolled up a sizeable popular vote.

The last person to be portrayed is a professional man, not on our list of top leaders. He is an executive secretary of one of several civic planning associations in the community. His salary is nearly ten thousand dollars a year, which in Regional City is considered good for that kind of work. This man is Denny North. He is in his middle thirties. He has considerable following among the town's professional personnel and has some contact with a few of the top people in the community. His job is dependent, to some extent, upon his convincing the top structure, through intermediaries, that he is "all right," because many of the projects in his office are concerned with civic improvement, and the top leaders are watchful that no reformer or agitator be long in the job. Threatening experiences with two or three persons in the job, before North took it, have made the power leaders a little suspicious of any incumbent of this position, but they are convinced half-heartedly that the organization should be continued under careful supervision. The lack of trust on the part of the top leaders makes North uncomfortable at times, because he is hit from above and below. Regional City does need improvement in the areas which come under the planning jurisdiction of North's office, and he is constantly organizing citizens' groups to "study and remedy" conditions. Many of the conditions which need remedy are expensive propositions and are long held in abeyance by the men who could really make decisions to move toward solutions of the various problems. Objective study of housing conditions and other pressing social problems made by North and the professionals around him convinces him of the needs which should be met in the community, but it is a slow and painful process to get his ideas across to the right people. If he organizes too well, and sells his program too effectively, he is in danger of becoming what is known as a controversial figure in the community and of meeting the same fate as his predecessors who were considered reformers. His organization constantly runs afoul of real estate and other powerful interests. The volunteers upon whom he relies are fairly low in the power hierarchy; and, if violent disapproval of any proposed program of change is met, they are liable to run out, leaving North to hold the bag, as they have done on occasion in the past. The questions tackled by the agency are in many respects technical, and the planning process usually involves North's "taking volunteers along" on the technicalities; but final plans have to be drawn up by him. If the plans go sour at any point, North is liable to be blamed.

All of these pressures have made Denny North a cautious young man, and he feels impelled to give the appearance of being anxious to please. He is privately rebellious toward the superstructure of power in the community but likes the income from his job. He therefore does not come to open warfare on issues which are constantly arising. He feels keenly the burden and responsibilities of his office.

In a letter written to a close friend, soon after a local crisis in planning activities, he set down his feelings in the following way (changes made only to disguise places and identities of persons):

September, 1950

DEAR JOHN:

Things are simmering here. The difficulty is not personal—but you know the suspicion which planning evokes in certain quarters —in Georgetown, Regional City, and I daresay everywhere else in this free nation of ours. I remember swearing never to get back into this kind of agency again—that was in Georgetown in 1942. Well, I'm still of the same opinion; no money can quite compensate for the tensions and anxieties which this job provokes. The thing becomes personal in that the general suspicion of what the agency tries to do deteriorates into suspicion of you personally. One never knows what the correct course is—whether to fight for social principles and face the loss of budget for the agency, or "knuckle under" and compromise the principles in order to retain the opportunity to fight again and under better circumstances. Of course, you know which course I prefer; but the former course requires some support, and in Regional City I'm afraid we're woefully lacking in agency executives with professional attainments or a "sense of profession." In a crisis, the "professionals" (so-called) will drop off, just as they have always done.

We are being compelled, in effect, to move into the Harvester building—and the whole project is unsavory from the start to the finish and involves an ultimate threat to the independence of our agency. You move or you are "uncooperative" and face a sure budget slash. That's the situation. Under the circumstances, you can perhaps draw a big sigh of relief that you're not here.

The lot of the liberal is becoming increasingly hazardous, involving personal trials and deprivations. One tries to avoid discussion of world and domestic events these days, because only complete and perfect unanimity of opinions is permitted. To question or to criticize is to be traitorous. The kids asked me the other day about telling the truth. What can one say? To tell the truth throughout life is to subject oneself to all manner of difficulties and indignities. One has to learn how to lie—which includes telling part of the truth only, not all the truth as one sees it—in order to survive economically if one is in a position such as this is. Sometimes it seems to me that the most desirable status one can ever achieve in this culture is that condition of independence which will permit one to call the shots as he sees them. I know you've done a lot of thinking on this problem. Perhaps one day you can write something on it. . . .

I'm enclosing some clippings on sundry odds and ends. We now have two kids in school. Harry will enter next year. Let me know if anything turns up in research or allied fields which would be of interest to me and where I could make a contribution. Given the right kind of opportunity, I would leave here rather quickly. Give my regards to the family—we long to see them all again. Write when you can.

Yours,
(signed) DENNY

Denny North is one of the under-structure professionals as contrasted with the upper-structure. His position is a relatively unstable one, even to the point that he feels the need for moving on. Professionals in civic jobs seem prone to be nomadic; and North has reached a point in his thinking when anywhere else looks better to him than Regional City. He has worked in several other cities, and his moves have stemmed, in at least two instances, from dissatisfaction with his role in community life. The professionals in Regional City, in their social gatherings, are rather likely to discuss their frustrations and dissatisfactions in terms of hopeless or resigned despair. Much of their discussion centers around disparaging remarks concerning the powers that be and the feeling that they have little opportunity to help in matters of community policy and decision, in which they feel they have definite contributions to make. Many of the professionals may be termed intellectuals, in a broad sense of the word.

Harold Farmer, a lawyer, has some contact with these professionals. He says of them: "I sometimes think they ought to go to work at something else rather than the 'do-good' stuff they engage in. Some of the things they do are just downright silly. They are always out to raise money for some fool thing, and half the time it's something to keep these guys in a job. They get on the 'hind teat' and won't let go. But it *is* the *hind* teat, mind you. Some of them are smart enough, and if they were in honest work they would make a lot better living, and best of all they would stop pestering people!"

He went on to cite as examples a man and his wife who are both engaged in social work in the community and who have moved from one activity to another within the town. Currently one of them is engaged in raising funds for one of the many health agencies that have sprung up in Regional City in recent years. The other is "fighting juvenile delinquency." Before taking on these obligations they were active in sponsoring a home for young girls. They make a modest living at whatever they do, and they get support for their various projects. Not all men in Regional City feel about them the way Farmer does.

There is, however, a definite distinction drawn between this under-structure of professional personnel and the upper-structure. The professionals in the civic and welfare associations feel the distinction and react to it in a variety of ways, often by withdrawal and consequent movement to another community where they hope conditions will be more favorable. In contrast, though upper leaders may drop out of positions of power, this fact alone does not entail removal from the city. For example, Epworth Simpson may not become an outstanding leader when the flurry of his present success in attaining national recognition is over, but he will more than likely retain a secure economic base in the city. His father's position makes that probable, and his own position is not one which is easily threatened if he behaves with a fair degree of conformity to the customs of the community. But members of the professional under-structure do not usually have community roots in either family background or economic security. They are dependent upon salaries, which may be terminated almost immediately or at best within a year's time.

Out of the fourteen professionals interviewed, only one was born in Regional City. Two were born in the state, five in the region, and the remaining six were born outside the region, one in a foreign country. None is financially independent. Three have savings bonds or other small investments. Twelve are paying off mortgages on small homes. In the top leadership group questioned on economic assets, twenty-five out of twenty-seven persons giving such information own farms and other real estate, over and above their own homes, or they own stocks and bonds, the major portion of a large business, or other investments, as the case may be. Thus the differentiation in economic status is apparent as between the professionals and the top leaders.

Another measure of difference may be gained from listing the number of persons under the immediate supervision or direction of the top leaders and comparing these figures with those for the professionals (Table 1). With the exception of only two professional persons, less than fifty individuals are under their direct control and supervision in an employment situation. In the top-leadership group many control hundreds and even several thousand employees. The difference in power between the two groups is obvious, if we take as a definition of power the ability of men to move goods and services toward goals designated by persons of authority. At least, within the realm of everyday work, the top leaders can move more men than the professionals, and their resources would indicate an ability to move goods as well.

To sum up the matter of what kind of men the leaders are, it is first of all clear that such descriptions of the leaders as have been given are only a part of the story that needs to be told about community power structure. The purpose of these descriptions, as mentioned earlier, has been to add human

TABLE 1

NUMBER OF PERSONS UNDER DIRECT ADMINISTRATIVE CONTROL
OF LEADERS IN REGIONAL CITY, 1950-51

Number Employed	Top Leaders	Professionals in Civic and Welfare Associations
Less than 50	7	11
50-99	1	1
100-149	0	0
150-199	1	1
200-249	2	0
250-299	1	0
300-349	2	0
350-399	0	0
400-499	1	0
500-999	2	0
1000-1999	4	1
2000-2999	0	0
3000-3999	0	0
4000-4999	3	0
5000 and over *	3	0
All leaders	27	14

* Two of these men have more than 50,000 employees under their administrative control.

interest to the structure of power in Regional City and to the placing of these men in their structural relationships. It has seemed undesirable to discuss such men without giving some account of their actions, but the actions used for illustration have obviously been of a random nature. The following chapter will tie together some of the relationships of these men into a clearer pattern as we turn to a closer scrutiny of the structural relationships of power personnel in Regional City.

4 THE STRUCTURE OF POWER IN REGIONAL CITY

O NE of the first tasks in making a theoretical analysis of the community is that of delimiting and defining it as a structure.[1] The task of delimitation may take into account four basic elements, namely (1) personnel (members), (2) test(s) of admission and membership, (3) distinctive roles or functions of the members, and (4) norms regulating the conduct of the personnel.[2] The physical limits of the structure with which this study is concerned have been set, or at least an awareness of such limits has been indicated. We shall presently be concerned with all of the elements suggested here, and most particularly with the first three, but only in relation to a segment of the community—the power element. The fourth item, norms regulating conduct within the community of Regional City, presents problems with which the present study does not deal, except in a passing fashion. All of the norms of behavior of power personnel in Regional City are not known, but some specifications of men which may indicate norms will be outlined.

The personnel with which the current discussion is concerned represents but a minute fraction of the community in which it moves and functions. It does represent a definite

1. E. T. Hiller, "The Community as a Social Group," *American Sociological Review*, VI (April 1941), 191-92.
2. *Ibid.*, p. 189.

group, however, and a very important one in Regional City. No pretense is made that the group to be discussed represents the totality of power leaders of the community, but it is felt that a representative case sample is presented, and that the men described come well within the range of the center of power in the community.

It will be recalled that the leaders selected for study were secured from lists of leading civic, professional, and fraternal organizations, governmental personnel, business leaders, and "society" and "wealth" personnel suggested by various sources. These lists of more than 175 persons were rated by "judges" who selected by mutual choice the top forty persons in the total listings. These forty were the object of study and investigation in Regional City. Some data were collected about the total number. Twenty-seven members of the group were interviewed on the basis of a prepared schedule plus additional questions as the investigation proceeded. Any figures used in the study will need to be tied fairly rigidly to the twenty-seven members on whom there are comparable data. Thirty-four Negro citizens are included in the study, and this group will be discussed later. The fourteen under-structure professionals in civic and social work who were interviewed have also provided data which may be considered comparable.

The top leaders, the under-structure professionals, and the Negro community leaders represent community groups. They are identifiable groups. Since they are definitely groups, I shall rely to a considerable extent, in this portion of the discussion, upon George C. Homans for certain hypotheses he has put forward on group structure.[3]

The system of power groups which is being examined may not be called a closed system. The groups are links in a total pattern, which may offer suggestive clues to total power patterns in the operating system of Regional City. There are gaps in the power arc which investigation may not be able to close.

3. *The Human Group* (New York: Harcourt, Brace and Company, 1950).

Actually the discussion here is primarily concerned with the structuring of power on a policy-making level. Only a rudimentary "power pyramid" of Regional City will be presented. One may be content to do this because I doubt seriously that power forms a single pyramid with any nicety in a community the size of Regional City. There are *pyramids* of power in this community which seem more important to the present discussion than *a* pyramid. Let me illustrate this point.

In the interviews, Regional City leaders were asked to choose ten top leaders from the basic list of forty. The choices of the twenty-seven persons answering this question showed considerable unanimity of opinion. One leader received twenty-one votes out of a possible twenty-seven. Other leaders received nearly as many votes. Some received no votes at all. One could pyramid the forty leaders on the basis of the votes cast for them, as has been done in Table 2, but the pyramid is not a true expression of the existing relationships between the top leaders of the community. George Delbert, for example, was chosen eight times more than Charles Homer, and Homer is consequently six places down the scale from Delbert. Delbert is considered a "big man" in Regional City affairs, but he is not as big as Homer, according to most of the informants in answer to the simple question, "Who is the 'biggest' man in town?"

The question on which Delbert came to the top of the voting poll was phrased, "If a project were before the community that required *decision* by a group of leaders—leaders that nearly everyone would accept—which *ten* on the list of forty would you choose?" Delbert came out on top in this question, but not on the one related to who is the biggest man in town. Thus the pyramid scheme suggested by the voting poll of leaders, related to making projects move, must be modified in relation to the factors which weigh in Homer's favor in other areas related to power. Quite possibly some of these factors are Homer's wealth, his social position, and his

TABLE 2

REGIONAL CITY LEADERS RANKED ACCORDING TO NUMBER OF VOTES
RECEIVED FROM OTHER LEADERS IN LEADERSHIP POLL *

Leaders	Number of Votes
George Delbert	21
Cary Stokes	19
Ray Moster	18
Peter Barner	17
James Treat	15
Fargo Dunham	14
Charles Homer	13
Adam Graves, Joseph Hardy, Luke Street, Harry Parker, Jack Williams	12
Avery Spear	11
Elsworth Mines	10
Percy Latham	9
Mabel Gordon, Arthur Tarbell	5
Truman Worth, Edna Moore, Mark Parks	4
Harvey Aiken, Epworth Simpson, Bert Tidwell, Grover Smith, Edward Stokes	3
Phillip Gould, Harold Farmer, Brenda Howe, Gary Stone, Ralph Spade, Herman Schmidt	2
John Webster, Samuel Farris, Norman Trable, Claudia Mills, Horace Black, Howard Rake	1
Hetty Fairly, Gloria Stevens, Russell Gregory	0

* Code numbers used in analyzing data and corresponding to fictional names of leaders are as follows:

1. Latham	14. Delbert	28. Mills
2. Graves	15. Farris	29. Spade
3. Dunham	16. Stevens	30. Gregory
4. Mines	17. Trable	31. Parker
5. Smith	18. Schmidt	32. Williams
6. Fairly	19. Moore	33. Black
7. Webster	20. Farmer	34. Tidwell
8. Worth	21. Barner	35. Tarbell
9. C. Stokes	22. Parks	36. Moster
10. Stone	23. Gould	37. Treat
11. Simpson	24. E. Stokes	38. Street
12. Aiken	25. Gordon	39. Rake
13. Howe	26. Spear	40. Homer
	27. Hardy	

business position. Homer is from an old family of wealth in Regional City. He is the wealthiest man in the community according to most reports. He is chairman of the board of the community's largest industry in volume of sales. Delbert, on the other hand, is the president of a large corporation but is a salaried man—with a very large reputed salary. There is a distinction made between salaried personnel and owners of enterprises in Regional City whether the salary be large or small. Delbert's family background is also not comparable to Homer's.

This is not to say that Delbert is not a powerful man. He is. He can command the services of more than 50,000 employees, and he has a very large voice in community matters—a larger voice perhaps than Homer's, since he uses it oftener. Delbert is willing to serve on top-flight community committees and boards. Homer is not. Homer says of himself, "I will work on no boards or committees. I work entirely through other men." His attitude on this matter is well known in the community, and consequently he was chosen fewer times than Delbert on the question under discussion. In spite of his methods of work he was chosen by almost half the men voting on the question.

The validity of the question concerning who might be chosen to "decide" on a community project cannot be measured purely in terms of a pyramid-structuring. Its validity for this study lies in the fact that the question determined, in some degree, "how near the center" this group was that could "move things" in the affairs of the community. Each man interviewed was asked to add names of persons he considered as powerful as or more powerful than the men listed. Sixty-four names were added to the list. Thirty-seven of the additional names were mentioned but once by informants. Sixteen were mentioned twice; five, three times; five, four times; and one, five times. Eleven informants added names, but there was general agreement that the list was a fairly comprehensive one as it stood, with the exceptions mentioned.

The high consensus regarding the top leaders on the list of forty, plus the lack of any concerted opinion on additional individuals, would indicate that the men being interviewed represented at least a nucleus of a power grouping.

The question was also put to interviewees, "How many men would need to be involved in a major community project in Regional City 'to put it over'?" The answers to this question varied from, "You've got the men right here on this list—maybe ten of them," to "fifty or a hundred." One informant said, "Some of the men on this list would undoubtedly be in on getting the project started. After it got moving, perhaps six hundred men might be involved either directly or indirectly." This was the largest figure any informant gave. The informant elaborated on the answer by saying that a large fund-raising campaign was the thing he had in mind, and he illustrated the point by speaking of a fund drive for a hospital building program that had recently been completed in Regional City. He said that he could count the men on his hands who had "sparked" the drive, but hundreds of volunteers had been used from the civic associations and the general community to "put the drive over the top." He felt that any project for civic improvement would likely involve the same type of organization.

In the above illustration of structured action, the "men of independent decision" are a relatively small group. The "executors of policy" may run into the hundreds. This pattern of a relatively small decision-making group working through a larger under-structure is a reality, and if data were available, the total personnel involved in a major community project might possibly form a pyramid of power, but the constituency of the pyramid would change according to the project being acted upon.

In other words, the personnel of the pyramid would change depending upon what needs to be done at a particular time. Ten men might, for example, decide to bring a new industry into the community. Getting the industry physically established and operating might take the disciplined and coordinated action of a few more men or several hundred men, depending on the size of the project. Some of the same decision men in another instance might be involved in starting a program for some local governmental change, but another group of men would be involved in carrying out the decisions reached. Both projects are power orientated, but each requires different personnel in the execution. The men in the under-structure may have a multiplicity of individual roles within the totality of the community structure which can be set in motion by the men of decision.

As I became familiar with the list of forty names through the interviewing process, it became evident that certain men, even within the relatively narrow range of decision leaders with whom I was dealing, represented a top layer of personnel. Certain men were chosen more frequently than others, not only in relation to who should be chosen to decide on a project, as has already been indicated, but the same men interacted together on committees and were on the whole better known to each other than to those outside this group. Through analyzing the mutual choices made by those interviewed, it will be shown that there is an *esprit de corps* among certain top leaders, and some of them may be said to operate on a very high level of decision in the community; but this will not necessarily mean that one of the top leaders can be considered subordinate to any other in the community as a whole. On specific projects one leader may allow another to carry the ball, as a leader is said to do when he is "out front" on a project which interests him. On the next community-wide project another may carry the ball. Each may subordinate himself to another on a temporary basis, but such a structure of subordination is quite fluid, and it is voluntary.

In a scale of mutual choices among twenty of the top leaders (that is, when two leaders chose each other in the leadership poll), there is indication of a selective process in leadership choices made by the men of decision. Again, these choices were made on the basis of "who might best decide on a project." The fact that the mutual choices remain well within the upper limits of the ranking scale (Table 2) indicates definite selectivity.

A sociogram, adapted from Lundberg and Lawsing's work in a Vermont community, was constructed to show graphically the interrelationships of the choices indicated in Table 3.[4] The Vermont study indicated "friendship choices" made by 256 persons interviewed and showed in sociometric form both single and mutual choices of friends of the respondents.[5] Our sociogram shows only the mutual choices among forty persons who were asked to choose ten top leaders from the list of forty. Figures 2 through 5, to follow, are drawn from data collected from twenty-seven of the total list of forty. With one exception,[6] the leaders receiving a high number of votes as

TABLE 3

LEADERSHIP AS DETERMINED BY NUMBERS OF
MUTUAL CHOICES AMONG 40 POWER LEADERS

Leaders	Number of Mutual Choices
Delbert, Hardy	6
Barner, Moster, Street, Dunham	5
Graves, Homer, Mines, Williams	4
Latham, Tidwell	3
Parker, E. Stokes Parks, Spade, Stone, Tarbell, Webster	1

leaders were interviewed, and scheduled data were gathered from them. The group receiving the largest number of votes will be designated an upper-limits group in contradistinction

4. George A. Lundberg and Margaret Lawsing, "The Sociography of Some Community Relations," *American Sociological Review*, II (June 1937), 318-35.

5. *Ibid.*, pp. 328-29.

6. This man was out of the city for an extended period working with the Federal Government on defense mobilization plans.

to a lower-limits group which received fewer votes from the leaders interviewed. Mutual choices of leaders are shown only among the twenty-seven persons interviewed and do not in-

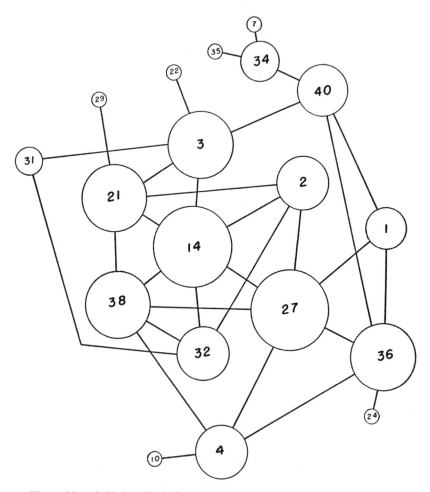

Fig. 2. Mutual Choices Made by Leaders in Regional City Leadership Poll. (Each circle represents a leader involved in one or more mutual choices with another leader. Size of the circle in each instance indicates a relative number of choices received by the individual leader. For key to numbers, see footnote to Table 2, p. 63.)

clude their choices among the forty leaders. The sociogram of the mutual choices of twenty-seven leaders is illustrated in Figure 2.[7] The usefulness of the sociogram lies in the fact that it does indicate that the leaders who were most frequently

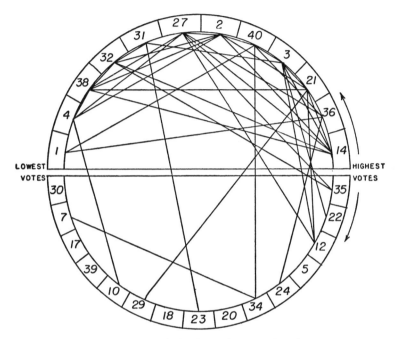

Fig. 3. Mutual Choices of 27 Leaders in Regional City Leadership Poll. (For key to numbers, see footnote to Table 2, p. 63.)

chosen as the very top leaders tended to choose one another more frequently than they chose persons who received the fewest number of votes. Aside from this point, the sociogram was not found to be particularly useful.

The principal objection to the sociogram may be illustrated in this way: Number 14, George Delbert, in the sociogram

7. The numbers used in all figures correspond to code numbers used in analyzing data.

may be considered the "star," since he has the highest number of mutual choices. However, the study of Regional City was convincing on the point that number 40, Charles Homer, was

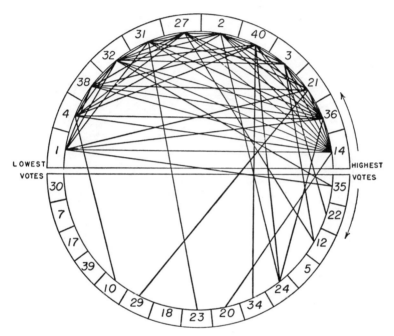

Fig. 4. All Choices of Upper-Limits Group of 12 Leaders in Leadership Poll. (For key to numbers, see footnote to Table 2, p. 63.)

the more powerful man. Thus the same objection obtains that was found to hold true in pyramiding the total votes cast for all leaders. It was also felt that any one of the men who surround the "star," number 14, could be just as powerful and influential in initiating and carrying through a particular project in the community. The sociogram does not show a true working relationship between the persons described. F. Stuart Chapin, in discussing "star isolates," has voiced some of the same objections.[8] The dimension of status is lacking in the flat-surfaced sociogram presented.

The leaders named in mutual choices as indicated in Table 3 do, however, represent a majority in the upper limits of the

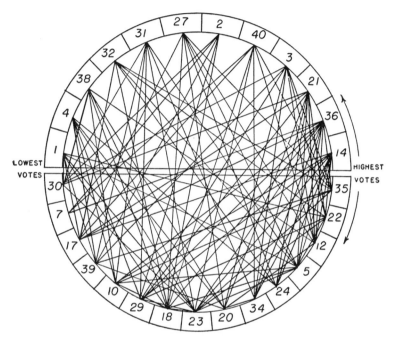

Fig. 5. All Choices of Lower-Limits Group of 15 Leaders in Leadership Poll. (For key to numbers, see footnote to Table 2, p. 63.)

group of forty men and women in the Regional City decision-leader group. By using this group as an upper-limits group, and comparing it with the remaining leaders interviewed in relation to committee interaction, the hard core of leadership represented by the former group may be shown more clearly. And for clarity, it may be repeated that here an attempt is

8. "Sociometric Star Isolates," *American Journal of Sociology*, LVI (November 1950), 263-67.

being made to isolate decision leaders from other elements of personnel in the community, in order that they may be discussed as a structural grouping.

In order to present another visual picture of the differentiation of choices among the leadership group interviewed, Figures 3, 4, and 5 have been prepared.[9] The top half of the circle in each figure shows by code number those leaders who received the highest number of votes from other leaders for their position as a leader. The bottom half of the circle shows the leaders who received the lowest number of leadership choices.

Figure 3 represents the mutual choices among all leaders responding to the question on this item. It may be clearly seen that most of the mutual choices occur among members of the upper-limits group. This clustering of choices obtains also in Figure 4, in which all choices of the upper-limits group of leaders are shown. Relatively few times did the top leaders go outside the upper-limits group to choose leaders. Contrariwise, Figure 5 shows that the lower-limits group often looked to the upper group in choosing top leaders.

The question was also asked each person interviewed, "Indicate how many persons (in the list of forty) you have worked with on committees within the past five years?" The upper-limits group indicated that they had worked with an average of twenty-nine persons on the list. The lower-limits group indicated that they had worked with an average of only twenty-one persons on the list. The professional under-structure of civil and social workers were asked the same question and indicated that they had worked with an average of only ten persons on the list. There is a definite drop, therefore, in the rate of interaction between each of the three groups and the group of forty leaders. Each group has access to the other, but those in the upper-limits group are in contact with other

9. These figures were adapted from schematic diagrams used by Seymour Louis Wolfbein in depicting "interlocking directorates" in a field study of a mill community. See Wolfbein, *The Decline of a Cotton Textile City* (New York: Columbia University Press, 1944), pp. 93-95.

leaders more frequently, in committee work, at least. The under-structure professionals, with few exceptions, interact with persons immediately above them and with other professionals close to them in the power scale.

Another index used to discover the degree of relationship existing between the leaders interviewed and the total group of forty leaders was based upon a question which asked, on a six-point scale, how well known each person on the list of forty was to the interviewee. The scale read: "How well do you know each person (on the list of forty): (1) related_____, (2) know socially_____, (3) know well_____, (4) know slightly_____, (5) heard of him_____, (6) not known_____." By again utilizing the upper-limits and lower-limits groups of leaders, and through comparison of these two groups with the professional under-structure personnel, we see a definite differentiation between the groups. In order not to present too confusing an array of figures, we shall indicate only the average number of persons known well or better in each group.

The upper-limits group knew well or better an average of thirty-four persons in the list of forty. The lower-limits group of top leaders knew an average of 28.7 leaders well or better. The professional under-structure averaged only 7.3 persons for this same degree of acquaintance. Obviously the upper-structure is better acquainted with the total group of top leaders, in addition to having a higher rate of committee interaction with this same group. The professional persons who carry out the decisions of the policy-making group are definitely differentiated from the top leaders in rates of interaction and in degree of acquaintance with the top leaders.

Our rudimentary statistical conclusions on the degrees of relationship among the persons named were borne out in qualitative interviewing. Over and over, the same persons were named as influential and consequently able to "move things" in Regional City. The significance of a high degree of interaction is suggested by Homans' hypothesis, "The more nearly equal in social rank a number of men are, the more frequently they will interact with one another." [10] Our findings bear out this hypothesis.

One other index was used to determine how closely integrated the upper-limits group was in relation to the lower-limits group. By ranking the leaders according to the number of leadership choices received from other leaders and analyzing how far up the scale or how far down the scale each went in making his choice, one finds a differentiating picture of the two groups. Members of the upper-limits group would go both up and down the scale from their own position in their choices, but not very far. They would go up an average of 5.4 places. They would go down an average of 4.9 places in their choices. These figures indicate a tendency to choose persons as leaders who are fairly close to the choosers in the scale.

The lower-limits personnel, on the other hand, tended almost entirely to choose men above them in rank. They would go up the scale an average of 13.1 places, and would go down only 0.6 places in their choices. It would seem from this evidence that the under group defers to the upper group, and that there is some solidarity in the upper echelons of policy-makers.

As shown earlier, power has been defined in terms of policy leadership, and the data given in the present chapter make a beginning at defining structural power relations. A group of men have been isolated who are among the most powerful in Regional City. It has been shown that they interact among themselves on community projects and select one another as leaders. Their relations with one another are not encompassed in a true pyramid of power, but some degree of ranking, even in the top-level policy leadership group, has been indicated. Let us now look at policy personnel patterns in another way.

In sizing up any individual one often asks, "What do you do for a living?" The reply to this question allows one rather

10. *Op. cit.*, p. 184.

quickly to rank another in a rough scale of social values. The men under discussion hold commercial, industrial, financial, and professional positions in Regional City that tend to classify them in the minds of any observer. In order to make a beginning at seeing the relations among the men of power in more personal terms than statistics will allow, let us examine a list of positions held by some of the leaders of the policy-determining group in Regional City (Table 4).

It can be seen at a glance that most of the leaders hold positions as presidents of companies, chairmen of boards, or professional positions of some prestige. Generally speaking, the companies represented in the listing are of major enterprise proportions. More than half the men may be said to be businessmen, if the term is used broadly. The major economic interests of the community are overwhelmingly represented in the listing. The pattern of business dominance of civic affairs in Regional City is a fact. No other institution is as dominant in community life as the economic institution, and this phenomenon will be dealt with at greater length under an appropriate heading.

Figure 6 represents those leaders who are related to one another as directors on boards of corporate enterprises in Regional City. The figure is intended to show that the economic interests of the leaders are in some measure coordinate. Again, one cannot rely too heavily upon a schematic diagram to understand the interrelations of leadership patterns, but such configurations as have been shown cumulatively tend to lend credence to the fact that there are structural relations among the members of the leadership group. All interviews with leaders helped to fill in some of the structural gaps. The sources of data for this figure give only a partial sample of existing corporate board relationships. Comparable data could be obtained only from fifteen out of the total leadership group of forty.

One of the first interviews had in Regional City was with

TABLE 4

Policy-Making Leaders in Regional City by Occupational Position

Type of Occupation	Name of Leader	Name of Organizational Affiliation	Position
Banking, Finance, Insurance	Hardy	Investment Company of Old State	President
	Mines	Producer's Investments	President
	Schmidt	First Bank	President
	Simpson	Second Bank	Vice-President
	Spade	Growers Bank	President
	Tarbell	Commercial Bank	Executive Vice-President
	Trable	Regional City Life	President
Commercial	Aiken	Livestock Company	Chairman, Board
	Black	Realty Company of Regional City	President
	Delbert	Allied Utilities	President
	Dunham	Regional Gas Heat Company	General Manager
	Graves	Refrigeration, Incorporated	President
	Parker	Mercantile Company	Executive Manager
	Parks	Paper Box Company	Chairman, Board
	Smith	Cotton Cloth Company	Manager
	C. Stokes	Oil Pipe Line Company	President
	Webster	Regional City Publishing Company	Managing Editor
	Williams	Mercantile Company	Chairman, Board
Government	Barner	City Government	Mayor
	Gordon	City Schools	Superintendent
	Rake	County Schools	Superintendent
	Worth	County Government	Treasurer
Labor	Gregory	Local Union	President
	Stone	Local Union	President
Leisure	Fairly	None	Social Leader
	Howe	None	Social Leader
	Mills	None	Social Leader
	Moore	None	Social Leader
	Stevens	None	Social Leader
Manufacture and Industry	Farris	Steel Spool Company	Chairman, Board
	Homer	Homer Chemical Company	Chairman, Board
	Spear	Homer Chemical Company	President
	E. Stokes	Stokes Gear Company	Chairman, Board
	Treat	Southern Yarn Company	President
Professional *	Farmer	Law Firm	Attorney
	Gould	Law Firm	Attorney
	Latham	Private Office	Dentist
	Moster	Law Firm	Attorney
	Street	Law Firm	Attorney
	Tidwell	Law Firm	Attorney

* Attorneys' affiliations not given. Without exception they are corporation lawyers.

James Treat of the Southern Yarn Company. He gave a great deal of information concerning power relations in the community. Among other things, he supplied a clue to certain

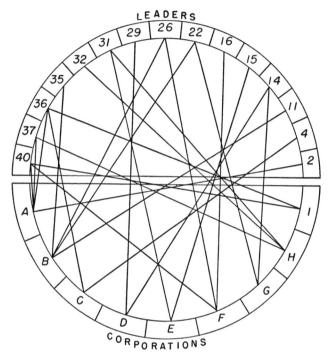

Fig. 6. Interlocking Directorates of Corporate Leaders in Regional City. (For key to numbers, see footnote to Table 2, p. 63.)

existing clique relationships and considerable information about them which was later verified. Several times in his conversation he had used the term "crowds" in describing how certain men acted in relation to each other on community projects, and he was asked to explain the term. His reply ran in this vein:

"I simply mean that there are 'crowds' in Regional City— several of them—that pretty well make the big decisions. There is the crowd I belong to (the Homer Chemical crowd); then there is the First State Bank crowd—the Regional Gas Heat crowd—the Mercantile crowd—the Growers Bank crowd—and the like."

Mr. Treat was asked to give the names of some of the men who were active in each crowd, and he said:

"Sure! The biggest man in our crowd is Charles Homer. I belong to his crowd along with John Webster, Bert Tidwell, Ray Moster, Harold Jones, James Finer, Larry Stroup, and Harold Farmer. There are others, but they would be on the edges of this crowd. These would be the ones to be brought in on anything.

"In the State Bank crowd there would be Herman Schmidt, Harvey Aiken, Mark Parks, and Joseph Hardy. Schmidt used to be the biggest man in that crowd, but young Hardy is coming up fast over there.

"In the Regional Gas Heat crowd there is Fargo Dunham, Elsworth Mines, Gilbert Smith, and Percy Latham maybe. George Delbert might be said to belong to that crowd, but he is a pretty independent fellow. He moves around [from crowd to crowd] quite a bit.

"The Mercantile crowd is made up of Harry Parker, Jack Williams, Luke Street, Adam Graves, Cary Stokes, and Epworth Simpson.

"The Growers Bank crowd would be Ralph Spade, Arthur Tarbell, and Edward Stokes. They are kind of a weak outfit, but they come in on a lot of things. Spade is probably the most aggressive of the lot, but he's not too much at that!"

With this information given, Mr. Treat was asked to tell how these crowds would operate in relation to one another on a community-wide project, and he outlined the procedure very clearly. This type of action will be given in fuller detail in connection with the techniques of power wielding, but it may be said here that representatives from each crowd are drawn into any discussion relative to a major community decision.

Each man mentioned as belonging to a crowd also belongs to a major business enterprise within the community—at least the clique leader does. His position within the bureaucratic structure of his business almost automatically makes him a community leader, if he wishes to become one. The test for admission to this circle of decision-makers is almost wholly a man's position in the business community in Regional City. The larger business enterprises represent pyramids of power in their own right, as work units within the community, and the leaders within these concerns gather around them some of the top personnel within their own organization. They then augment this nucleus of leadership by a coterie of selected friends from other establishments to form knots of interest called "crowds" by Mr. Treat. The outer edges of any crowd may pick up such men as Percy Latham, the dentist, who in turn picks up others in relation to any specific activity in which the crowd may be interested. The top men in any crowd tend to act together, and they depend upon men below them to serve as intermediaries in relation to the general community.

The crowds described by Mr. Treat were also mentioned by numerous other informants. These crowds did not, however, exhaust the possibilities of clique relations within the larger group of policy leaders. Twenty-one distinct groupings were picked up within the forty persons on the list, as the study proceeded, but the crowds mentioned by Treat seemed to be the most generally recognized groupings. Several of the top leaders within the crowds would "clear with each other" informally on many matters. The older men, as mentioned earlier, tended to get their heads together on most matters, as did the younger group, but such relationships were not completely stable. Each man at the top of a "crowd pyramid" depended upon those close to him in business to carry out decisions when made. An older man, for example, could not command another older man to do something, but within his own crowd there would be a hierarchy he could put to work.

In most instances decision-making tended to be channeled through the older men at some point in the process of formulation, but many things may be done on the initiative of any combination of several powerful leaders in the crowds named. None of the leaders indicated that he could work alone on any big project, nor did any feel that there was any man in the community with such power. The individual power leader is dependent on others in Regional City in contrast to mill or mining company towns where one man or one family may dominate the community actions which take place.

Society prestige and deference to wealth are not among the primary criteria for admission to the upper ranks of the decision-makers according to the study of Regional City. The persons who were included in the listing of forty top leaders purely on the basis of their wealth or society connections did not, with three or four exceptions, make the top listing of persons who might be called upon to "put across a community project." As has been mentioned before, a distinction is made between persons of wealth and social prestige who engage in work and those who do not. The persons of wealth are perhaps important in the social structure of the community as symbolic persons. They may be followed in matters of fashion and in their general manner of living. Their money may be important in financing a given project, but they are not of themselves doers. They may only be called decisive in the sense that they can withhold or give money through others to change the course of action of any given project. Gloria Stevens spends large sums of money on Regional City projects, but the expenditures are made through her lawyer, Ray Moster. She does not interact with any of the top leaders whom we interviewed, other than Moster, so far as could be ascertained. Hetty Fairly, another woman of wealth, spends her charitable monies through a foundation handled by a lawyer not on the list of leaders. The lawyers may be vigilant in serving the interests of their clients in both instances, and a part of the vigilance exercised is in keeping abreast of possible tax incursions on the "frozen wealth" of the foundations. In this there may be some connection with power, but it is rather obscure in terms of the definition of power as being the ability of persons to move goods and services toward defined goals. If there is power in the charitable foundation structures, it resides in the lawyers who operate them, rather than in the donors who are largely inactive in the affairs of the foundations.

Political eminence cannot be said to be a sole criterion for entry into the policy echelons of Regional City's life, generally speaking. The two exceptions to this statement are embodied in Mayor Barner and County Treasurer Truman Worth. Both Barner and Worth were successful businessmen before becoming involved in local politics to the point of seeking public office. Their interests may be said to be primarily business in the strict sense of the word. Both have a popular following that has kept them in office, but their close associates are businessmen. Mayor Barner had only one picture in his office—that of Charles Homer, the biggest businessman in the community. Both Barner and Worth look to businessmen constantly for advice before they make a move on any project concerning the whole community. Furthermore, they do not ordinarily "move out front" on any project themselves, but rather follow the lead of men like Delbert, Graves, or any one of the other leaders of particular crowds.

The point made at this turn of the discussion is not a new one. Businessmen are the community leaders in Regional City as they are in other cities. Wealth, social prestige, and political machinery are functional to the wielding of power by the business leaders in the community. William E. Henry puts the matter this way:

The business executive is the central figure in the economic and social life of the United States. His direction of business enterprise and his participation in informal social groupings give him a significant place in community life. In both its economic and its social aspects the role of the business executive is sociologically a highly visible one.[11]

The "visibility" suggested by Henry is a highly applicable concept in connection with an analysis of Regional City leadership. One need not labor the point. This study has already shown that business leaders take a prominent position in Regional City civic affairs.

In the general social structure of community life social scientists are prone to look upon the institutions and formal associations as powerful forces, and it is easy to be in basic agreement with this view. Most institutions and associations are subordinate, however, to the interests of the policy-makers who operate in the economic sphere of community life in Regional City. The institutions of the family, church, state, education, and the like draw sustenance from economic institutional sources and are thereby subordinate to this particular institution more than any other. The associations stand in the same relationship to the economic interests as do the institutions. We see both the institutions and the formal associations playing a vital role in the execution of determined policy, but the formulation of policy often takes place outside these formalized groupings. Within the policy-forming groups the economic interests are dominant.

The economic institution in Regional City, in drawing around itself many of the other institutions in the community, provides from within itself much of the personnel which may be considered of primary influence in power relationships. A lengthy discussion on institutions per se is not proposed. Their existence as channels through which policy may be funneled up and down to broader groups of people than those represented by the top men of power is easily recognized. Some of the institutions would represent imperfect channels for power transmission, however. For example, the family as an institution

11. "The Business Executive: The Psycho-Dynamics of a Social Role," *American Journal of Sociology*, LIV (January 1949), 286.

is not a channel of itself for bringing about general community agreement on such a matter as the desirability of building a new bridge across Regional River. On the other hand, the church might represent a more potent force on this question. The preacher could preach a sermon on the matter in any given church, and the members could sign petitions, attend meetings at the behest of the church bureaucracy, and go through a whole series of activities motivated by the institution in question.

It may be noted here that none of the ministers of churches in Regional City were chosen as top leaders by the persons interviewed in the study. The idea was expressed several times by interviewees that some minister *ought* to be on the listing, but under the terms of power definitions used in the study they did not make "top billing." It is understood, however, that in order to get a project well under way it would be important to bring the churches in, but they are not, as institutions, considered crucial in the decision-making process. Their influence is crucial in restating settled policies from time to time and in interpreting new policies which have been formed or are in the process of formulation. Church leaders, however, whether they be prominent laymen or professional ministers, have relatively little influence with the larger economic interests.

One cannot, in Regional City at least, look to the organized institutions as policy-determining groupings, nor can one look to the formal associations which are part of these institutions. But let us briefly be specific concerning the role of organizations. There is a multiplicity of organized groups in Regional City. The Chamber of Commerce lists more than 800 organizations from bee-keeping societies to federated industrial groups. The membership lists of some of these organizations often run into the hundreds. In this study organizations were considered as being influential in civic affairs and some ranking of the most important was deemed necessary. Consequently, all persons interviewed were asked to give their opinion on a

selected list of supposedly top-ranking organizations in the
community. An initial selection of thirty organizations was
made by a panel of judges from lists supplied by the Chamber
of Commerce and the local Community Council. The persons
interviewed in the list of forty leaders narrowed their selections
of organizations to seven—organizations to which the majority
of these top leaders belonged. They were (in rank order of
importance) the Chamber of Commerce, Community Chest,
Rotary Club, Y.M.C.A., Community Council, Grand Jurors'
Association, and Bar Association. There was a scattering of
votes for the Christian Council and for one of the larger labor
organizations. The Retail Merchants Association was added
to our list by two merchants. The under-structure professional
personnel in civic and social work who were interviewed indicated that they recognized the influence of the same organizations chosen by the top leaders. It may be noted that they
generally belonged to only the Community Chest and the
Community Council in conjunction with the top leaders.

Some of the top leaders may hold board positions within
the associational groupings to lend prestige to the organization,
but such members are more noted for their absence than for
their attendance at meetings of the respective boards. They
can be called upon in an organizational crisis or emergency,
and at such times they may function decisively. One leader
explained his position in this way: "If I attend meetings too
regularly, I am asked to be chairman of this or that committee.
I don't have time for that kind of work, but you hate to refuse
before a bunch of people. There are usually two or three
listening posts, people who can keep me in touch with things,
on these boards. I get reports from them from time to time and
that way keep a hand in. I also read the minutes of important
meetings. Most of the time I know about where any board I
belong to stands on various matters. I attend meetings only
when I'm really needed."

Occasionally a top leader will take the presidency of one of the associations, but such position is usually unsought and avoided if possible—particularly by the older leaders. The younger leaders may be pushed to take some of the top associational posts as training assignments. They take on such duties, they say, with reluctance and make feeble protests of being terribly busy and pressed for time. The less powerful understructure associational personnel may scramble (in a dignified way, of course) for the top positions in these groupings.

In crisis situations, such as during World War II, many of the older leaders were called to active duty on civic boards. This was particularly true in the large fund-raising organizations where campaign goals were doubled or tripled over previous ones and the prestige of the older leaders was needed to insure the success of particular drives. During the crisis of depression in the 1930's several of the older leaders served on the local welfare board, but as the economic situation improved, they were replaced by "second-rate" and "third-rate" community leaders.[12]

Many of the persons interviewed belonged to many more organizations than those previously indicated, but the groups listed represent those that the power leaders consider most important in carrying out or interpreting a community-wide project. Two formal organizations were mentioned which are not generally known to the community at large but which are considered quite influential by the men of power. One is called the "49 Club" and the other the "Committee of 101." The 49 Club is a highly selective group organized in Regional City at the turn of the century. It is composed of a group of men who are prominent in community life and who have in some instances inherited a place on the membership roster. The club discusses major issues before the community and the general body politic seeking agreement on general policy matters. Its meetings are not formal and are often held in the homes of members. When a member dies, his vacancy is not filled for a

12. This classification is explained later in the chapter.

considerable time. The one chosen to fill the vacancy is highly honored. Several of the top men on our list belonged to this club.

The Committee of 101 is almost exclusively devoted to a discussion of political matters. It discusses candidates and issues but takes no action on any matter which comes before it, nor are any formal records kept of the meetings. These latter stipulations also apply to the 49 Club. Membership in the Committee of 101 is considered a privilege, but it does not rank as high as the 49 Club. Both have high dues, the proceeds of which are spent on entertainment of the members.

Comparable data were gathered on twenty-four Regional City leaders concerning club memberships. Figure 7 shows the interlocking nature of these memberships. Attention may be called to Club C. This club is comparable to Club B. Both are civic luncheon clubs, but Club B has a higher status in the community than Club C, as indicated by its apparent popularity among the top leaders. Clubs A, D, and E are social clubs of prominence. None of the under-structure professional personnel interviewed belonged to any of these clubs.

None of the men interviewed considered any of the associational groupings crucial in policy determination. Their role, like that of the organized institutional groupings, is one of following rather than leading. They may provide a forum for discussing and studying community issues, needs, and policies; but, when decision is called for, another structure must come into play before action becomes the order of the day. The organizations may serve as training grounds for many of the men who later become power leaders. Most of the leaders had "graduated" from a stint in the upper positions of the more important organizations. Most associational presidents, however, remain in the under-structure of the power hierarchy. The organizations are not a sure route to sustained community prominence. Membership in the top brackets of one of the stable economic bureaucracies is the surest road to power, and this road is entered by only a few. Organizational leaders are prone to get the publicity; the upper echelon economic leaders, the power.

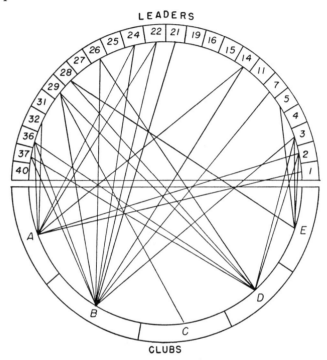

Fig. 7. Interlocking Club Memberships of 24 Regional City Leaders. (For key to numbers, see footnote to Table 2, p. 63.)

It was indicated at the beginning of this chapter that there would be a discussion of leadership groupings in a framework developed by E. T. Hiller, and by implication, at least, two of his criteria for analyzing community structure have been touched upon, namely, personnel and tests of admission of members. In a sense the third criterion has been bordered upon, that is, the distinctive roles of members. It has been said that the leading personnel in community power situations in Regional City tend to be businessmen. The personnel factor has been isolated to a definite group. One of the critical tests of membership in the policy-making group is prior membership in one of the commercial or industrial bureaucracies in the community. Kingsley Davis has indicated that because a man occupies a certain status and office, he enjoys power.[13] The men under discussion for the most part hold offices within powerful economic units in Regional City. Definite roles are played by these men in moving goods and services within each of the enterprises of which they are a part, but if their roles were limited to only one community unit we would be speaking of economic power and not community power. The composite power relations of men in the community are the primary object of this study.

Neither the institutional, associational, nor economic groupings comprise the totality of the power scheme in Regional City. The difference between policy-making and policy-execution has been stressed and it has been shown that the various organizations in the community may be very important in carrying out policy decisions. Segments of structure including individuals and cliques, particularly those related to the upper decision-making groups, have been identified. One more organizational component must be analyzed before tying together the units of the community structure. This component is what may be termed a fluid committee structure.

The committee is a phenomenon which is inescapable in organized community life in American hamlets, villages, small cities, and great metropolitan centers. Almost every activity of any importance in our culture must be preceded by committee work, carried on by committee work, and finally posthumously evaluated by a committee. Regional City is no exception to the general rule. Day after day the hotel, club, and associational meeting rooms are packed with men going

13. "A Conceptual Analysis of Stratification," *American Sociological Review*, VII (June 1942), 316.

through the familiar motions of calling meetings to order and dismissing them. Committees may have short lives or they may go on for years. An example of the latter is the Committee of 101 previously discussed. Committees may be quite formally organized, utilizing parliamentary rules of order, or they may be loosely organized and informal in their procedures. They may be accompanied by food and drink or they may be devoid of such amenities. They may have serious or light purposes, and consequently solemn or gay occasions as the case may be. Withal, each is accompanied by a certain degree of ritual befitting the occasion. Men used to committee work are sharp to detect poorly conducted meetings. No meeting, for example, can be said to have amounted to much if at least one motion is not put, passed, or put down—that is, in the more formally organized meetings. Men trained in conducting meetings are in demand, and such a person may display rare skills in ordering a group as it goes about its business.

Meetings are often a substitute for group action. As one Regional City professional phrased it, "There are those who believe in salvation by luncheon!" There is great faith manifest in certain quarters of our society that if people can just be got together in a meeting all problems will be solved. And there is some justification for this faith, since so many matters of community business, as well as private transactions, are brought to successful conclusions in meetings.

Meetings have the functions of clarifying objectives of a group and of fixing and delegating responsibilities for action on any matter. They may in like manner hold action in abeyance. Decisions reached in meetings may be solemnly binding, or they may not be. Decisions arrived at in one meeting may be changed in the next meeting. Responsibilities may be shifted and membership changed according to the will of the group as a series of meetings proceeds. Rarely are committee meetings bound by "constitutional" prohibitions or heavy legalistic trappings which characterize so many associational and institutional gatherings. The outstanding characteristic of the ordinary committee meeting is its fluidity and its adaptability in adjusting to changing conditions, which are so essentially a part of our modern urban culture. The importance of the committee in power relations cannot be overstressed.

While it is important to stress the fluidity of committee structure, it must also be pointed out that there is a stable base of personnel who are seen time and again in a variety of committee meetings. There are men in any community who devote large portions of their waking hours to attendance at one meeting or another. Public-relations men in industry and associational secretaries are paid to devote considerable of their time to meeting attendance. It becomes commonplace among this latter personnel group to see one another at committee meetings, and such personnel become familiar with community leaders who operate on a similar level with them. There is a tendency to judge the importance of these meetings by who is in attendance.

Most of the top personnel of the power group are rarely seen at meetings attended by the associational under-structure personnel in Regional City. The exception to this general statement may be found in those instances in which a project is broad enough so that the "whole community needs to be brought in on the matter." Such meetings as bring in the under-structure personnel are usually relatively large affairs, rather than the smaller, more personal meetings which characterize policy-determination sessions. The interaction patterns of the two groups discussed here have shown a much higher rate of interaction among the top group than between the top and lower groups.

In matters of power decision the committee structure assumes keystone importance. The committee as a structure is a vital part of community power relationships in Regional City. Let us illustrate graphically in Figure 8 the place of two hypo-

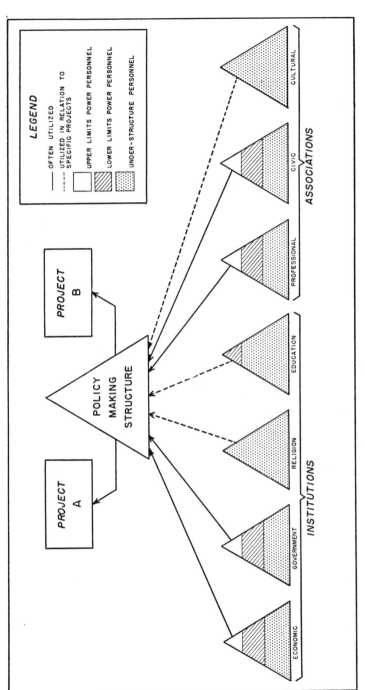

Fig. 8. Generalized Pattern of Policy Committee Formation Utilizing Institutional and Associational Structures.

thetical policy committees in relation to institutional, associational, and corporate groups.

Not all the institutions and associations in Regional City were identified as being related to the power leaders studied. For example, none of the leaders in a power relationship could be identified as representing the institution of the family or a cultural association. This does not mean that either of these groupings was unimportant for some of the top leaders, but in the specific power relations studied no identification could be made of persons within these groupings as such. Because of this, in Figure 8 the cultural association is indicated as a pyramid grouping for under-structure power personnel only. No family institutional pyramid is shown. On the other hand, some of the institutions and associations could be identified with both upper-limits and lower-limits power personnel, and these pyramids show this by contrasting shaded portions for the two types of power leaders. We have also indicated in the figure that some institutions and associations are more frequently drawn upon for power personnel than others. The dotted lines represent those groups that are potential contributors to the policy-making structure. The cultural association group has been so designated, for example, since policy is formulated around some cultural activities which may have bearing on power relations. As an illustration, the status factor operating when a leader becomes a patron of the arts may have some relation to his general power position.

A few generalized remarks may be made concerning Figure 8, using a hypothetical example, after which it will be illustrated concretely how the structure worked in relation to a specific community project in Regional City.

If a project of major proportions were before the community for consideration—let us say a project aimed at building a new municipal auditorium—a policy committee would be formed. This may be called Project Committee A. Such a policy committee would more than likely grow out of a series of informal meetings, and it might be related to a project that has been on the discussion agenda of many associations for months or even years. But the time has arrived for action. Money must be raised through private subscription or taxation, a site selected, and contracts let. The time for a policy committee is propitious. The selection of the policy committee will fall largely to the men of power in the community. They will likely be businessmen in one or more of the larger business establishments. Mutual choices will be agreed upon for committee membership. In the early stages of policy formulation there will be a few men who make the basic decisions. As the project is trimmed, pared, and shaped into manageable proportions there will be a recognition that the committee should be enlarged. Top-ranking organizational and institutional personnel will then be selected by the original members to augment their numbers, i.e., the committee will be expanded. The civic associations and the formalized institutions will next be drawn into certain phases of planning and initiation of the project on a community-wide basis. The newspapers will finally carry stories of the proposals, the ministers will preach sermons, and the associational members will hear speeches regarding plans. This rather simply is the process, familiar to many, that goes on in getting any community project under way.

Project B might be related to changing the tax structure of the community. Much the same organizational procedure will be repeated, but different associations may be drawn into the planning and execution stages. The policy-making personnel will tend to be much the same as in Project A and this is an important point in the present discussion. There will be a hard core of policy leadership on Policy Committee B that was also present on Project Committee A. This relative stability of the top policy-making group is a pattern quite apparent in Regional City civic affairs. A similar pattern of stable committee membership exists in the under-structure of the associational and corporate bureaucracies in the community which interact in a chain of command with the top power leaders on given projects.

It must be stressed that the same policy leaders do not interact repeatedly with the same under-structure personnel in getting projects put over. The interaction is based entirely upon a given project that is under consideration at a given time. The under-structure personnel may be likened to a keyboard over which the top structure personnel play, and the particular keys struck may vary from project to project. The players remain the same or nearly so, however.

A variation in the pattern of structuring a top-decision committee may be found in those policy committees in which the decision is made by individuals who are not to be out front on the project. In other words, the men of policy may wish to remain anonymous in relation to the action phases of the program in question. In such cases, the policy group remains informally intact, and "second-rate" or "third-rate" men are advertised as the sponsors of the particular project. This pattern may occur when a project is somewhat questionable as to its success. The policy-forming group is just as real, however, as if it were named publicly. The men upon whom falls the burden of carrying the project into its action stages are well aware of the persons who chose them.

Projects that are not originated in the policy-determining group are often allowed to proceed with a tentative blessing of a few of the men of decision if their interests and dominant values are not threatened by the proposed activity. If such a project goes sour, the men of decision cannot be blamed. This is another variation of structure and represents a real behavioral pattern in civic affairs in Regional City.

The leaders interviewed indicated that one of the projects which has current top priority in the community is known as "The Plan of Development." This project will be outlined in more detail in the chapter on projects and issues. Here we are interested in two things: (1) Which community leaders were identified as related to the project on the level of policy decision; and (2) which community leaders were identified with activating the project. It can be seen in an examination of Figures 9 and 10 that a different group was concerned with policy from that concerned with activating the project. Both the power leaders we have been discussing and the secretary for the official Committee for the Plan of Development were interviewed in relation to leadership utilized in formulating and activating the program. Consequently, it is clear that the leadership identified with this project represents a relatively closed and inclusive group.

The Plan of Development has been a controversial project in the community. It is a project that has a history of some ten years. One of the top policy leaders was quite active over a period of time in getting the interest of other leaders in this particular case. The leaders he interested on a policy level are indicated by code numbers in Figure 9. These numbers correspond to the upper- and lower-limits groups of personnel earlier identified. No under-structure personnel, so far as could be determined, participated in the informal policy committee which laid the groundwork for the program and determined its major outlines.

As the program moved toward the action stage, however, the structural picture changed. Three of the power leaders, numbers 31 and 1 in the upper-limits group and number 5 in the lower-limits group, were designated from the policy group as a nucleus around which an official operations committee was to be built. These leaders are subordinate to number 14, the leader who largely initiated the project.

The dominance of the business leaders may be noted. Out of thirteen policy leaders active in the project, nine were identified as belonging to the business group, six of whom were in the upper-limits category and three in the lower-limits group. The government leader identified with the movement was very

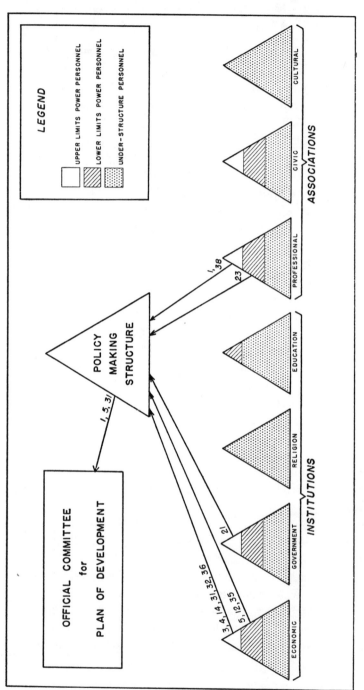

Fig. 9. Pattern of Participation of Three Strata of Institutional and Associational Personnel in Policy Formulation of Regional City's Plan of Development.

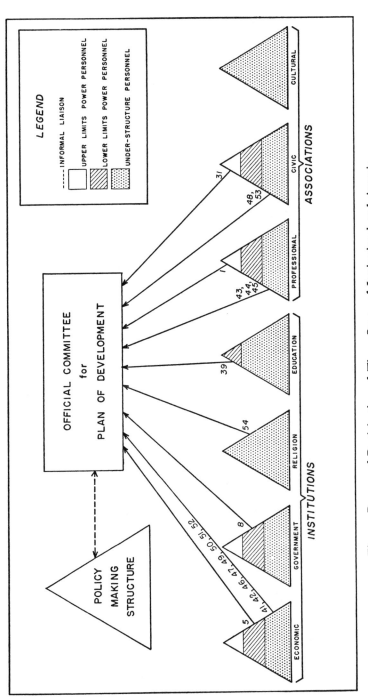

Fig. 10. Pattern of Participation of Three Strata of Institutional and Associational Personnel in Activating Program of Regional City's Plan of Development.

anxious to see the program get under way and succeed. He had a personal power interest in the matter, but his interest could not be made public. Publicly he maintained a hands-off policy in relation to the project, but in policy formulation he was quite active. In the professional group, numbers 38 and 23 were legal advisors to the policy group as a whole. Number 1, in the professional category, acted as an informal liaison person between several organizations and the policy-makers.

After the policy line had been set and before the project could be activated, it was necessary to go to the state legislature for enabling legislation. In this process the legislators bargained with the policy group concerning the membership of the proposed official committee. During the horse-trading, some of the names proposed by the policy-makers were dropped in favor of local politicos agreeable to the state political leaders. The local "politicians" might be classified as semi-politicians. They have business connections which are their primary interest, but in at least four instances these businesses involve contracting or motor transport in which it is profitable to have good political relations with state officials.

Figure 10 identifies the institutions and associations with which the leaders were involved in getting the project activated. With the exception of numbers 1, 5, 8, 31, and 39, the leaders named to the official committee operate outside the policy-making power group. These men have been given code numbers above 40 to distinguish them from the policy-making group. None of them operate businesses that can be favorably compared in size or influence with the policy leaders'. The remaining business leaders operate small establishments that might be compared in size to local insurance or auto sales agencies. The religious leader in this group is a minister of one of the larger churches in Regional City. He is a man who may be characterized as a community gadfly and a person upon whom the policy leaders depend for a certain amount of civic information.

Two of the persons identified in the professional association grouping, numbers 43, 44, are lawyers from the outlying sections of the city. It was considered good strategy to have these men identified with the official group concerned with activating the project, since the areas adjacent to Regional City were affected by the proposals. Number 45 in the professional grouping is a secretary of a local dry cleaning association. The reasons for his inclusion on the project committee are not clear. It was mentioned by one informant that he had "good labor connections," but I could not ascertain the scope of these connections.

One labor representative from a relatively weak union was put on the committee. He was chosen because he was identified with a joint union committee on community affairs devoted to interpreting welfare projects to the various labor groups. It does not seem desirable or necessary to describe all of the leaders of the activating committee, but mention will be made of one more individual, since his position in the scheme of project operation seems significant. This leader is identified with code number 31.

Number 31 is a top policy leader. He represents the upper-limits power leaders in the policy group. He is also a person identified with big business in the community. When the Plan of Development project was to be officially launched, number 31 was asked to take the presidency of one of the more powerful civic associations for a year to "swing that group into line." He was given an impressive build-up by the newspapers for his broad civic interests and for a year he devoted a great deal of time to getting the Plan of Development under way. His leadership was well received generally, and apparently he was well supported, for the project has been put across successfully.

By comparing Figures 9 and 10, it may be clearly seen that the policy-makers generally move out of the picture at the stage of project execution. This pattern holds true generally for major community projects. The men in the under-structure of power become the doers and are activated by the policy-makers—the initiators.

The project discussed above is one related to Regional City *as a community*. Of course the affairs of the community do not stop at its borders. There are relationships between personnel in the city and persons in state and national power groups. Robert K. Merton observed in a recent study that community leaders fall into "cosmopolitan" and "local" groupings.[14] This generalized concept seems to hold true in Regional City. Some men tend to confine their activities almost entirely within the community, while others are active on state and regional matters.

Homer, Parks, Hardy, Aiken, Parker, and Rake appear to be the men in Regional City who act largely as liaison persons between the communtiy and national policy-making groups. These men average three committees each on the national level, in comparison to 1.2 for the group as a whole. Hardy claims to belong to the most national policy-making boards and committees, with ten as his total. Homer and Aiken are definitely more interested in national than in local affairs. This fact came out strongly in interviews with them. Aiken said, "There are plenty of men who can keep an eye on things here at home. Some of these matters like inflation and national defense need to be got at in Washington, and my interest is in these things."

On the state level of operations in relation to the city, Hardy is also active along with Stone, Rake, and Parker. These men average four state committees each in comparison with an average of 1.3 for the remainder of the group. Stone confines his policy-making committee work entirely to the state. He belongs to a few local committees but is not active on them. The other persons interested in state affairs tend to divide their

14. Paul Lazarsfeld and Frank N. Stanton (eds.), *Communications Research* (New York: Harper and Brothers, 1949), p. 192.

remaining committee time between local and national groups. The majority of the top leaders belong to an average of six policy-making boards or committees in comparison to an average of 1.3 in the state and 1.2 nationally.

The professional under-structure persons belong to fewer local committees and boards on a policy-making level than do the top leaders, but they compare favorably with the leaders on the national and state levels. They average 4.7 local committees, 1.0 state committees, and 1.3 national committees. Qualitatively their committees and boards differ from the upper power group. They most generally belong to professional association groupings which are different from the trade and other economic groupings of the top leaders.

The community politicians almost entirely operate locally on boards and committees, but the Mayor has many individual contacts with the two levels of government above him on a less formalized basis than boards and committees of policy would imply. During an interview with the Mayor he was interrupted by a phone call which he had put through to Washington regarding a project which concerned the community, and one cannot say that he is not an influential man in national and state affairs. On the phone he sounded influential. He is not the most influential man in Regional City in local-national policy matters, and when the dynamics of the power structure is elaborated upon, this will become apparent. The Mayor denies much influence in state matters. When questioned on this area he said, "I was saying to Rafferty Jones [a state politician] the other day, 'Rafferty, I'll bet that I could not be elected to the lowest job in state government!'" State and local politics are differentiated, but not entirely distinct. As in other states where a large metropolitan center is located there is much friction and conflict of interest between the two political groupings. The two are joined often at that point at which major economic interests are involved, and the leaders of economic bureaucracies have much personal influence in bridging the formal structural gaps between the levels of government on specific matters.

In one of our postulates it is stated that, "Power is structured socially, in the United States, into a dual relationship between governmental and economic authorities on national, state, and local levels." In the light of the present analysis, there is less of a "dual" relationship than had been assumed. This is particularly true in Regional City, where the dominant factor in political life is the personnel of the economic interests. It is true that there is no formal tie between the economic interests and government, but the structure of policy-determining committees and their tie-in with the other powerful institutions and organizations of the community make government subservient to the interests of these combined groups. The governmental departments and their personnel are acutely aware of the power of key individuals and combinations of citizens' groups in the policy-making realm, and they are loathe to act before consulting and "clearing" with these interests.

Brady is enlightening on this point when he says that the same interests tend to dominate politics and business, particularly in the realm of policy. "The same individuals, the same groups and cliques, [and] the same interests dominate each sphere [of property and politics]," he says.[15] One is compelled to agree with him from observations of the two groups in Regional City. There is evidence, too, that the local economic interests tie into larger groupings of like interests on the state and national levels which tend to overshadow the policy-making machinery of government at all levels. The structure is that of a dominant policy-making group using the machinery of government as a bureaucracy for the attainment of certain goals coordinate with the interests of the policy-forming group. The description of the structure of the "third house"

15. R. A. Brady, *Business as a System of Power* (New York: Columbia University Press, 1938), p. 314.

mentioned in the discussion of Gary Stone, a labor leader, may be recalled in this connection.

The structural relationship between the economic policy-determining groups and the operating units of government have often been looked upon as inherently immoral. The ethical implications of the domination by one set of men in manipulating government for specific and limited purposes may be avoided, but some concern must be expressed in relation to a functional difficulty which such domination presents in our society. "Common to all the national, social, and economic crises of our day," says von Beckerath, "is the fundamental problem of rebuilding a constant workable connection between the political structure... and its economic structure."[16] A consistent and workable connection between the political and economic structures appears to be an extremely pertinent concept, which highlights a weakness of the power structure of Regional City as it relates to other units on the political level. There are gaps in the power arc which are closed on many issues by the narrower-interest groups. In other words, it has been pointed out that the power personnel do not represent a true pyramid of political power. The power personnel may decisively influence most policies that concern legislative groups, and they are acutely aware of their own interests in such policy matters. However, on many issues they are not interested, and there is consequently no continuing structure which may transmit to the legislative bodies the general interests of the underlying groups within the body politic. This is no new problem, but it is a structurally significant one. If the formalized structures of government are under the domination of a group of policy leaders who are isolated from direct responsibility to the mass of people in a democratic society, then, values aside, the scheme is at best dysfunctional. No pat-

16. Herbert von Beckerath, "Economics and Politics," *Social Forces,* XIV (October 1935), 42.

ent remedy is suggested in this writing but there is a structural weakness in the policy-making machinery and power-wielding mechanism as it has been observed in a particular locality. Correction of the difficulty may come from an open recognition of actual operating elements in power relations unobscured by abstract value descriptions which do not fit reality. Simply put, power structure is looked at here, not from the point of view of what one may think we have, or what one may think we ought to have, but rather in terms of what we've got. Although in the concluding chapter there will be a brief discussion of ways in which community democratic processes may be strengthened, the central intention of the entire study is to describe what actually *is* in community power relations.

The Mayor of Regional City says, "We have got a citizen-run town here." And one can agree with him, but policy is controlled by a relatively small group of the citizenry. In such a situation an obvious question is, "What holds the system together?" This question was asked of our informants. The question was put in this way: "It is evident that we are dealing with a small group of policy leaders in this study, but the whole community of Regional City is comprised of some half million persons. What holds the whole group together in relation to the influence exerted by so few leaders?"

Boiled down, the more significant answers ran along the following lines: "It is a sense of obligation which some men have toward others which keeps the system operating." "It is obligation plus confidence in the ability of some men to get things done, while other men cannot get things done." "Some men are interested in working on community projects, others are not." "Money holds them together." "Some people just naturally work together better than others." "You get to know certain people and when anything comes up you tend to call on the same men over and over to work on community projects." "You watch to see who is moving—when you see a man on the move, pick him up. He'll work for you!"

There is merit in all of these answers. Within the primary groups, or separate crowds clustered around specific interests, it is evident that similar interests and resulting common sentiments have a great deal to do with holding the groups together. Men who work together over a long period of time become comfortable in their working relationships with one another. Mutual sentiments of liking will grow up between them, and these sentiments in turn will lead to further interactions.[17] The ability of a top leader to retain a position of prestige depends to some extent on how well he conforms to the norms of the group he leads. The men of Regional City tend to be exponents of the "common man" in appearance and manner of speech, at least during the workday. Some of the men of top wealth and position are spoken of as "common as an old shoe." Their private lives hidden from the general mass of people may be uncommon, but their everyday behavior tends toward a confirmation of what one Regional City professional in the understructure has called the "patched pants theory." "The biggest ones act like they have patches on their pants," he said. "The higher the rank of the person within a group, the more nearly his activities conform to the norms of the group," says Homans.[18]

Common interests, cutting across the lines of all separate crowds, tend to hold the community structure intact. James Treat said, "If you want to know what is going on, you have to be where the money is. It is capitalism, I suppose you would say. The men who make things move are interested in the larger issues—making money, keeping power." Joseph Hardy and Harvey Aiken agreed with Treat, but Aiken modified his statement by saying, "Money is only good so long as it is backed up by material goods. Inflation can ruin money, and it can ruin all the people who have money." He told of being in France recently where he inquired of some of the banking men

17. Homans, op. cit., p. 112.
18. Ibid., p. 141.

who lived along one of the old boulevards whether their neighbors had suffered from post-war inflation. They indicated that most of their neighbors were the newly rich who had profited in the black markets resulting from World War II, and many of the new men of power were those who had been able to hold goods during the inflation rather than depend upon income from securities. The writer shares Aiken's caution about money as a sole source of power. It represents power in a stable economy when it is backed by tangible resources. With this limitation noted, it must be admitted that money still has meaning in power terms in Regional City. It is an important element.

Force is also an element of power but it is not an independent element. Von Beckerath says, "A state built upon *mere* force of a minority against the will of the majority is never possible in the long run." [19] One must look deeper than the elements of money or force to analyze adequately the power structure of Regional City. Both of these elements have their place, but both are interconnected with a complex set of habitual relationships of men which are described in terms of group relations.

Homans says, "The higher a man's social rank, the larger will be the number of persons that originate interaction for him, either directly or through subordinates." Also, "The higher a man's social rank, the larger number of persons for whom he originates interaction, either directly or through intermediaries." [20] The actions indicated are a two-way process. The men of high social rank—in this discussion, policy-makers—are acted upon and they act upon others, and because of their position they influence large numbers of people. Homans also says that high social rank presages a wide range of interactions. If Homans were to leave the matter at the latter

19. "Economics and Politics," *loc. cit.*, p. 52.
20. *Op. cit.*, p. 145.

point, I should have to disagree with him, since I found that the men of power tended to act within a limited range of contacts in Regional City, but Homans has an answer to this:

An increasing specialization of activities will bring about a decrease in the range of interaction of a person ... and will limit the field in which he can originate action. ... Thus an increase in the size of the group and in the specialization of activity will tend to increase the numbers of positions in the chain of interaction between the top leader and the ordinary member [in our case, citizen].[21]

The group of men dealt with here have a specialized function, namely, policy-making. It would not be physically possible for the men of decision to interact with great numbers of citizens on a face-to-face basis in Regional City. The contacts with the average citizen must be limited, but there must be channels of interaction open for decisions to flow down, and for issues to rise, at times, from the underlying population. These channels are open through the institutions and associations previously outlined in this chapter. The men of decision will not go far up or down the scale of leadership to choose others with whom to work, and these findings are in conformity with another of Homans' theories: "If a person does originate interaction for a person of higher rank, a tendency will exist for him to do so with the member of his own subgroup who is nearest him in rank."[22]

The tendency works the other way, too. Persons in the higher ranks most often work with persons close to them and rely on men immediately below them to originate interaction with persons in turn below them. As a matter of custom and practice, the person of higher rank originates interaction for those below him more often than the latter originate interaction for him.[23] This process has the following results:

21. *Ibid.* p. 406.   22. *Ibid.,* p. 184.   23. *Ibid.,* p. 145.

Channels of interaction will become established, and the leader will not become overburdened with interaction. The relative frequency of interaction with immediate superiors and interaction with the top leader must differ from group to group according to the number of circumstances, two of which are the size of the group and the severity of the environment.... The more severe the environment in which the group must survive—ships and armies [for example]—the more likely it is that interaction will be strictly channeled.[24]

The channels of interaction are established in Regional City to conserve the time of the men of power. Even with the channels that are opened, there is still considerable burden of responsibility placed upon these men. In discussing this point with George Delbert, the question was asked, "With so few men in policy positions, isn't there a tendency to choke off many projects which may be of equal merit with those being given consideration?" He thought the question over for a moment and replied, "Yes, I suppose that may be true; but there's only so much time in a year, and we can only handle a certain number of things. Then there's not money enough to go around for everything that comes up. There is always anywhere from one to two million being raised in this community for one purpose or another. It takes time to get around to everything!"

The power leaders do get around with considerable facility in the area of economic activity. When a new corporation is started, as for example a new television company, or a multi-million dollar apartment building project recently established in the city, one or more of the leaders were observed to "find time" to be identified with such developments. Certainly, the top leaders would appear to have time for policy considerations of such economic projects, if one takes into account the reports in the business section of the local press. The day-to-day working arrangements of the corporations are put into the hands of

24. *Ibid.*, p. 184.

trusted under-structure administrative personnel. The pattern of power implicit in the situation matches that of civic enterprises in formation and development.

"If two institutions," says Hughes, "draw upon the same people . . . they may compete in some measure, for people have but a limited amount of time and money to expend." [25] The leaders of Regional City tend to protect themselves from too many demands by channeling policy execution through an under-structure on matters of policy. This under-structure is not a rigid bureaucracy, as has been pointed out, but is a flexible system. It has elements of stability and tends to operate by levels. The men at each level are spoken of as first, second, third and fourth rate by the power leaders, who operate primarily in conjunction with individuals of the first two ratings. The types of personnel which may be found in each rating by a sample classification are as follows:

EXAMPLES OF PERSONNEL FROM FIRST TO FOURTH RATE IN REGIONAL CITY

FIRST RATE: Industrial, commercial, financial owners and top executives of large enterprises.

SECOND RATE: Operations officials, bank vice-presidents, public-relations men, small businessmen (owners), top-ranking public officials, corporation attorneys, contractors.

THIRD RATE: Civic organization personnel, civic agency board personnel, newspaper columnists, radio commentators, petty public officials, selected organization executives.

FOURTH RATE: Professionals such as ministers, teachers, social workers, personnel directors, and such persons as small business managers, higher paid accountants, and the like.

25. Everett C. Hughes, "Ecological Aspects of Institutions," *American Sociological Review*, I (April 1936), 186.

These ratings might be expanded. They are given simply to indicate a suggested ranking of selected personnel who operate below the policy-making leaders in Regional City. The first two ratings are personnel who are said to "set the line of policy," while the latter two groups "hold the line." The ratings are very real to the under-structure professional personnel. One of these men said: "I know that the top boys get together on things. This community is divided into tiers. You can't get the first-tier men to work on anything originating in the second- and third-tier level. The top ones may put their names on second- and third-tier projects, but you cannot get them to work with you. They will not attend your meetings, but you know they are attending their own meetings all the time." The top leaders are conserving their time and energies for the primary role they play—policy-determination. They are also interested in holding a balance of power in the community.

In discussing the men in the lower group of the top leadership hierarchy, one of the informants said: "When you see one of the little fellows move, you know he is not moving on his own. Somebody is moving him, and it is the bigger fellow who is moving him that you need to watch, if you want to know what is going on.

"My father, who was a farmer, used to chop wood with me. He'd say, 'Son, when you see a chip in the woodpile move, look under the chip. You probably will find something interesting under it.' I've always remembered that. I've always looked to see what makes the 'chips' move."

The "little fellows" are continually moved to perform their proper tasks by those above them. The roles defined for the under-structure of power personnel are carefully defined in keeping with the larger interests. Their movements are carefully stimulated and watched at all times to see that their various functions are properly performed.

Stability of relationships is highly desirable in maintaining social control, and keeping men "in their places" is a vital part of the structuring of community power. Andrew Carnegie expressed the idea of every man in his place in this manner: "It is the business of the preacher to preach, of the physician to practice, of the poet to write, the business of the college professor to teach...." [26] Each of these professions also has a role to play in the community activities consistent with its economic or professional role. Such roles do not ordinarily include policy-making. If one of these under-structure men should be presumptuous enough to question policy decisions, he would be immediately considered insubordinate and "punished," first by a threat to his job security, followed possibly by expulsion from his job if his insubordination continued. To quote Homans:

A social system is in a moving equilibrium and authority exists when the state of the elements that enter the system and the relations between them, including the behavior of the leader(s), is such that disobedience to the orders of the leader(s) will be followed by changes in the other elements tending to bring the system back to the state the leader(s) would have wished to reach if the disobedience had not occurred.[27]

There may be isolated dissatisfactions with policy decisions in Regional City, but mainly there is unanimity. The controversial is avoided, partly by the policy-making group's not allowing a proposal to get too far along if it meets stiff criticism at any point in decision-making. A careful watch is kept for what "will go" and for what "will not go." Luke Street says, "Most of the carping comes from people who are envious of some of the bigger crowds. When there is such envy, the crowds are talked about and criticized." Such criticism usually is not open. When criticism is open it is generally directed toward some of the under-structure men who are fronting for

26. *The Empire of Business* (New York: Doubleday, Page and Company, 1902), p. 189.
27. *Op. cit.*, p. 422.

the larger interests. If criticism is directed toward the top leaders, the critic is liable to job dismissal in extreme cases or more subtle pressures in less flagrant cases. The omnipresent threat of power sanctions used against recalcitrant underlings is recognized by the lower echelons of power, and they generally go along with most decisions, grumbling in private with close associates, if at all. Most of these third- or fourth-rate leaders rationalize their behavior—particularly when upper decisions are in conflict with their professional or private value systems.

There is one more element in Regional City's power structure which must be discussed. It is the element of power residing in the Negro community of the city, and it is such an important element in this study that I propose to analyze its structure in a separate chapter. The Negro community represents a sub-structure of power as well as a sub-community. As a community grouping it calls up many issues which tend to mobilize the total power structure. As a sub-community power structure it is inextricably interwoven with the elements discussed in the present chapter, but for analytical purposes it calls for special treatment. After a restatement of the concepts discussed in the present chapter, I shall analyze power relations in Regional City's Negro community.

Two of the hypotheses of the study have been discussed in some measure in the preceding analysis. These hypotheses, restated, are as follows:

1. The exercise of power is limited and directed by the formulation and extension of social policy within a framework of socially sanctioned authority.

2. In a given power unit a smaller number of individuals will be found formulating and extending policy than those exercising power.

A corollary of the latter hypothesis was also touched upon: All policy-makers are men of power, but all men of power are not, per se, policy-makers.

The top group of the power hierarchy has been isolated and defined as comprised of policy-makers. These men are drawn largely from the businessmen's class in Regional City. They form cliques or crowds, as the term is more often used in the community, which formulate policy. Committees for formulation of policy are commonplace, and on community-wide issues policy is channeled by a "fluid committee structure" down to institutional, associational groupings through a lower-level bureaucracy which executes policy.

It has been pointed out that intra-community and extra-community policy matters are handled by essentially the same group of men in this city, but there is a differentiation of functional activity within this policy group. Some men operate on different levels of policy decision, particularly in matters concerning governmental action. Some structural weaknesses in the power structure have been touched upon but at no great length. Finally, it was found that the structure is held together by common interests, mutual obligations, money, habit, delegated responsibilities, and in some cases by coercion and force.

R EGIONAL CITY'S Negro community hugs the heart of its business and commercial districts. As in many cities, it is characterized by poor housing, sub-standard community facilities, unpaved streets—all of which are used by a highly concentrated population. It is a segregated community—a fact of which most of its citizens are acutely aware. It is a functional community within the whole metropolis, furnishing the manpower which keeps much of the commerce of the town moving and which provides through its laboring force a sizeable proportion of the services demanded by all classes in the larger community. It is also an organized community. Its organization is of particular interest —especially its structure along lines of power.

As a preview to the materials to be presented in this chapter, it may be said that the pattern of power leadership within the Negro community follows rather closely the pattern of the larger community. The method of turning up policy-determining leadership was the same as used in the larger community, but in this sub-community, Negro judges were used, seven of them, to give a basic list of leaders who might be questioned on leadership patterns.[1] The questionnaire to leaders was

1. Sub-community, as the term is used here, does not necessarily mean inferior, although many features of the sub-community could be so classified. It means rather that this is a community operating within a larger community.

mailed, but a series of interviews was conducted to augment the data collected by correspondence.

As in the larger community, the Negro leaders tended to pick the same persons within their own community on policy matters, and there was a high rate of committee interaction among the top leaders. There was a clear differentiation between top organizations and lower ones on a scale of choices. A total of twenty-two organizations of top influence were selected by Negro leaders from a listing of more than 350. This figure alone represents the high degree of social organization within the Negro community.

The twenty-two organizations are structures through which policy decisions may be channeled. Many of them may be characterized as religious, fraternal, and welfare in nature. Two are economic organizations paralleling the Merchants' Association and the Chamber of Commerce in the city proper. Both of these groups are considered "weak and struggling" by leaders of influence. The Organized Voters' Association has much more influence, generally, than the business associations. The union organizations, with the exception of the Pullman Car Porters Union, are also considered weak.

While I do not wish to go into too much detail in describing individual leaders in the sub-community, I do wish to present a structural picture of leadership patterns and relate this pattern to the larger community power structure. Let us turn, therefore, to such an analysis, picking up more detailed data on organizational patterns as we proceed.

In a poll of the top leaders of the sub-community, twenty-three schedules give comparable answers in identifying persons of power and influence. The ranking of leaders in Table 5 gives a leadership array which may be compared with that found in the larger community as illustrated in Table 2.[2] In

2. See p. 63, above. All names as well as organizations with whom leaders are identified are disguised, as in the discussion of the larger community.

examining the occupations of the Negro leaders one finds them
falling into the following categories: nineteen professionals;
eight commercial enterprisers; three banking and insurance
operators; two leisure persons (social leaders); one civic

TABLE 5

Sub-Community Leaders Ranked According to Number
of Votes Received from Other Negro Leaders
in Leadership Poll *

Leaders	Number of Votes
Calvert Smith	19
Courtney Jackson, Hedley Ryan	18
Myron Lake, Fortney Todd	17
Georgia Cravens	15
George Green	13
Cecil Bardon	12
Morris Elam, Claude Jones, Sidell Rumley	11
John Last	9
Gideon McKay, S. T. Story	8
Samuel Judson, Maude Lynde	7
Foster Ledder	6
Paisley Brown, Eva Trulowe	5
Elbert Johnson	4
Roy Clayton	3
Hyram Jasper, Maimie Stanton	2
Harvey Aberdeen, Nelson Hanson, Dolphan Greer, Blanche Keys, Mrs. John Last, Edmond Whitney	1
Myron Crookshank, Grant Missler, N. L. Norris, Gertrude Tylor, T. C. Whitlock	0

* Code numbers used in analyzing data and corresponding to names of
leaders are as follows:

1. Trulowe	12. Missler	24. Keys
2. Mrs. J. Last	13. Aberdeen	25. Whitney
3. Last	14. Cravens	26. Rumley
4. Bardon	15. Elam	27. Tylor
5. Ryan	16. Lynde	28. Jasper
6. Whitlock	17. Hanson	29. Greer
7. Johnson	18. Crookshank	30. Smith
8. Brown	19. Ledder	31. McKay
9. Green	20. Story	32. Norris
10. Todd	21. Judson	33. Clayton
11. Stanton	22. Lake	34. Jones
	23. Jackson	

worker (a retired postal employee); and one politician. This occupational listing differs markedly from that for top personnel in the larger community, where leadership is recruited largely from commerce and industry. Among the Negro professional workers are included a lawyer, a doctor, four educators, six ministers, and seven social workers. These professionals all work on top policy-making committees and boards with the community business leaders. Their advice on policy matters is sought and taken by the leadership group as a whole. This pattern does not hold true in the larger community where the majority of the professional personnel are found only in the under-structure supporting the power elements.

The fact that six ministers were included on the list of leaders differs from the situation in the larger community where no ministers were chosen. It is interesting to note, however, that although the ministers were included on the list they were not considered top leaders in a policy-making sense by those within the leadership group itself who voted on them. Only one minister was voted into the upper-limits group of top leaders in the poll. This is interesting, because there is a belief abroad in the large community that if anything is to be done through leadership in the Negro community, the ministers, the educators, and possibly the undertakers should be contacted in about that order. The top policy leaders turned up in the study were found to hold, in order of rank, the following positions: publisher, banker, minister, educator, politician, social worker (2), insurance executive, civic worker, and lawyer. The other ministers (including two bishops), the educators, and the undertaker were subordinate to the persons holding the above positions.

Inquiry was made about this matter in the interviews. The answers may be summed up in the words of Morris Elam, civic worker, who said, "The ministers and the undertakers are mostly selfish in their approach to most community situations. They either want to get more for themselves or to increase the size of their own organizations. People catch on to that sort of thing and when they are asked to choose leaders, they think of people that are not so much out for their own benefit. The doctors here are in the same category. They are interested in making money, but they are withdrawn from community life. They could not lead anyone."

It was asked if the ministers would be drawn in on projects to help secure agreement of opinion in the community—that is, after policy had been determined by the top leaders. One reply to this question was as follows: "Yes, the ministers have a part in getting projects under way and they can be helpful. You certainly would not leave them out, but I would not go to them *first* on a community-wide matter, because I would know that they would see a lot of reasons why they should not try to move the people. They would be thinking that any money-raising scheme, for example, would hurt their own contributions. They will go along on most things, if they think a lot of powerful people are behind a project."

From interviews with sub-community leaders the conclusion is clear that the process of decision on matters of policy rests with the top leaders, as it does in the larger community. The individual ministers representing church associations are utilized as channels of communication to apprise large numbers of people of these decisions. The civic associations stand in the same relationship to the leadership group. The process of decision within the upper group is called "getting it straight," that is, policy is informally cleared between top leaders, and the line is set, before it goes to the underlying mass of people.

An examination of the mutual choices of leaders in our poll indicates a pattern similar to that of the larger community. The persons making the highest number of mutual choices are shown in Table 6.

As in the larger community, there is a definite correlation between the number of votes received by a person as a top leader and the number of mutual choices he made and received. Figure 11 shows graphically the mutual-choice pattern. There is a slight tendency for the top leaders to go down the scale more in their choices than was true in the large community, as can be seen by comparing the pattern shown here with that illustrated in Figure 4.[3] By illustrating all mutual choices, as in Figure 12, it is clear that the mutual choices tend to remain in the upper-limits leadership group. The lower-limits leaders tend to pick leaders above them in the scale. This pattern is shown in Figure 13 and compares closely with the pattern of the larger community illustrated in Figure 5.[4]

TABLE 6

SUB-COMMUNITY LEADERSHIP BY NUMBERS OF
MUTUAL CHOICES BETWEEN LEADERS

Leaders	Number of mutual choices
Smith, Lake	8
Jones	7
Cravens, Green	6
Bardon, Todd	5
Jackson	4
Brown, Judson, Last, McKay	3
Elam, Norris	2
Jasper, Ledder, Stanton, Trulowe	1

In ascertaining the degree of interaction by top leaders on committees it was found that the upper-limits leaders interacted with an average of six more persons in the total group than did the lower-limits leaders. The upper group interacted with an average of 17.8 persons in the total group of leaders during the past five years, while the lower group averaged 11.7 persons. The evidence at hand indicates that the policy-making group tends toward closure. A total of 90 per cent of the leaders know each other either "well" or "socially." Only six

3. See p. 70, above.
4. See p. 71, above.

persons indicated that they knew another leader by hearsay, and only three admitted not knowing three different leaders in the group.

The leaders of the sub-community, like those of the larger community, live apart from their followers. Figure 14 (p. 123)

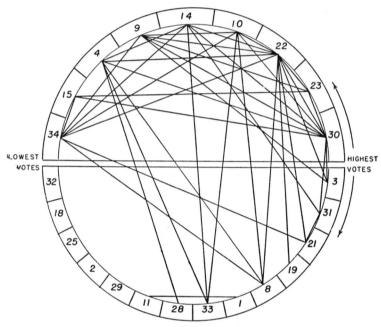

Fig. 11. Mutual Choices of 23 Leaders in Sub-Community Leadership Poll. (For key to numbers, see footnote to Table 5, p. 116.)

shows the areas in which the Negro leaders live. The leaders occupying dwellings in the northeast section of the sub-community represent families who have lived in the area for many years. This particular section is becoming less desirable as a neighborhood because the western section of the community is being built into a substantial dwelling area. Some of the homes in the latter district are as fine in appearance and luxury of appointments as many of the finest in Regional City. There is tacit agreement in the community as a whole that the westward movement of Negro dwellers shall proceed unabated.

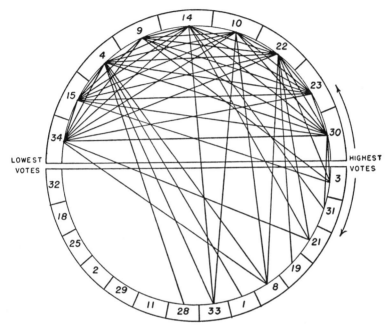

Fig. 12. All Choices of 9 Upper-Limits Group of Sub-Community Leaders in Leadership Poll. (For key to numbers, see footnote to Table 5, p. 116.)

This movement represents a "black belt" development, but to the sub-community it represents a way of breaking through the bonds of a ghetto-like existence that has plagued the area for many years.

Some other general characteristics of sub-community leaders may be mentioned before discussing in more detail the interrelations among them. The average age of these leaders is 54.3 years. The youngest leader was forty years old and the oldest seventy-three, with the median age at fifty-one. Few of these leaders were born in Regional City in contrast to their counter-group in the larger community. Only three were born locally. Five others were born in smaller communities in Old State,

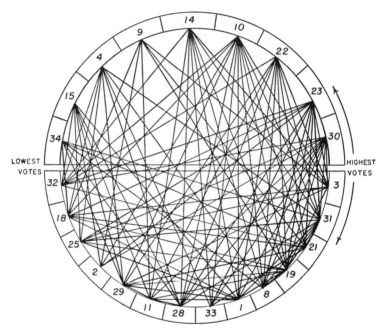

Fig. 13. All Choices of 14 Lower-Limits Group of Sub-Community Leaders in Leadership Poll. (For key to numbers, see footnote to Table 5, p. 116.)

while eleven were born in other states and five of these out of the region. It would appear that Regional City attracts Negroes of leadership capacity rather than developing them locally within the sub-community.

The religious affiliations of the sub-community leaders follow the pattern of the Protestant tradition of the larger community and the region. Of those from whom comparable data were obtained, eight were Methodists, seven Congregation-

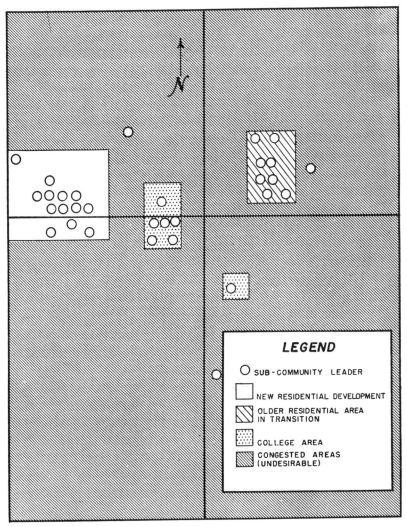

Fig. 14. Residential Areas Occupied by 31 Sub-Community Leaders.

alists, five Baptists, and two Episcopalians, the two last being
born outside the region.

Of twenty-two persons upon whom there is comparable
data, twenty-one owned their own homes. The non-owner was

an educator living within his educational institution. Four of these leaders owned their own businesses and other property besides. Nine others also owned property besides their homes. Most such properties consisted of additional real estate. On the whole it may be said, both from the data presented here and from observations of the group under discussion, that they represent a substantial element of the sub-community citizenry.

On the question of how many employees were supervised by the leaders, the answers ranged from a top figure of 1800 down to none. One bishop supervises 850 ministers in the region. Two educators have respectively 200 and 138 faculty members under their jurisdiction. Four leaders have between 50 and 100 employees working for them. Three have between 25 and 50. Compared with the thousands and hundreds of employees under the jurisdiction of some of the larger community leaders, these figures are not impressive, but they do show strength in organized economic and professional activity within the sub-community. The operators of the larger economic and cultural establishments are looked up to as leaders in this community, as comparable leaders are in the larger community.

The business owner who supervises 1800 employees compares favorably in status, within the sub-community, with the owner of the largest corporation in the general community. This man, Nelson Hanson, like Charles Homer in the white community, is a substantial contributor to charitable enterprises. His annual gross income is reportedly around $200,000. He is not a person who is active on committees and in the civic associations. He "operates through other men." Two of the other Negro leaders act as front men for Mr. Hanson and often make charitable contributions for him. Many community decisions are quietly cleared with him before the line is set. His business represents about a twenty-million-dollar capital investment which grosses two millions for the company annually. Mr. Hanson is the only member of the sub-community group of leaders who inherited his position from his father. The present business has its roots in real estate but it has expanded into other areas. As with the majority of other sub-community business enterprises, Mr. Hanson's activities fall within the commercial field.

Hanson is not well known to the leaders of the larger community. He does not interact with any of the white leaders. He feels quite strongly concerning some of the issues that confront the group with whom he lives and has threatened on occasion to move his business from Old State if conditions become less tolerable. Few believe that he would carry through this threat since Regional City is so well located for his business operations.

Six other leaders in the top group of the sub-community do not generally work through formal policy committees and on boards of civic agencies to achieve their ends, but the majority do. Out of twenty persons answering a question related to policy committee and board memberships, fourteen indicated that they each belonged to an average of 3.0 national groups, 1.2 state groups, and 3.0 local groups. The sub-community memberships in national groups thus equal the local memberships—a pattern that is quite different from that in the larger community. This possibly reflects the fact that many of the problems which affect Negroes locally have relatively strong national associational groupings. Three of the five local organizational groups which were considered top influential associations in the sub-community were organizations having strong national affiliations. The listing of the upper-limits organizations is presented in Table 7.

It was learned that besides the formal organizations there is also an elite association known as the "23 Club," which corresponds to the 49 Club and the 101 Committee in the larger community, previously described. The 23 Club has been in existence for more than a decade and most of the upper leaders belong to it. The members play golf together, have dinner meetings, and engage in what they term "chew sessions," which help to clarify group thinking and provide the basis of group solidarity on major problems or community issues. Membership in this club is carefully selected.

TABLE 7

NEGRO ORGANIZATIONS RECEIVING THE HIGHEST NUMBER OF VOTES IN SUB-COMMUNITY LEADERSHIP POLL

Organization	Number of Votes
N.A.A.C.P.	23
Y.M.C.A.	21
Organized Voters Association	18
Luncheon Club	17
Urban League	15
Fraternal Order	11
Welfare Organization	10
Business League	9
Social Fraternity	7
Y.W.C.A.	4

The preconceived notion was carried into the study that the social fraternities were powerful organizations. There are a great number of Greek letter societies in the sub-community. Only one of them, however, was considered influential in civic affairs, and it comes almost at the bottom of our listing of top organizations. Some of the social fraternities on the list in the questionnaire received no votes at all as top influence organizations. The role of the fraternities seems to be in the area of social rather than power relations.

In general it may be said that the top associational groupings identified in the sub-community have a political content not found in the larger community. This is true even in the welfare and recreational associations. It may also be said that the leadership within the associations, while entertaining discussion on political matters, tends to a conservative approach to issues. For example, during the formation of a Progressive party in Regional City there was considerable discussion on what part

Negroes should play in its activities. There was much open discussion of the matter in the associational meetings but the leadership was dedicated to remaining loyal to the traditional local parties of a more conservative nature. The Progressive party was stressing equal rights for Negroes in its platform in direct opposition to the older parties. This plank had considerable appeal to many of the citizens and the leaders did not openly oppose discussions of the issues presented by Progressive party candidates. They quietly worked against the movement, however. The process was described by one leader in these words:

"Many of us [the leaders] were in sympathy with the aims of the Progressive party, but we felt that more could be gained ultimately by sticking to the older parties. We discussed the matter of alignment very carefully among ourselves [the top leader group], and decided to play a waiting game. We knew that the Progressive party was scaring the leaders uptown and we thought the fright was good for them. If the party gained strength we could always threaten to go along with it, but we would wait and see.

"All of the leaders [in the sub-community] have one or two white men they can go to and discuss various matters that concern us. Whenever there is a threat of trouble or when the police get too brutal, we can get help from some of the men we know personally. At the time of the Progressive party activity the white men got in touch with us. They wanted to know how our people were reacting to the propaganda being put out by this party. They said they were very much against the party and hoped we were. They said they had helped us in the past and they wanted our help now.

"We discussed this among ourselves and agreed to let the uptown boys dangle a little. We finally told them, however, that we were not for the Progressive party ourselves and we would do what we could to discourage it in the community here. We said we could not act openly, but we would do what we could. We figured that we would really gain more by such a move on our part. As things turned out the Progressive party was a flop. I definitely think we gained something by not going too radical. Our strategy is to get places for ourselves in the older parties." [5]

The sub-community leadership is here taking a position characterized by Oliver C. Cox as that of "protest within the *status quo* (desire to be 'counted in')." [6] This position, so succinctly summarized by Cox, would seem to describe the general tenor of the demands for recognition made upon members of the larger community by the top leaders in the sub-community.

The relationships between sub-community and larger community leadership are well illustrated in the description of actions taken relative to the Progressive party. The conversations between white and Negro leaders reported above were informal in nature. The telephone was utilized in most instances. The leader quoted met a leader of the larger community in a meeting of the Community Council and had an informal discussion with him afterwards. Sub-community leaders never rate inclusion on the white upper-policy-strategy committees but are approached informally to get their opinions. This process is a relatively fixed pattern. The exception may lie, to some extent, in the realm of partisan politics.

Some of the top leaders in the sub-community do have access to the elected officials of the city, and on one or two occasions within the past five years some of the more progressive candidates for public office have visited the sub-community leaders in their offices. These visits are described as

---

5. The Progressive party will be referred to again as it relates to the dynamics of politics in the state and in the Regional City community. We are not concerned with describing the total program of this party, but only such parts of its activities as may illustrate specific points in our discussion, e.g., the dynamics herein illustrated.

6. See "Leadership Among Negroes," from *Studies in Leadership*, edited by Alvin W. Gouldner (New York: Harper and Brothers, 1950), p. 270.

stealthy. None of the other top policy leaders of the larger community have ever made personal visits to the private offices of the sub-community leaders, but some of the top leaders have entertained visits from delegations of Negro citizens in their own offices—sometimes at the request of the sub-community leaders and again upon invitation by the white leader. Such interchange of visits keeps the top leadership informed concerning sub-community opinion on selected issues, but the practice is considerably restricted and formal. There cannot be said to be a free flow of information in most situations affecting the sub-community and requiring policy decision. Usually crisis situations are involved when the two groups meet. For example, the sub-community may have reached a point where they are *demanding* better school facilities or recreation facilities or housing. At such a point there is much withholding of information on both sides in order to maintain bargaining advantage.

Many of the larger community leaders expressed interest in the fact that a study of leadership patterns was being made in the sub-community. They were particularly anxious, it appeared, to know who the real leaders were in the sub-community, indicating that they knew one or more Negro leaders, but that they were unsure of such leaders' position in the sub-community. One top leader in the white community asked that the field worker return for a second interview in order that he might discuss his own views regarding relations with the sub-community. No information was volunteered in such situations, but some pertinent material was picked up by allowing the larger community leaders to give their views concerning the pattern of inter-community relationships. Much of the information so gathered fell into stereotyped statements regarding Negro behavior, e.g., his love of churches that have emotional appeal, or the belief that the Negro wants to be left to develop his own patterns of life, etc. But some leaders were apparently honestly concerned with inter-community relations and were fumbling for ways to strengthen community ties.

Three leaders in the larger community were extremely impressed with the showing the sub-community had made in the Community Chest drives during the past three or four years. It had come to their attention that the Negroes were dissatisfied with the fact that none of them were invited to the progress report meetings during the campaign. One white leader suggested that perhaps next year a table at the luncheons might be set aside for some of the Negro leaders so that they might make their own reports. To this leader such a move would be a progressive step—a real concession. It would not satisfy the leaders of the sub-community, according to their own statements, but it does illustrate the fumbling for answers on the part of the larger community leaders. A few years ago, perhaps, such a concession would not have been even considered or discussed.

Another white leader said he felt that the housing demands of the Negro citizens were justified. He thought it a shame that the maids working in his neighborhood had to travel across town to their work. He favors a housing project for Negroes within easier commuting distance from his own home. Certainly the man's interest may be said to be selfishly motivated, because he has sometimes had to drive his maid across town to her home, but somehow he has become aware of the fact that there is a demand on the part of the sub-community for better housing arrangements.

The sub-community leaders who answered a question pertaining to larger community leadership chose seven men above others as leaders they felt they could depend upon in crisis situations. It is significant that five of these men are persons who have an active interest in partisan politics. Three were found to be upper-limits leaders in the larger community. Qualitatively the relationships with these men have not been close. The pattern of contact described earlier in this connection would be applicable. Many of the leaders chosen by the sub-community leaders have been prominent in fund-raising campaigns, and the sub-community leaders may have attended a general meeting in which the top leader of the larger community participated.

Generally speaking, it is safe to say that the sub-community leaders are not sufficiently acquainted with the top leaders of the larger community to make valid choices among them. Only ten sub-community leaders answered the question on this point. One sub-community leader illustrated the point by stating: "Complete segregation of racial groups in a community makes it impossible for a member of one racial group to evaluate the effectiveness of an individual in another racial group. Therefore, the names of the influential persons listed are somewhat meaningless to the Negro group. If, on the other hand, minority group representation had at all times been included on policy-making bodies, a better evaluation could be made of an individual's influence. In short, influence and effectiveness can only be measured by having had a personal or working relationship with the person measured."

In order to get some objective criterion of the working relationships existing between the white and Negro leadership groups in Regional City, the Negro leaders were asked to choose from a list of top leaders in the community those persons "with whom they had worked on community projects within the past five years." All the leaders in the larger community were not asked the same question, since it did not come to mind until after an analysis of the sub-community had begun. A total comparison of choices would be desirable, but this writing is necessarily limited, in large degree, to the choices made by Negroes of white leaders with whom they had worked. There is some qualitative information from the white leaders, but it cannot be adequately compared with the data gathered in the sub-community.

If the recognized political leaders in the larger community

are excluded from the choices of the sub-community leaders, the working relationships which Negro leaders have with top leaders in the larger community are confined for the most part to the under-structure of the top power group, i.e., the lower-limits leaders.

Figure 15 illustrates the fact that the leaders in the sub-community tend to work more frequently with the lower-limits group in the larger community and that the white leaders tend to work with lower-limits Negro leaders. The two groups are ranked in the figure according to the number of leadership votes they received from other leaders of their particular group. In twenty-seven instances on this chart a Negro leader had worked with a white leader farther down on the leadership scale than he was; in eighteen instances the reverse was true. We find further that six of the top white leaders had eleven contacts with Negro leaders; of the top ten Negro leaders, only four had contacts with white leaders. Only one of these was in contact with the top community leadership in the white community. He is Barden, a man connected with a financial institution in the Negro community. He has had frequent contact with white leaders in relation to community-wide charitable fund campaigns.

Three upper-limits partisan politicians in the larger community are excluded from Figure 15 in order to simplify it and to show some differences in patterns of working relationships that exist in the political and non-political areas. As has been indicated, the leaders in the sub-community do have contact with the elected officials and a few of their advisors. They also have contact with two of Old State's top-ranking political factional leaders. Figure 16 shows the choices of Negro leaders who indicated a working relationship with three of the partisan political leaders. Here it can be seen that top Negro leaders work with top white leaders. The top Negro leaders tended to work with all three of the white political leaders from whom they could choose. This is less true of the lower-

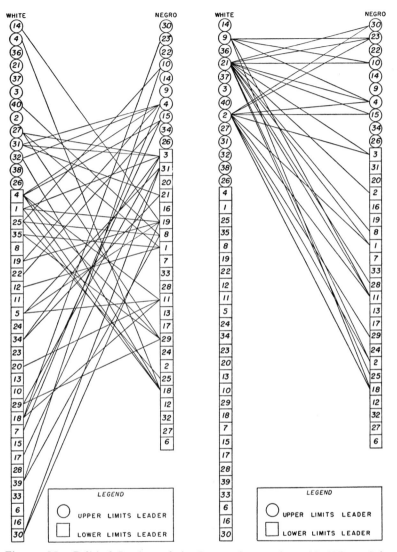

Fig. 15. Non-Political Leaders of the Larger Community with Whom Sub-Community Leaders Have Worked. (Exclusive of the Mayor and two leaders of Old State political factions, numbers 27, 31, and 32 represent larger community leaders who have been prominent in welfare fund campaigns. For key to numbers, see footnotes to Tables 2 and 5, pp. 63 and 116.)

Fig. 16. Upper-Limits Political Leaders from the Larger Community with Whom Sub-Community Leaders Have Worked. (For key to numbers, see Tables 2 and 5, pp. 63 and 116.)

limits Negro leaders. The top Negro leaders averaged 2.4 working political relationships as compared with 1.6 relationships for the lower-limits Negro leaders. The reverse case is true for the non-political activities, as was seen above. There the upper-limits Negro leaders averaged 2.8 working relationships with white leaders, while the lower-limits Negro leaders averaged 3.4 such relationships.

These figures are presented with some caution. "Working relationship" is not rigorously defined, and in some cases the sub-community leaders indicated that they had worked with some of the persons in the larger community who are not actively engaged in civic affairs in the community. Some of the non-political choices of the Negro respondents were made from society leaders, with whom there is little possibility of any kind of contact. Other choices were made of men who have been active in large-scale community enterprises such as the Community Chest or Red Cross campaigns. These choices of working partners may be the result, in some cases, of random selection on the part of the respondents. The distinction shown between political and non-political choices, however, seems generally to be a valid picture.

Within recent years there has been a growing recognition on the part of more of the leaders in the sub-community that a united stand must be taken on common issues. The task of welding together the Negro leadership in the community has not been an easy one. The jealousies and striving for individual recognition on the part of many leaders in the sub-community have required tact and finesse on the part of those who have been instrumental in bringing about much of the unity on policy matters that seems to exist today. One of the Negro social workers in a community organization agency had this to say in writing:[7]

"Regional City has been an awfully difficult community in

7. Paraphrased to disguise identification.

which to get concerted community action. This is especially true in the Negro community, and yet in the past ten years we have had unusual success. It should be borne in mind that there is terrific pressure for individual power and a great amount of friction and jealousy between leaders which has defeated many community projects.

"A few of us several years ago decided that we would try to break through this difficulty and bring together dissident people, who as individuals had considerable power as leaders in the community and yet by uniting with others would be far more effective. Since the Community Association was sort of neutral grounds, much of this has taken place through this organization, but with the organization remaining as much in the background as possible. The most significant instance of this was the formation of the Organized Voters League bringing together Calvert Smith and Courtney Jackson who stand out as the two most significant leaders in the Negro community of Regional City and possibly Old State. A few of us have continually kept in mind, however, that in order to achieve unity of action great care had to be taken to divide recognition, not only among the two leaders mentioned above but at other points with other leaders who have been equally difficult. All of the groups listed in the questionnaire have been instrumental in working together on community projects.

"One of the most difficult areas to secure cooperation has been the Negro Church, and yet in no list can they be omitted. I think very properly, however, this survey is using the names of ministers rather than churches, but here again the fusing of individuals to a common community project has always been difficult and has always required constant understanding of the individuals involved.

"Several of the people included on this list, in my opinion, are extreme individualists and sometimes have to be avoided if the project is to go forward. Some on the list are so interested in personal recognition, either for themselves or the

organization or both, that the project has to be pretty well
under way or at least developed quietly in its formative stage
so that these difficult people would not destroy it even before
it was born."

The role of the professional Negro worker is well illustrated
in the above statement. It is a role of leadership. In the main,
the professional workers have been acutely aware of the problems confronting their community and most of them have
guided their agency programs along lines of "community organization" endeavor. Politics has not frightened them and
they have been in the middle of many political issues affecting their community. The Negro agency programs seem to
have a more secure base in community participation by larger
numbers of citizenry than is true in the larger community.

The Negro professional persons named as leaders are comparable in job placements to the white professional under-
structure with which the top power leaders in Regional City
were compared, but in the sub-community they are consulted,
as has been indicated, and have a great part to play in formulating policy for the total Negro group. This is not to say that
they are not outranked in wealth and in other appurtenances
of social status within their own community. They are sub-
ordinated to several of the persons mentioned, but they, unlike
the professionals in the larger community, have a voice in
policy decisions affecting their life arrangements. They are a
part of what is called in the Negro community the "Big Links."
The Big Links represent the group of leaders in the top influence brackets who have for many years dominated civic affairs
in the Negro community much as the top leaders dominate in the larger community. Some of the power leaders mentioned are also links to the general community.

Even with some familiarity with the larger social patterns
operative in this sub-community, many of the more subtle lines
of communication and behavior in relation to community

affairs and power are beyond the writer's present knowledge. It was deemed highly important, however, to include such facts as have been gathered concerning this community because it is an area of study that has been neglected more often than not in general community studies. Such relationship patterns as have been observed to exist between the sub-community and some members of the larger community will therefore be presented here.

Some of the under-structure professional personnel in civic and social work in Regional City seem to have established a fairly good working relationship with several of the top leaders in the sub-community. In the field of health-welfare planning the interrelationships are particularly strong. Yet, from a power point of view, the health-welfare planners of the community are a relatively weak group in the area of policy. This fact is recognized by the leaders of the sub-community. One sub-community leader stated that he had been a board member on one of the social planning groups for several years, but he stopped attending the meetings because he felt that there was too much discussion in the group that culminated in too little action. He has since turned his attention to political activities within his own community.

Another sub-community leader stated that he had attended meetings held by one of the welfare groups for a long time. This particular group was "liberal" in its thinking and decided to hold a series of luncheons in which total community problems might be discussed. No Negroes attended these luncheons, even though they were invited, because they felt that even though the welfare group was sincere in its desire to have them attend, it was such a weak group in the community that they would ultimately be embarrassed by having interracial luncheons. No Negroes were invited to the sessions in which the luncheons were planned, this man said, or they would have stated their objections rather than failing to appear at the luncheons. He said, "My wife insisted that I should attend in spite of the possibilities of a community uproar over the matter, but I just couldn't bring myself to do it." A few professionals do attend a regular luncheon meeting in the sub-community. Many of them are dedicated to a change in racial relations, but they are a small and weak minority at present. The top policy leaders in the white community are vigilant that the pattern of "fraternization" between under-structure professionals and sub-community personnel be kept within bounds of the existing mores as interpreted by them. However, they uneasily tolerate the fact that some white professionals do attend Negro community functions.

Some of the leaders of the larger community to whom the sub-community leaders look for help are not actually sympathetic to aspirations of this group. They mock the sub-community privately, even as they solicit money from them in their community-wide campaigns. They believe they can flatter some of the sub-community leaders, and they apparently do so enough to get their money. On the basic issues revolving around segregation, the top leaders in the larger community are adamant in maintaining the present alignment of relationships. As one white leader put it, "It is not what they want—it is what they are going to get that counts!" The man who said this is considered a friend by some of the sub-community leaders. He was dumbfounded when told that some of the Negro leaders had chosen him as a top leader in the larger community. He said, "I don't need their votes. Of course, I'm a true friend of the Negro and will be as long as he keeps his place."

Under the existing patterns of segregation and social exclusion operative in the general community of Regional City, Negro leaders, as well as followers, have to adapt themselves to the situation. Let us be somewhat more specific on this point by discussing, first and briefly, two sub-community leaders, and then turn to some generalizations concerning power relations and the sub-community.

Two of the leaders named in this study, Calvert Smith and Courtney Jackson, represent the strongest leadership in the sub-community. Mr. Smith has been discussed before and was described as a sub-boss in Regional City affairs. What has been said about him need not be repeated, but it should be stressed that he is considered a powerful person both within and outside his immediate community.

Courtney Jackson is a banker who is highly favored by the general community as a quiet and effective man. He acts as a liaison person between the Negro community and the larger community. He likes to operate quietly. He will not engage in the protest type of meeting in which demands are occasionally put forward to the political and other under-structure leaders of the general community, but as he puts it: "I lie low till things have quieted down some; then I get to two or three key people in the other community and we usually work things out all right." He thinks of himself as "operating behind the scenes." The contacts he mentioned in the general community, with but one exception, were second- or third-rate men in the opinion of their own peers. None of the leaders in the Negro community may operate in the same echelons of power as the top leaders in the total community, and herein lies a basic difference between the power wielded by the top Negro leaders and the top leaders of the general community.

The definition of power as the ability of personnel to move goods and services toward defined goals gives some Negro leaders power, but within limits. Within their businesses and professions they have power. They have power of decision within these limits. They have certain power within their own community to organize services on a sub-community-wide basis, and this is done much in the same order as community projects are initiated and carried through in the larger community. Committee structures are utilized and many of the same rituals of inclusion and exclusion come into play. Organizations and certain institutions, particularly the religious, educational, and economic institutions, play an important role in civic projects—but on a limited scale.

When larger issues or projects must be tackled, the leadership of the larger community is often consulted and it is appealed to for help. Recently a building program was contemplated for the Community Association. The cost of the project was prohibitive in terms of the resources of the Negro community. The aid of the larger community was solicited and received. The general community was sold on the project on the basis that such an institution as the Community Association helps to keep down unrest and that it plays a vital role in quelling delinquency, which is considered a pressing problem by the community at large. The leaders are willing to use the notion that they are able to "quiet unrest" among the Negro population, but it is not entirely clear how they would go about this, nor is there any accurate measure which has been found to ascertain how much unrest there may be in the sub-community. There is indication that there is much dissatisfaction with certain policies which spring from the segregated status of the Negro community. The point here is that the Negro leaders maintain themselves in semi-power positions, in some instances, by appealing to the fears of the general community concerning the unrest of their community, while on the other hand they appeal to their people on the basis that they are actively working out the problems which may be defined as causing the unrest they say they would assuage. They are apparently sincere in most instances, but it is also evident that the Negro leaders work under certain structural handicaps in attaining their goals.

General community policy is determined by persons with whom the leaders in the Negro community have little contact. The most potent contact between the Negro community and the larger community is that between the political leaders of both communities. The Mayor of Regional City was once considered anti-Negro in his public pronouncements. With the advent of Negro voting on a large scale, the Mayor is less vociferous concerning his views. The Negro leaders are well aware of his change of heart, and they see progress in the situation. Many of the Negro leaders pin great hope on the fact that their votes count heavily in municipal elections. They have been able to demand and receive certain concessions. They have a few Negro policemen on the municipal force. They have been able to get two parks and other recreational facilities where none existed a few years ago. They are getting concessions in school building facilities, and the teachers are being paid on an equal basis with other teachers in the community. These concessions are all traceable to the power of the ballot, and Negro leaders point them out to their constituents and take credit for them as real achievements. The top leaders are still operating in connection with a lower echelon of power in Regional City, because they must deal with the elected political leaders who are not the top policy-makers in the community. The importance of such working relationships in achieving the goals indicated cannot be denied, but the fact that the contacts of the Negro leaders are limited to such a degree indicates a community structural weakness.

The lack of any but a superficial relationship between Negro leaders and the men of top decision in the larger community is a serious handicap in over-all policy arrangements. Observation of the community and interviews related to this subject with several top leaders in the larger community lead one to believe that the real leaders in the sub-community are not generally known to the top white policy-makers. Only two men who rated high among the leaders in the sub-community were selected by the top white leaders with whom the matter was discussed. They were Morris Elam and Myron Lake, neither of whom is considered an aggressive leader in his own community. The aggressive leaders are considered to be those men who put the interests of the Negro community before their own and who are willing and able to speak forcefully to mixed audiences in which the interests of the Negro group are put forward. The acceptable leaders in the larger community tend to be less acceptable in the Negro community. The one exception to this statement may be that of the leadership of the banker, Courtney Jackson.

The aggressive leader, Calvert Smith, is recognized as a real leader by the white policy-makers, but they do not accept his leadership in terms of a person with whom they would choose to work. Their rejection of him as such a leader does not appear to trouble Mr. Smith, who recognizes that he may antagonize some of the people in the larger community, but the rejection does remove him from any kind of close working relationship with the top community leaders as a group. By the totality of community circumstances, he is forced into a position of working on a political basis with politicians in the community at large, politicians who themselves are subordinate to larger powers. The structural relationship to the sources of power and policy decision must accordingly be indirect for most of the top Negro leaders.

Some of the professional leaders in the Negro community are acceptable on the boards of certain civic and charitable organizations in the larger community, and their position on these boards offers them an opportunity to place before this segment of the larger community many of the problems and issues which face them as leaders within their own community; but again they are placed in an under-structured position in relation to the men of power in the larger community. It has been pointed out that the associations in Regional City are considered a part of the "bureaucratic" under-structure which carries out policy in most instances rather than initiating and formulating it. The associations which do have Negro membership on their boards are often somewhat questionable in the eyes of some of the top community leaders, but they do offer a source of information to the top leaders concerning certain projects considered essential for "quieting unrest." There is certainly value in this contact, indirect as it may be.

Within the Negro community there are two points of view as to how issues should be brought before the whole community. The conservative leaders are prone to say, "Now is not the time to act." This philosophy is the familiar pattern laid down by Booker T. Washington. Education, as he conceived it, and a gradual approach to solving problems appeal to this group. On the other hand, the aggressive leaders are more militant and are unwilling to let much time elapse before seeing progress in meeting their demands. These conflicting interests make the Negro leadership "walk a tightrope," as one leader put it. They are constantly having to mediate between the two groups, but they have, in the main, been able to satisfy both factions and thus retain a position of prominence in the community. The stability of the leadership in the Negro community is a functional necessity for the leaders in the community at large; and consequently, through the channels described, a relationship does exist between the total community and the sub-community, however unsatisfactory to all concerned.

Some of the business leaders of the sub-community expressed the idea that progress in race relations can come for the minority group only through integration into the economic spheres of community activity. They point out that "trade knows no barriers," and they feel that they are making substantial progress in building potent economic enterprises. Looking at their business establishments from the point of view of size and comparing them with some of the business establishments of the larger community, one can safely say that the sub-community businessmen have a long way to go to catch up with their giant neighbors. Power is a relative matter, of course, and the men in secure economic positions in the community feel their influence and prestige mount as they are successful within their own community. Yet there are constant reminders, even to these men, that they are in a sub-status within the larger community. The police, if no one else, so remind them.

Naked power in the form of force is practiced on the recalcitrant members of the underlying population by the police of the larger community. Negroes are arrested on slight provocation, and their fines amount to a substantial portion of the revenues of the municipal police budget. With the advent of increased political power, the situation has perhaps improved somewhat, but according to observations made during the progress of this study there is still much to be desired in this area. Many Negro professionals will not venture forth at night for fear of being picked up by the police and subjected to indignities. Night meetings of the larger community associations of which Negroes may be a part are usually poorly attended by the latter group. If Negro women do venture out, they are escorted by men companions because of fear of attack by the police or hoodlums in the community who prey on unescorted Negro females. Many of the meeting places in the community are closed to interracial groups, which highlights another structural weakness in the community.

For many years the policy of moving Negro riders to the back of busses and street cars was held in force by settled habits of the people in Regional City. There may have been grumbling and dissatisfaction with the practice in normal times. It is known that with the advent of World War II there was a heavy burden placed upon the public transportation facilities. Cars were overcrowded with many riders, white and Negro, standing in the aisles. The familiar pattern of movement of Negroes to the rear became a very real physical problem, and the enforcement of the policy fell upon the trolley conductors as a difficult social problem. The conductors or motormen were for the most part uneducated men, untrained in handling the human relations involved. There was serious question in the minds of many white people in the community as to whether segregation on common carriers could long hold as a social pattern. But since the "Negro question" has long been a potent Old State party political issue, the policy was kept in force. The Old State party was a Democratic party faction with a "white supremacy" plank in its platform. Newspaper writers upheld the traditions of the region on the matter, and the Klan and other groups discussed the matter in terms of "keeping things as they had always been." Inflammatory speeches made in these meetings were common gossip. Professional and middle class people would say to one another privately, "I am personally for doing away with segregation on the cars, but it is too hot an issue to become involved in. Now is not the time to do it. It would merely give an issue to the outs in Old State party politics upon which they could ride back in." (Incidentally, the Old State "outs" got back "in" in spite of the cautious approach of the groups who generally call themselves the liberals in Regional City. How they got back in is to be discussed later in relation to Traverse Simpkins' campaign for the post of governor.)

All the while this informal discussion of policy was in progress, the car operators were finding it more and more difficult to enforce the rules for "proper" racial conduct on the cars. Several fights occurred between operators and Negro riders. One such altercation was reported by a Negro rider as follows:

"I was on the X car going home. I did not ride the trolley often because of the crowded conditions, but on this particular night, I had to. At one of the stops a working man got on the car, which was extremely crowded. He was in overalls, and they were covered with the dirt of his trade. As the car started, he failed to move to the rear. The motorman stopped the car in the middle of the block and demanded in an angry tone that the man move rear. The man replied in a lower tone, but with some emphasis, that he was too dirty to 'move through all those people.' The motorman in rising anger ordered the man to the rear and loosened an emergency tool of the car threatening the man with violence if he did not obey him.

"More angry words followed, accompanied by cursing on the part of both men. The cords on the necks of both men had risen," said the informant, "and I saw before me the loosening of so many tensions of race that affected us all in varying degrees. Suddenly the motorman struck his adversary a hard blow on the head with the iron tool. The men grappled, and the Negro wrenched the weapon from the motorman and beat him almost to death to the horror of the onlookers. There was a wild milling within the car to get out. Someone managed to open the front door, and the Negro who had been fighting kicked the body of the motorman to the ground before fleeing into the darkness. Many on the car fled likewise. The police came, and held some witnesses, but the Negro man was never located. No one recognized him."

Following this episode all car operators were deputized as special police and armed with revolvers. There was very little publicity on this action, but periodically the papers carried back page stories of Negroes who had been wounded or killed by the trolley operators. Violence is in this case a concomitant of policy, and policy within our definition is determined by the wills of men and is sanctioned within the social structure. Threats and statements designed to intimidate were followed in this case by the power-practice of violence.

Violence usually comes into play when threats, subtle coercion, and veiled intimidation fail. Regional City has experienced its share of house bombings by hoodlum groups who try to keep the Negro community "in its place," that is, keep it from encroaching on white areas. Early history records a major race riot and a long series of lesser flareups. The police, the trolley car conductors, the "patriotic" organizations, and the local Ku Klux Klan units are some of the instruments of violence. There is insufficient information on the total pattern of linkage between the upper echelons of the power structure and these groups, but there are hints among some of the professional groups and townspeople that these groups of violence are financially supported by the "big boys," as the top leaders are called. At least two persons, however, are known as links between top leaders and the mobile under-structure of violent force. There is an uneasy acquiescence on the part of the governing groups in firm measures taken by the police, trolley operators, and some of the patriotic organizations in keeping order. The Klan is looked upon with disfavor by many. Newspaper editorials occasionally condemn the actions of the Klan, and an ordinance has been passed prohibiting masked meetings and parades. The "public will," that is, the decision of many organized groups, is turning against such open measures of violence as those acts carried out by the Klan, or in the name of the Klan.

The Mayor admitted in an interview with him that there is still considerable Klan activity in Regional City and that many of the police, firemen, and trolleymen are members. He attributes their interest in the Klan to the fact that so many of them are "country folks come to the city" and that they are organized to "keep the way of life they knew in the country." There are other organized groups which we have not mentioned, but the groups indicated are the most active in the use of controls of a violent nature. Two informants indicated that the gamblers helped finance some of the operations of the major repressive organizations.

In summary, the Negro community in its structural patterning of power relationships with reference to the larger community, occupies a place roughly comparable to that occupied by any one of the larger associational groupings in the community, with the exception that no members of the Negro group are called upon to contribute to top policy-making in the larger community.

Structurally a community participation scheme would appear something like that presented in Figure 17. It may be readily seen that this structural pattern follows the scheme illustrated in Figure 8.[8] The essential difference lies in the inclusion of Negro citizens in the lower brackets of the structure and the indication by broken lines within the institutional and associational pyramids that there is a bar to their rising to the apex in either of these groupings. The bottom structures of all pyramids are theoretically open to all groups of the population. In no case may the Negro citizen break out of the pyramids into the upper echelons of policy-making groupings at the top of the total community structure. This is the general pattern of participation of the Negro community in the power pattern in Regional City. Negroes can rise higher in the government group through voting rights, and in the civic association groups through more widespread acceptance of participation there.

In a certain sense organized labor in the larger community is held within similar bounds in the power structure. The associational channels are generally closed to the labor leaders and to the underlying labor personnel, and top labor personnel is absent from most of the highest ranking policy committees. But organized labor cannot be said to be a community. Thus, the sub-community we have been describing stands alone in its isolation from the sources of power as no other unit within the metropolitan area. Its channels of communication in most of its power relations with the larger community are partially blocked, if not totally closed. This stands in contrast to the sub-community of Websterville, the outlying suburb of Regional City previously mentioned. The citizens of Websterville may participate freely in most of the city's associational

8. See p. 91, above.

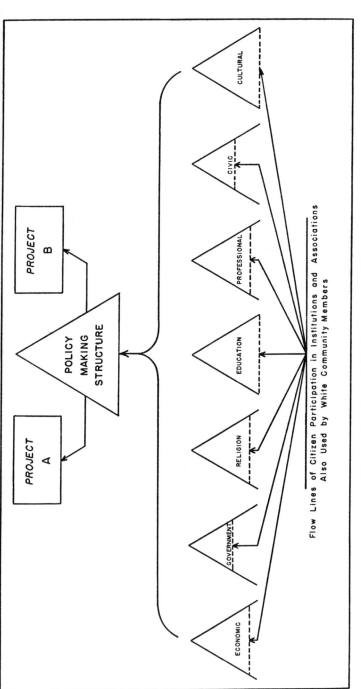

Fig. 17. Relation of Sub-Community Citizens to Policy-Making Structure in Regional City.

and institutional structures with the exception of government in the city proper.

Regional City's Jewish "community," a sub-community only in a special sense, will merely be mentioned here. Many limitations exist in general community participation for this group—yet compared with the Negro community, the Jewish community enjoys great freedom of privilege and movement. Four of the top policy leaders in the large community are of the Jewish faith.

6 REGIONAL CITY IN POLITICAL PERSPECTIVE

NO community is an isolated entity—particularly when it is as large and complex as Regional City. The policies of Regional City are inextricably bound up with state and national policies and, to some extent, with international policies. They are also inextricably bound up with politics. The first part of the present discussion will therefore concern itself with politics in Old State, and, as we shall see, politics in Old State is dominated to a large extent by the "Negro problem." The so-called Negro problem of the state spills over into Regional City through an influx of rural Negro migrants, and, in other ways, from the outlying territory of the community and state. Neither the state nor the community of Regional City has developed adequate provisions for meeting the many problems presented by this large minority group. The traditional methods of suppression and coercion are failing.

The Negro, as an issue, has dominated Old State politics for many decades, but there are voices in the state that are protesting other issues. These voices belong to city men who are concerned with pressing organizational problems that have not traditionally troubled the politicians of rural areas. Consequently, there has been a growing struggle for a balance of power favoring the urban as over against the rural areas. Gradually the urban areas, through the dominance of various

152 COMMUNITY POWER STRUCTURE

corporate groupings, have gained power, *de facto*, and to retain and legitimize this power candidates are sought who can command a large following in the rural areas and at the same time be sympathetic to the urban and corporate interests. The survival of the latter interests is of paramount importance to the leaders in Regional City. Because of the dominance of Regional City in the state, no other community group of leaders is quite as interested as they in the outcome of state elections.

Historically the selection of gubernatorial candidates has been of major interest to the leaders in Regional City. In some measure they have been able to exercise control over state politics by holding key posts in one or another of the factions in the major political party of the state and from these positions using influence to name gubernatorial candidates. All candidates are financed largely by the big business interests who control the elected governors. These facts of political life in the state are carefully kept from the rural electorate—as carefully kept as possible. The rural people are under the impression that they control state politics and in some measure they still do. At least an appeal must be made periodically to the rural electorate for their support of chosen candidates. The tried and true formula for a successful campaign that appeals to the rural voters has been to raise the "race issue."

The race issue has been a convenient one. It appeals to the rural people, and it detracts from many of the real issues that beset the larger cities. As an issue, race has far less appeal in Regional City than it has in the rural communities. There is, consequently, difficulty in choosing candidates who will appeal to both the urban and the rural electorate. The balance in choosing candidates is currently on the side of picking a man who can appeal to the rural voters, since they can out-vote the urban districts through a coalition of rural counties.

The discussion of state politics will be followed by mention of two other political areas, national and international, that impinge on the community. This mention will be very brief in contrast to the materials presented on Old State, but it seems necessary, for in total perspective both national and international politics are highly important, if not generally recognized, aspects of community life. There is a tendency for extra-community politics to be played down in community life—particularly among the lower strata of the voting population. Action on state, national, and international matters of policy is made to appear foreign to what one should be doing as a community citizen. The ordinary citizen who gets too vitally interested in political affairs outside the community runs the chance of being considered a little queer, if not radical. There is an unwritten and unspoken code of conduct abroad in communities which would allow only the leaders to be vociferous and active in political affairs beyond community borders. Such perspective of community participation seems to be askew when measured in democratic terms.

The manipulation of the voters of Old State is carried on to some extent by the ability of candidates to speak to rural voters in "folksy" terms in contrast to what has appeal to the urban residents. To elect state officials, the rural people must be appealed to in language they understand.

One of the difficulties in choosing a man who is in sympathy with the goals of the larger interests in Old State, and who can also appeal to the people of the state, is that most corporation executives and attorneys are city-bred men who cannot speak the language of the people. For several years this difficulty was surmounted in Old State by the selection, by the corporate interests, of a man called Traverse Simpkins. Mr. Simpkins early acquired the nickname, "Old Hoss." Simpkins had been a wheel horse in the legislature; and as his party regularity and leadership capacities became appreciated, the nickname was given to him and it stuck.

The frame of reference employed in examining Regional City's structural connection with Old State politics may be found in Howard W. Odum's exposition of "folkways" and "technicways." [1] Regional City represents the technicways of the state society of Old State, that is, it represents maximum achievement in industry, in manipulation of the state apparatus, and in centralization of power. It is, furthermore, a center of learning, technology, and intellectualism. The values of such a community are in conflict with the rural "folk" of Old State whose ways of behavior represent the opposite pole from "state society" as embodied in Regional City culture. Appeal to the voters in Old State must be made to the people in the rural districts in their own terms. "Old Hoss" Simpkins was a man who could perform this feat, as can be demonstrated. Let us begin a campaign speaking tour with him.

Old Hoss, sitting on the speaker's platform listening to an introduction of himself, appeared to be a confident man. His campaign manager, Ray Cockle, was speaking. [2] Thumbs shoved into his famous silk waistcoat, Simpkins peered out over his heavy-rimmed glasses, recognizing with a smile and a nod some of the "common-folks," his wheel horses. He appeared impatient for his turn at the stage, but Ray Cockle was wound up and appeared loath to relinquish the pleasure of playing up to an appreciative audience. The band was tuned up to play "Dixie," and the crowd was listening in good-humored disbelief as Cockle said, "Mr. Simpkins is engaged in no mudslinging campaign.... He is letting me and some of the others do the hell-raising...." (laughter)

The "red-necked" men in faded clothes had gathered early in the day, coming to town in their clay-spattered old cars. They had stood around in little groups discussing crops, weather, and politics, while their women-folks shopped with

1. *Understanding Society* (New York: The Macmillan Company, 1947), pp. 260 ff.
2. Notes of the speaker's words were taken from the newspapers *Regional City Star* and *Afternoon Sentinel*.

the kids. While the men waited, they would break into small groups and go into the back alleys "for a chance at the bottle," and come out laughing at "the good ones" they had heard. These men were now waiting for "the main show."

But Ray Cockle continued, "They [the opposition] claim there is nothing they can do toward restoring the white primary.... If they feel that way, they ought to get off the nest and turn it over to someone who thinks he can do something about it!" (yells, whistles) The band strikes up "Dixie."

Then, Old Hoss!

The crowd, worked up to a pitch of excitement, yells, stomps, whistles, "Yahoo-o! Give it to 'em, Hoss! Tell 'em about it! Whoo-ee!" And he told them many things—many things his crowds wanted to hear and in a language they understood.

"I am counting," Simpkins began, "on the man in overalls." The countrymen would look quickly around them. "I've talked to the city folks, asking that they challenge the votes of thousands of Negroes who are registered to vote, but it is the man in overalls, out in the country, who is going to really do things to stop them from voting.... If the men in overalls don't help me get control of this situation, then I don't know who can!" As he spoke, a group of Negroes near the railroad station listened.

This theme was a major recurrent one throughout the campaign. The issues exposed here are used to pose the rural man in overalls against the city man who, by Simpkins' definitions, would belittle the former in dress and manner and, by "trickery," would remove his "superiority" over the Negro in voting rights. Control of the countryman's vote is a functional necessity for control of the cities in Old State by the men of power who reside primarily in the cities, and in Regional City in particular. The countryman is traditionally conservative in his thinking, while the townsman is more radical.[3] Support of the more conservative elements in the rural areas of Old State helps the policy-makers of Regional City to balance power in their own conservative interests.

"I have been telling county officials all over the state to purge their lists of Negro voters," Simpkins continued, "cut them down with a fine-toothed comb! I certainly couldn't be consistent if I advised our Negroes not to vote, and then went out and solicited their support. If I get a single Negro vote, it will surely be an accident."

Later, however, Simpkins became aware that, among some classes of white voters, his opposition was making political capital out of what was termed "Simpkins' hate for our Negro citizens," and he said soothingly, "Oh, how they are spreading the propaganda. I hear it in barbershops and in the stores I go into over the state [appeal to the familiar], and they ask, 'Why do you hate the Negro?' Goodness knows, we do not hate the Negro [taking his listeners with him].... We have the greatest respect for the Negro [pause] in his place!" (Yahoo-o!)

"No Negro will vote," Old Hoss would promise, "during the next two years in Old State!"

"How you gonna stop 'em?" someone in the crowd would yell, "when the Supreme Court says they can?"

Old Hoss would pretend to cogitate on that one; then he would drawl, "A lot of people have asked me how I'm going to get around the Supreme Court decision against segregation. There are plenty of ways to stop a law, even if you follow a law. Many a time I've seen an old cow leaning over the fence to nip the grass—but she didn't leave the pasture!" So had his listeners seen this. (Whoo-ee!)

There was, however, a crack in the solid wall of bigotry in the campaign. Even though the Negro issue carried the day for Simpkins, his opponents were leading away from that sub-

3. Howard B. Woolston, "The Urban Habit of Mind," *American Journal of Sociology*, XVII (March 1912), 612.

ject. The real issues, those related to social and economic life, in Regional City, cannot be assuaged by appeals to folk prejudice. The ability of the men of power in Old State to cope with some of the pressing problems in the large cities will in the end, perhaps, determine whether or not they maintain their power. The Negro, as an issue, is a false approach to policy determination. In the campaign described here, both of Simpkins' opponents were forcibly pointing out this fact.

Concerning corporate domination of the state legislature, several sources indicated that the X Company of Regional City held a great deal of power within that organ of government. The president of the X corporation was asked if this were true, and his reply to this question and to subsequent ones is quoted:

"I have been connected with the legislature since I was twelve years old . . . as a page boy, and later as a member of the house. . . . I do not believe the X Company dominates the legislature . . . my father was a man who damned the X Company for all he was worth. I heard this kind of thing as I grew up . . . maybe there was some domination in the early days when the company was trying to get franchises—just like the railroads in the early days, but that's pretty well over, and now we are pretty well out of open politics."

A worker asked, "What if there was a tax bill before the legislature not in the interests of the Company?"

Answer: "Well, that would be a different situation. We would fight for our legitimate rights, but we would not do it alone. We would get together with other corporations whose interests would also be threatened. We would appear before committees and do anything else to keep from being taxed out of existence."

Worker: "Would some legislators be bought in this process?"

Answer: "There might be a few who would sell their votes, but a man like that does not last long. His usefulness is limited.

There are an awful lot of gullible businessmen who fall for the line that some person can swing a bloc of votes. My experience would lead me to believe that these fellows for the most part could not deliver, but nobody takes the time or trouble to check up on them, and year after year they hang on—milking gullible businessmen—and very reputable ones sometimes at that."

Worker: "How about electing men to the legislature?"

Answer: "Some of our men do get elected, but they are always good men in their own right, and fairly independent, except where the interest of the Company is concerned. Of course, they would go along on matters like that."

The domination of Old State politics by the men of power in Regional City is a functional necessity so far as these men are concerned. The region beyond the borders of Old State stands in a somewhat similar position to the city but in a less marked degree. The men of power in the city have economic interests in all the neighboring states. They may have, in many instances, some ties with regional trade associations and with similar organizations with their network of attorneys and bureaucratic personnel, but the next higher power groups with which the power personnel interact on matters of governmental concern most frequently are on the national level.

The present chapter is fundamentally concerned with what the men of power *do*. It has been suggested that the use of a controlled politician in the state setting—the use of a man who can garner votes to secure executive power in sympathy with the interests of the power structure—is a common practice. Political parties are mainly, although not exclusively, concerned with *who* shall exercise power.[4] Pressure groups and the men of decision are also concerned with *how* power shall be exercised.

4. Joseph Roucek, "Political Behavior as a Struggle for Power," *Journal of Social Philosophy*, VI (July 1941), 343.

The policy-making group in Regional City is primarily interested in how power shall be exercised and consequently is concerned over who shall be in governmental positions in the exercise of public power. Public power has the sanction of "legitimate force." There are many other ways in which the men of power in Regional City may intimidate or coerce the under-structure personnel to do their bidding by direct or indirect methods, but once in a while force becomes necessary. Two illustrations will be given.

Within Regional City there are two factions of the one-party political machinery of Old State. Such of our men of power as Elsworth Mines, Truman Worth, Epworth Simpson, George Delbert, Harry Parker, Ray Moster, James Treat, and Charles Homer belong to the faction which now controls state politics. Their candidate for governor has for years been Traverse Simpkins. James Treat is the man who has the direct control over Simpkins. Simpkins has been in and out of office, since no governor may succeed himself for more than two successive two-year terms in Old State. He has failed of re-election twice in the past three decades, but in those instances he has been defeated by a candidate put forward by such men of power in Regional City as Adam Graves, Fargo Dunham, Cary Stokes (who was a candidate himself in the campaign just described), Harvey Aiken, Arthur Tarbell, and Gary Stone. The campaigns are accompanied by heated rivalry, and after the defeat of one or the other of these factions, there is much fanfare accorded the winning faction. Offices in the State Capitol turn over, and new governor's aides are sworn in— aides whose greatest claim to fame is the ability to display low license-plate numbers with "Governor's Aide" printed on them. The new crowd is editorialized in the papers and a plea is made for letting by-gones be by-gones. The state quickly settles down to normal, and the average citizen is unaware of much basic change in his government. Within Regional City, in the business establishments of the power leaders of both

the victorious and the defeated factions, life goes on much as
it had previously. Contracts out of state largess are awarded to
some of the winning firms, of course; and once in a great while
one faction will decide to "punish" leaders of an unusually
aggressive losing faction.

On any issue that tends to threaten all of the interests alike
there is usually joint action in the manipulation of the machinery of state. When the Progressive party was formed in
Regional City, threatening to bring to the fore issues inimical
to the power interests, private force, intimidation, and threats
were called forth. The persistent aggressiveness of the Progressive party was a troublesome thing to all the interests.
There was no legislation on the state books to handle the matter of putting down the party in Regional City. The use
of police action to harass members of this party was questionable in the minds of many of the local citizenry, even among
those who could not be called sympathetic to the movement.
The right to petition for inclusion on local ballots, a right
which included Negro candidates, was the issue. A coalition of
both factions came into being quickly to meet the crisis, and
a special session of the legislature was called to change the
election laws to deny local ballot rights to the new Party.

At least six of the men on the list of leaders may be identified with the movement to call the state legislature into session,
but suffice it to say that George Delbert of one faction and
Fargo Dunham of the other were the chief instruments in
bringing about the action. The legislature acted quickly—at a
cost of almost a quarter of a million dollars to the state tax-
payers—and laws were passed, repealed, and juggled, which
made it impossible for the Progressive party to get on local
ballots in the general election in the state. The constitutionality
of the law was in grave question at the time of its passing, but
as one man in the power group put it at the time, "By the time
the courts get around to passing on the question of constitutionality, the election will be a thing of the past, and who will

then care what the courts say? If they say the wrong thing, we can always pass another law!" With the new law in effect, the power leaders in the state were in a position to use legal force, if necessary, to achieve their ends. The state machinery of government, as well as that of local and national government, represents legitimized power which is highly important to the policy-makers in Regional City. The city had thrown up the elements of a threatening political force—elements almost wholly confined to the urban areas—and the city leaders used the rurally dominated state machinery to quell the uprising. The importance of keeping a firm hold on state machinery of government cannot be overstressed in Old State so far as the larger interests are concerned.

The fact that the Progressive party did not represent a real threat to the positions of the established political leaders in Old State was not evident in the initial stages of its development. No attempt will be made here to analyze the pros and cons of this abortive movement, but it can be used as an illustration of the fact that the power groups in Old State will move with alacrity at the first wind of opposition. In keeping a power balance in their favor they must depend upon speed in spotting and isolating dissident elements in the body politic. The closing of ranks, on the part of the power leaders, in face of the Progressive party threat was immediate and effective.

Interpersonal relationships have much to do with power-wielding, as all politicians seem to know. The personal connections between some of the men of power in Regional City and those in power in state offices are often quite close. The point may be illustrated in this way. In the study the question was asked, "If a decision was to be made that affected Regional City in which the Governor of the state might be involved, who would be the best contact man?"

It became apparent from the answers received that James Treat, of the Southern Yarn Mill, would not only contact the

Governor but that he was a power behind him. Having established this fact, we then asked informants, "Would Treat go to see the Governor, or would the Governor come to Treat on an important matter?" The answers were in several instances, "The Governor would come to Treat if the matter were important enough."

James Treat represents a sizeable industrial establishment in Regional City. It is widespread rumor that Treat had come out for the Governor when others had held back. His contributions to the Governor's campaign were also substantial, according to political gossip. It is well known that it requires over a half million dollars to elect a governor in Old State, and consequently contributions of the size which Treat could give, or obtain from others, are highly regarded in political circles. Treat is therefore a desirable political acquaintance.

Treat's position in the corporate structure of the community makes him a man of wide influence and power. Besides his business connections, he sits on charitable foundation boards. He is a trustee of the largest bank in Regional City. His name appears on numerous letterheads as a sponsor of many projects of top priority in the community. In short, he is a man well integrated into the most powerful formal organizations in Regional City. His advice is often sought informally. During an interview with him he was interrupted twice on matters pertaining to community affairs outside the jurisdiction of his business. As an individual he has wide powers, but as a person he would seem very ordinary—a man who might be overpowered physically quite easily by one of average strength and pugnacity. His power lies in his ability to summon the services of others.

So far as was ascertainable, Treat was the only man with enough personal influence to manipulate the Governor in quite the manner in which he did. Having established the one-to-one relationship between the Governor and Treat, it was asked if others had the power to have the Governor come to them on important matters. The answers were negative. Treat seemed to be the only one with such power. It was understood that Treat himself was subordinate to at least two other men of financial power in the community, but Treat had the responsibility for contacts with the Governor, and this was understood by the Governor. He would not go over Treat's head in any matter.

So far as other individuals and groups were concerned in the community, they would go to the Governor for conference on policy matters. This was substantiated in essence by Arthur Tarbell, President of the Commercial Bank, who said, "It is true that the Governor would go to Treat. I do not think he would go to any of the others. Take for example the Steel Wire crowd. They would go to the Governor. They would have a lot of influence with him, but if it was a matter of very great importance, he would make the Wire crowd wait till he had cleared it with Treat. That's pretty well understood, I think."

Treat is a man of authority. His authority is drawn in part from the institutionalization of his activities. He can be said to be a man of power, since he is able to manipulate men who are in position to use force or any other of the elements of power to compel obedience to given commands. Treat is one of the men who stand near the apex of the power structure in Regional City. He does not stand at the very top, but he is not far removed from it.

There remains one other factor of primary importance in Treat's relationship with the Governor which was turned up in a second interview with him. It illustrates the personal side of political relations. Mr. Treat was asked, "We hear that you have considerable influence with the Governor—that on an important matter he might come to see you. Is that true?" Mr. Treat answered in mild surprise, as if he wondered that anyone would doubt the fact, "Why, yes, that is true. I have known the Governor's family for many years. I knew his father rather intimately in business before I knew the Governor. Yes, I guess you might say we would confer if the occasion arose." The personal relationship came to Mr. Treat's mind immediately rather than the fact that he was a man of organizational influence, important as the latter fact may be.

Mr. Treat was also asked if he had other influence in state government besides his relations with the Governor. He said, "It is hard to say. If you mean as some kind of lobbyist, the answer would be no. I am asked occasionally to appear before state legislative committees, but I am not registered as a lobbyist. I just happen to know a lot of people, and I get called in on a lot of things. Sometimes, I think, on too many!"

The exposition of the concepts of authority and influence in the illustration of James Treat's activities may help to clarify and bring into focus the differences underlying them. They are related concepts vital to each other. Both are elements of power, but they are not synonymous. Both Treat and other individuals were said to have influence with the Governor, but Treat had more than influence. He could evidently command the Governor's presence through personal and organizational prestige. This is a difference of no mean proportions. The other organized personnel of the community may have authority in many spheres, but only in those areas where they can command and be obeyed do they exercise unbridled power. Treat could bridle their power with the Governor. We are indebted to Bierstedt for the distinction between authority and influence and the connection between the concepts of organization, authority, and influence.[5] It is further suggested, recalling the definition of power, that authority, as institutionalized power, sits astride latent force. Force itself is manifest power.[6]

One more example of what the men of power in Regional

5. Robert Bierstedt, "An Analysis of Social Power," *American Sociological Review*, XV (December 1950), 733.
6. *Loc. cit.*

City do on a governmental level to achieve their ends will be given. The political activity to be described was transmitted in an interview with a top leader who was interested, not in party politics as such, but in how the power wielded by elected politicians should be exercised. The relationship between at least one leader of the community and individuals concerned with national legislative matters may be illustrated by Harvey Aiken's visit to Washington, D. C., regarding tax matters.

If there can be said to be any one rallying cry that will coalesce the power interests of Regional City it is, "Keep the taxes down!" Almost any proposal for public improvements must be looked at in the light of what it will do to the tax rates. But the actions of Harvey Aiken in our present illustration are contrary to this general principle. Aiken went to Washington to appeal for *raising* the tax rates. Aiken is a lay reader of economic theory, and it has long been his contention that inflation is the greatest evil that can befall a nation. In an interview with him he kept repeating his concern over the national crisis related to defense preparations, and he was asked by the investigator to indicate any action he had taken to put his points of view across either locally or in the nation's capital.

Aiken said that he had made several speeches to the local luncheon clubs, and that he had written a few articles for the trade journals which are related to his own business. He had been on panel discussions in his trade association regarding tax matters, and he had needled the board of one of the major national associations on various occasions relative to his points of view on current tax matters. His point of view is essentially that taxes must be increased, particularly in the lower brackets, during a time of large military expenditures in federal governmental operations. To remove money from the hands of the "little fellows" eases the threat of disastrous inflation, in the opinion of Aiken.

His views had found favor in many quarters, and Aiken stated that he was asked by one of the congressional committees to appear and give his views. The investigator asked, "Were you asked by the Congressional Committee, or by someone else?" Aiken replied, "I was asked by the Committee, but my trade association had arranged that I be asked."

The investigator then said that he would like to have a picture of all the subsequent actions of Aiken in his Washington experience. His reply was essentially as follows: "It took the better part of four days and nights in writing up a prepared statement for the Congressional Committee [which will be henceforth designated as Committee]. I used two secretaries in shifts of dictating, writing, and re-writing what I wished to say. I have appeared before these groups before, and I wanted to be ready with my facts. I've seen businessmen go up to the Hill and make fools of themselves. They stammer around, if they haven't got their facts down, and they turn to their lawyers too much, which indicates to me that they do not know what they are talking about."

The investigator asked if anyone else helped Mr. Aiken prepare his statement besides his secretaries. He replied, "No, I didn't think anyone else would know as much about the subject as I did. I did, however, take a copy of my final draft of the statement out to James Treat's house for him to look at. After he had read it, he advised me to take out certain phrases related to my contention that the legislation that was before Congress was headed toward the socialization of American industry. Treat said, 'Those Congressional fellows have heard that phrase so often that they do not scare easily when it is used.' I listened to his advice, but I did not take it. I felt too strongly about that particular subject."

It is evident that here are two men on an equal footing. Aiken will listen to Treat's advice, but he takes only that portion of it which fits his own ideas. He is not subservient to Treat.

Aiken was asked by the investigator what he did following this interview with Treat. He continued:

"We decided on our strategy. We decided we should get the advice of Charles Homer. When we called Homer, he said he would be glad to see us the following evening at his home, and suggested that Ray Moster, his attorney, should be in on the meeting with us. We met, the four of us, and laid out plans.

"We decided not to go up there [to Washington] flanked by a bunch of lawyers. As a matter of fact, we decided that the four of us should go. Moster was the only lawyer. We further decided to get in touch with the left wingers in Washington as a strategy. We knew that the Senators from Old State would be with us, and we knew that men like them would be with us, but we couldn't be sure what some of the radicals might do. So, we thought it good strategy to try to sell some of the men that might be the most vocal against us.

"When we got to Washington we contacted the leading Senator in the leftish group to sell him on the idea that American industry should not be socialized through some of the inflationary passages of the bill under question. We asked the Senator if he would have dinner with us in our hotel suite. He agreed. In the meantime we had discussed our strategy with our Old State Senators to let them know how we were operating, and they agreed with our strategy.

"When Jim Matson [the 'leftish' Senator] came to dinner he led off with a lot of talk about how he was elected by labor and the common man, and indicated that he might be hard to sell. We asked him to eat his dinner, and then read our material before he made up his mind. He did both of these things—spent about forty-five minutes reading through my material. He looked up after reading it and said, 'Gentlemen, this is an amazing document. It is clear and much to the point. I certainly could not be accused of wanting the socialization of American industry. I have never had the issue put to me quite in the manner in which you have put it. I would like to think it over and get in touch with you later.' We had asked him to come out on the Senate committee and on the Senate floor in favor of our proposals. He promised to get in touch with us later.

"Not more than an hour after he had gone home, he called on the phone and said he had been thinking about our proposals and would like to have us as his guests at breakfast to go into more of the details. We indicated that we could not be his guests the next morning, because we were having breakfast with John L. Lloyd, one of the big labor leaders whose offices are in Washington. We asked him if he would care to join this group, but he thought it expedient that he not do so.

"Well, to make a long story short, we saw a lot of people on this basis before appearing before the Committee—some of those we saw were on the Committee, like Matson, but we did not see all the members of the Committee. When we finally got to the Committee, we had a very cordial reception. I had decided by then not to put the members to sleep by reading a long prepared statement, and I opened my remarks by saying just that. I gave them copies of my prepared statement but talked extemporaneously for about twenty minutes, before asking for questions. They kept me there for about two hours asking questions.

"Two weeks later the bill was brought out on the floor containing most of the recommendations we had put to the Committee, and Matson made a forty-five minute address which supported our views."

The investigator asked, "Did you use the services of any of the lobby groups in Washington to help you during this time?" Aiken replied, "No, I'm against such tactics. Those lobbyists have worn their welcome thin in many cases, and they are just paid employees, in general. They can be more of a hindrance than a help on a thing like this. They have their place, but on a matter as vital as the one we're talking about, citizens from local communities carry a lot more weight. It's my opinion that more businessmen should do the very thing we did. Get to these fellows personally rather than relying on the lobbyists."

There are certain individuals in Regional City who in their actions are influential in matters that affect their particular community as well as the nation as a whole. They act as liaison persons between the local community and the national groups who set policy, and they are influential in doing so. They go to the national groups with no formal mandate of the body politic, nor are some of them particularly partisan in their views. They represent certain interests which coincide with the general interests of their community and with the major enterprises, often within particular communities. Strategy of action varies, possibly, with the individual situation. The interests of one group may not always be in accord with other interests of the community from which such policy-makers come, and to a certain extent it is the function of the professional politician to balance all interests appearing before them for political decision. That there may be a tendency for the politicians to favor the interests which speak with the most authority, namely, the larger economic interests, in any given community is a set of facts documented in this writing.

Let us pause to re-emphasize that the expression "larger economic interests," is not used in a sense derogatory to lesser interests, but rather in a functional sense coordinate with the structure described. The interests of economic power groups are often of necessity coincidental with the larger interests of the general community welfare. The men who hold the power structure intact through policy decision are firmly convinced that their decisions are correct more times than incorrect, and that their decisions are made with the whole community and nation, for that matter, in mind. That the system holds together and that the interests continue to dominate the political situation is the pragmatic test of the success of the policy-making group's ability to meet the minimum requirement for satisfying all interests in the community. The men who have been described have met such crucial "political" tests for many years. They furthermore meet these requirements not only in the formalized realm of politics but in informal ways, and the latter ways are often of greater importance than the former.

It has also come to the writer's attention that at least three of the men studied, whom one may call "junketeers," have political connections which extend into the area of international affairs beyond the level of national politics already touched upon. These men soon after World War II were engaged in extending the boundaries of their local economic interests into foreign areas—particularly into occupied areas. They went on junkets for the national government and for themselves. In a certain sense they appeared to operate much in the same way as the businessmen of the North who came into the conquered South following the Civil War. They carried no carpet-bags, so we cannot use that colorful term in relation to them. Their junkets were written up in the newspapers and this term may help to describe them in a passing note. The phenomenon is one that might be profitably explored in more detail than can be devoted to it here. Regional City's banks naturally have an interest in foreign markets, but there are no data readily available to show any activities on their part in the junketeering process. One bank official did mention that their bank has acted as a local business channel for more than one hundred foreign corporations, which naturally gives them an interest in foreign affairs.

Regional City cannot be isolated from state, national, and international affairs. To understand the community as a metropolitan entity this fact cannot be over-emphasized even though one can only hint at some of the structural relationships that exist in this perspective. The formation of an International Trade Council of Regional City would indicate that the extra-community activities are finding associational structuring a necessity. Thus, one is able to see how community structure becomes part of a greater whole.

7 THE MORE PRIVATE ASPECTS OF POWER

WHERE do public politics end and private politics begin? There is a very thin line between the two categories as they were observed in the study of power relations in Regional City. In the normal course of events the actions of the private citizen, at least on a policy-making level of power, are almost indistinguishable from those of formally designated officials. The dual relationship between government and economic operations tends to blur into one process. Yet many community activities which affect the total citizenry cannot be properly called processes of government. Community projects designed to "carry along" other elements of the community on a purely private basis may have elements of politics in them. Many informal decisions made by community leaders may have broad political implications. The formally elected officials may clear with private citizens on matters of political significance without taking into account the wishes of a majority of the population.

In the realm of administration of policy the lines of differentiation are more pronounced than they are in the policy-making process. When responsibilities are defined, the bureaucratic structure of government tends to a consistency of operation. But even here informal influences are operative and the most rigid bureaus are capable of some flexibility of program. In this chapter several of these more informal processes of power will be defined.

The informal relationships between power personnel described in the chapter on the structure of power and the examples previously related concerning the relations of Harvey Aiken to a particular incident in policy decision, seem to be of primary significance. The description of some of the processes and dynamics of relating the power structure to key problems within the community is a basic task in the present writing. James Treat has been quoted earlier in regard to his analysis of power relations existing in Regional City principally relating to the structuring of personnel. Mr. Treat will be quoted again on the processes employed in getting a major project under way, since his description is applicable to many similar situations in the community.

The situation which will be considered is that of getting an international trade council established in Regional City. The investigator had asked Mr. Treat to give an example of how the local power groups operated in getting a major project under way. Mr. Treat did not appear to get the meaning of the question in the way it was put, and the investigator elaborated upon it by saying, "If a major project, such as getting a new hospital, were up for consideration in Regional City, how would the men under discussion act in relation to each other in the matter? Who would contact which others? Would the community associations be drawn in on the project, and so forth?"

Mr. Treat answered the last question first. He said: "We would not go to the 'associations,' as you call them—that is, not right away. A lot of those associations, if you mean by associations the Chamber of Commerce or the Community Council, sit around and discuss 'goals' and 'ideals.' I don't know what a lot of those things mean. I'll be frank with you, I do not get onto a lot of those committees. A lot of the others in town do, but I don't. In a way, I guess I pretty much follow the lead of one other man in this town—the lead of Charles Homer. Let me give you an example.

"Charles Homer is the biggest man in our crowd. He gets an idea. When he gets an idea, others will get the idea. Don't ask me how he gets the idea or where. He may be in bed. He may think of it at breakfast. He may read a letter on the subject. But recently he got the idea that Regional City should be the national headquarters for an International Trade Council. He called in some of us [the inner crowd], and he talked briefly about his idea. He did not talk much. We do not engage in loose talk about the 'ideals' of the situation and all that other stuff. We get right down to the problem, that is, how to get this Council. We all think it is a good idea right around the circle. There are six of us in the meeting.

"All of us are assigned tasks to cary out. Moster is to draw up the papers of incorporation. He is the lawyer. I have a group of friends that I will carry along. Everyone else has a group of friends he will do the same with. These fellows are what you might call followers.

"We decide we need to raise $65,000 to put this thing over. We could raise that amount within our own crowd, but eventually this thing is going to be a community proposition, so we decide to bring the other crowds in on the deal. We decide to have a meeting at the Grandview Club with select members of other crowds.

"When we meet at the Club at dinner with the other crowds, Mr. Homer makes a brief talk; again, he does not need to talk long. He ends his talk by saying he believes in his proposition enough that he is willing to put $10,000 of his own money into it for the first year. He sits down. You can see some of the other crowds getting their heads together, and the Growers Bank crowd, not to be outdone, offers a like amount plus a guarantee that they will go along with the project for three years. Others throw in $5,000 to $10,000, until—I'd say within thirty or forty minutes—we have pledges of the money we need. In three hours the whole thing is settled, including the time for eating!"

Mr. Treat paused for a moment, then continued: "There is one detail I left out, and it is an important one. We went into that meeting with a board of directors picked. The constitution was all written, and the man who was to head the council as executive was named—a fellow by the name of Lonny Dewberry, a third-string man, a fellow who will take advice."

The investigator asked how the public was apprised of the action. Mr. Treat said: "The public doesn't know anything about the project until it reaches the stage I've been talking about. After the matter is financially sound, then we go to the newspapers and say there is a proposal for consideration. Of course, it is not news to a lot of people by then, but the Chamber committees and other civic organizations are brought in on the idea. They all think it's a good idea. They help to get the Council located and established. That's about all there is to it."

The investigator asked, "Suppose there was a political issue before the community that needed to be settled, what would be the line of action?"

Mr. Treat inquired, "What kind of a political decision?"

At the time of the interview there was much current discussion relative to the extension of the Social Security Act to include more participants, and this issue was suggested to Mr. Treat. He laughed and said, "Hell, we'd be against that, but there is not much we can do about it!" The investigator asked Mr. Treat if he could think of an example of political decision. He replied:

"If you are to understand Old State, you've got to know that about three companies are responsible for building it up to where it is today. Industry and agriculture are the main concerns in the state. The Homer Chemical Company, the Regional Gas Heat Company, and my own company are about as responsible for Old State development as any you could name. We know that industry must be undergirded with a sound agricultural program in the state. Right now we are interested in the development of the Regional City River project which will give Old State farmers cheap electricity. We want this to be a private company development, and we're working on that.

"The Governor, Traverse Simpkins, is a man devoted to Old State industry and agriculture. You may not like our Governor, but he is the man to see on what is being done along the lines I have given you."

The investigator did not know of Treat's influence with the Governor at the time of the first interview with him, but as the investigation proceeded, it became apparent that Treat was the power behind the Governor. Treat was then asked if the same methods would be employed in getting a new industry into Old State and Regional City as were employed in relation to other projects. He expanded on this theme as follows:

"We would probably ask the board of directors of any company we wanted to get into Old State to hold their next board of directors' meeting in Regional City, if they had shown some interest in locating here. The General Assembly Motor Parts Company and the Aluminum Can Company are two examples that I can think of right away. I spent several years in playing around with the Can outfit, before they finally decided to come here. When they were pretty well ready to come anyhow, we brought their boards of directors down by plane and train, and each of us in our crowd took one or two of them as guests. We took some of them hunting. Fed them all up well. They saw good farms and a lot of the better things we have in Old State. That's roughly the process. All the crowds do the same thing."

The investigator asked why the crowds would be interested in bringing other enterprises into the state? How would it benefit them? Treat replied: "Most of us are tied up with the banks, for one thing. We want the accounts these companies represent. Then, too, some of them are allied industries which help our own. In the past fifteen or twenty years we have brought perhaps a hundred such enterprises into this area in about the way I've told you."

The investigator asked if the banks were not in competition with one another for these accounts and if such a situation would not be something that might tend to pull the crowds apart. Treat replied, "No, we wouldn't pull apart on these things. It all about evens up. One bank will get a company, then another will get one." Mr. Treat went on to say that once a company was slated to come into the community, many of the under-structure personnel would be drawn into the planning stages for its entry, and the new enterprise would be integrated into the social and economic structure of the community commensurate with its size and the caliber of its personnel. The methods employed in all these processes have the common characteristics of being activated by a policy-determining group and of employing under-structure personnel in the execution of policy.

The combined use of power forms may be illustrated by another situation, that of Thaddeus Brown, a professional writer in Regional City, who ran afoul of a powerful personality in that community. Brown was an editorial columnist for a trade journal. At the time that price controls were to be lifted (a public issue following World War II), Brown wrote a piece unfavorable to the government's proposed action. His argument ran along the line that price controls were beneficial to the working population and that industry ultimately benefits if the large mass of consumers are benefited. Debbney Cruthers, a manufacturer of considerable means and influence, a reader and financial supporter of the trade journal, took exception to the article. His company was in a position to benefit by the elimination of price ceilings.

Brown reports his subsequent relations with Cruthers as follows: "Cruthers called me on the phone. He said, 'Brown, what the hell do you mean by this Communist piece you have in this month's Journal?' And before I could answer, Cruthers was off on a tirade about long-haired paid employees who thought they knew everything including how to run other people's businesses. When Cruthers stopped for breath, I tried to argue the point along a line of economic theory I espoused. 'New Dealish, I would call it,' he replied. This touched off another blast from Cruthers, who terminated the conversation abruptly by threatening, 'If you do not run a retraction on that story in the next issue of the Journal, or if your boss does not see fit to make you do it, I'm going to raise hell!' "

Cruthers, by shouting and threats, was attempting to intimidate Brown, who informs us that he was both frightened and rebellious. He had never had another man talk to him so bluntly before, and he determined that he would not follow this man's dictates, even if it did mean his job. His employer was called by Cruthers on the matter and tried to soothe the man's anger. Cruthers stated that Brown had talked back to him "in a very insulting and impudent manner," a fact which Brown stoutly denies. He insists that he felt that Cruthers had a perfect right to his opinion even if it differed from his own and he felt that Cruthers was completely unreasonable in his position. He began to feel that a principle of freedom of the press was involved and because of his humiliation and anger refused to write a placating article at the request of his employer. The employer was not insistent upon such a piece but suggested that if there were any way Brown saw to "back down some" on his point of view on price controls it might be wise to do so. The employer pointed out that strictly speaking there was no issue of freedom of the press involved in the matter, since the trade publication was subsidized to a large extent by the industry of which Cruthers was a member. The publication was not, therefore, a "public" journal.

The following month Brown wrote no retracting statement for either his employer or Cruthers, but did have an article on consumer prices, an article which was quite "toned down." It had no reference to price controls and was well within the rather conservative policies of the journal and in the field in which Brown habitually wrote. A week or so later a friend told Brown that Cruthers was calling him a radical, insisting that he was a nut on prices and that he should be removed from his job. "Cruthers is out to get you," his friend reported. Cruthers was resorting to indirect pressures.

Brown's relations with his employer began to deteriorate in the following weeks. It came back to Brown that he had become a controversial figure. His boss reported to him that he had seen Cruthers at a civic luncheon, and that Cruthers had stated that, "a little censorship is needed in that paper of yours." The boss cautioned Brown that he must be extremely careful in his writing and that he wanted to discuss each article with him for necessary revisions before publication. The boss, who had been rather tolerant, became less and less lenient and accused Brown of soldiering on the job, when he had overstayed his lunch period one day to do some shopping. He had done this before but had never been accused or reprimanded in any way. A series of minor altercations ensued. Brown admits a decided loss of interest in the job and was preparing himself for dismissal. He said: "I just did not seem to have the same spontaneity in my writing under the circumstances. Some of my friends in the office noticed that I wasn't on the ball. I imagined all sorts of slights from them, since I knew that they knew the trouble I was having, and a couple of them said they thought I was crazy for trying to stand up to Cruthers. The whole thing seemed like a melodrama to me. I couldn't figure how so little a thing could start such a chain of events, but I seemed helpless in the situation."

Soon afterwards Brown did secure another job. He was not fired from the trade journal, but he considered it only a matter of time until he might be. His new position dealt with writing straight copy for an advertising agency. He writes no editorial opinions now. He has heard no more from Cruthers.

Brown's case represents intimidation and indirect pressures applied by a man whose will was thwarted both by the actions and the refusal to act on the part of another. Brown was finally forced by Cruthers to move in a direction suitable to the latter. A part of the decision to move lay with Brown, but the action was initiated by Cruthers. Whether Cruthers would have continued to try to "get Brown" is problematical, but the feeling of persecution on Brown's part, set up by the chain of events, was as effective as any other pressure in forcing a move by him. Cruthers' actions fell short of violence, but it has already been shown that violence is not unknown in Regional City where, as in other communities, subordinate personnel are supposed to move according to prescribed modes.

At this point some positive things should be said about Debbney Cruthers. The position has been taken that the muckraking of personalities will not be a part of the present writing. Not all of Cruthers' actions in Regional City are negative ones to be criticized. Cruthers is a member of several local agency boards of directors devoted to civic improvement. He has done much good for the community. He has helped spark many fund drives for charitable purposes. He has carried his responsibilities in these areas with the same will and determination that motivated him to displace Brown. He did not, however, make the list of top leaders in our survey of leadership, although he was mentioned by several informants as being a powerful person, even if a somewhat erratic and irascible sort. One man said, "I think Cruthers might be right at the top of the list, but he is a little crude." He is a self-made man and not a person born in this area. He has no local family ties. His home is in the best residential area of the community, but it is referred to by many as the "wedding cake chateau," a home perhaps a little too pretentious to suit the taste of his peers.

Thus, some of his personal characteristics are looked upon with disfavor by his fellow citizens, but in spite of this he is recognized as a leader with a capacity for getting his way on the things he wants. When he wants things "for the town" he is a decided asset. Cruthers' case represents, in some degree, the lack of family background as a determining factor in his partial exclusion from the policy-making group.

The day-by-day operations of power wielding are accompanied by a host of related activities. The first is in relation to propaganda. In initiating this discussion, a word about fraud seems in order.

It is often suggested by writers on power that fraud plays an important role in power relations. This was not found to be true in the Regional City investigation—at least there was no outright indication that the relations between or the actions of men of power were based upon fraudulent claims. Nor is there indication that there is a group of men who scheme and plot frauds to perpetrate on an unsuspecting populace. The popular notion of men plotting behind the scenes is a fictional illusion except when one gets into the area of organized crime. The men of power usually operate openly with one another and on equal terms. They know full well that the manipulation of various factors in the community—such as the departments of government, the labor force, and the press—is to their advantage. The relation with these parts of the community is not one of deceit, in the main, but one of value agreement. If the little fellow comes out on the short end of affairs, or if he is "not in the know," as the popular expression goes, it is for reasons other than fraud.

The nearest the writer came to hearing a man say that he practiced guile was in a statement made by one of the power leaders when he said, "The way to manipulate men is to flatter them. The little fellow earning around $5,000 a year likes to feel that he is in on things. We do bring him in on certain projects like the Community Chest drive. He gets publicity, and he is flattered. The next time you ask him to do something he will fall all over himself to make good."

If propaganda is considered fraud, then it is practiced very widely in Regional City, but it is preferable not to enter into a philosophical discussion as to whether propaganda is fraudulent and deceitful. The impression gathered in the study is that many of the men who, in the early stages of a campaign, may know that propaganda tells only a part of the truth, begin to believe their own propaganda as it unfolds. Are such men deceitful? One must let social philosophers decide the question.

If one has been engaged in community work on any scale at all, he is impressed over and over with what might be termed the "principle of unanimity." When policy is finally formulated by the leaders in the community, there is an immediate demand on their part for strict conformity of opinion. Decisions are not usually arrived at hurriedly. There is ample time, particularly among the top leaders, for discussion of most projects before a stage of action is set. This is true for community projects. When the time for discussion is past and the line is set, then unanimity is called for. Pressures are put upon dissenters, and the project is under way.

On some subjects the press plays a major role in getting information to the public for discussion in the local associations; and the preachers can preach, and the speakers can speak. The line is tentatively set at this stage, for as has already been pointed out tentative decisions had been arrived at before they reached the lower echelons, but some decisions are not final until there has been thorough community discussion down to the level of the clubs and other associations. Once this process of "clearing all down the line" has been effected, and no serious objections have been voiced, then concerted effort is in order.

On some questions that are considered settled, there is a constant pressure for conformity. It is only on the unsettled issues that discussion is permissible. Such questions as land policy, private enterprise, and other matters dealing with the established interests are considered settled, and no discussion of a change of the rules is deemed desirable. On some of the unsettled issues such as labor relations and many matters of civic improvement there may be continuing discussion. In the area of labor relations the workers are free to engage in discussion of organization if they are already organized and if the discussion is carried on within the bounds of their own associations. Professionals retained by the policy-makers are not supposed to discuss labor matters, generally speaking. Their discussions are almost wholly bound up with minor issues affecting the community in areas where discussion is permissible—such as whether there shall or shall not be a new hospital or day nursery or the like.

"Don't rock the boat," describes the general theme of the propaganda which issues forth on the radio and is disseminated through the columns of the press in Regional City. The stories are usually not new, and they fit into the stereotype given to us by R. A. Brady in describing the propaganda put forth by the National Association of Manufacturers for the edification of the citizenry. It does not seem necessary to quote Brady at length, because the political and economic point of view of the association mentioned is quite familiar to most Americans in whatever community they may reside. Perhaps one statement from Brady will suffice:

All economic issues are transmuted [by the NAM] into terms of social and cultural issues, increasingly, as the political implications and military possibilities of cumulative economic power are realized. Propaganda then becomes a matter of converting the public—small businessmen, consumers, labor, farmers, housewives—to the point of view of the control pyramid. This accounts for the vast outpouring of the so-called "educational" literature of the NAM, now designed to enter into every nook and cranny of American life, economic, political, social, and cultural. It is a propaganda reaching the roots of the principles which underlie contemporary capitalistic civilization—that is to say, the propaganda is an ideological outpouring.[1]

Regional City has already been described as a city within the capitalistic culture of the United States, and one does not need to linger over the point that local propaganda reflects the general trend of the national pattern described by Brady. The more subtle phases of activities related to bringing about general conformity are of more interest than the propaganda content—important as it is—but it has been written about and described so often that it needs little elaboration in this discussion.

It is probably true that what does not get into the press is often more important than the materials that do. Much of the activity of the power group described here does not find its way into print. Many of the men with whom we have been dealing shun publicity and leave the credit to publicized individuals in the under-structure of leadership. It must be said that the men mentioned do share publicity on occasion, but the general rule holds true, and only on specific and well defined projects will their names appear as sponsors or men of action in the given situation. Adverse publicity is withheld by the newspapers, except in very extreme or extenuating circumstances.

Smoke-screen propaganda is often resorted to when issues are before the legislature. If a crowd or group is attempting to put through legislation particularly favorable to themselves, some hint of this might appear in the press, but such publicity quickly subsides and in its place the men so publicized will be put forward as the sponsors of a bill or project which has very positive social and civic implications. The build-up is a

1. *Business as a System of Power,* pp. 217-18.

continuing and vital process in propaganda favorable to the men of power, and the use of welfare projects and matters of civic improvement are a constant cushion for the shock of too obvious self interest.

The men in Regional City who hold power gather strength in many instances from association with their fellows on an informal and light-hearted level. The luncheon clubs provide a good place in which to exchange ideas, thus helping to keep a kind of like-mindedness. There is a camaraderie and a good-fellowship present in the atmosphere of the clubs which help greatly to cement the relations between the participants in these fairly select gatherings. One cannot resist calling the process of club action "ham, hocum, and horseplay" from some of the exhibitions observed in their meetings. This is not to say that there is not a serious side to the luncheon clubs, but the bulk of the programs are dedicated to speakers who say little new and who tend in many instances to be on the "hammy" side. Some of the speakers whom one may hear, indulge in the warmed-over lines of propaganda previously mentioned, which, boiled down, is in many cases pure hocum. But ham and hocum, while tending to unite men in common causes, are not as interesting, perhaps, as the horseplay that often goes on also.

Steiner describes the luncheon clubs as an integrating device in the following manner:

While the membership of these organizations is largely made up of business and professional men who individually would resent any imputation of sentimentality and emotionalism, yet collectively in their club meetings they lay great stress upon ritualistic devices as a means of securing unity of spirit and the proper degree of enthusiasm. Singing popular songs in which all are expected to join, snappy speeches full of platitudes reiterating the ideals of the group, stimulation of the spirit of comradeship by the use of nicknames, horseplay, and good humored badinage, and efforts to secure united action by the force of suggestion and emotional appeal are characteristic features without which it is felt that their meetings would be uninteresting and futile.[2]

Steiner wrote this in 1923, but three decades later the essential characteristics of the groups about which he wrote remain the same. The little fellows in the community who cannot make Rotary or Kiwanis or the "goodfellows" clubs, look upon the antics of these groups with mixed envy, ridicule, and contempt. The newspapers are prone to carry stories about the horseplay which goes on within these groups; and to the outsider, who is not cognizant of the value such activities have in holding the group together, the activities are liable to appear odd. Such phrases as, "He's a great guy and he is doing a swell job!" abound in these meetings.

Two or three examples of horseplay may illustrate our point. At one time there was an epidemic of "tie cutting" in one of the clubs. During a period when hand painted neckties were in vogue with some of the ties costing considerable money, some of the men in the Goodfellows Club of Regional City decided to shear some of the better ties off their neighbors with scissors. This was carried out amid great glee and approbation among those who were not victims but to the consternation and dismay of those who were. The tendency of a man to protest was quickly smothered by his overmastering desire to be a good fellow—to show that he could take it. There may have been the crude elements of the "potlatch" in the situation, too; that is, as in certain primitive tribes, some goods are destroyed methodically to show that the owner can afford the luxury of destruction. At any rate, the victim had the right to retaliate in kind, and for several weeks it was a badge of honor to be seen with one's tie bobbed. The craze died out rather quickly. It did not take hold in some of the lower echelon clubs, and there was a certain amount of ridicule in the papers concerning the practice.

2. Jesse F. Steiner, "Community Organization and the Crowd Spirit," *Social Forces*, I (March 1923), 222.

Such antics as printing special editions of newspapers in which a victim is charged with infidelity to his wife or is accused of some minor public offense are other examples of the horseplay that goes on in Regional City's luncheon clubs. On one occasion the sheriff was called upon to arrest a man publicly to the amusement of the onlookers. The jovial greetings, the laughter, the good feeling of belonging, and the horseplay give the participants in these club meetings a glow which comes with belonging to and being on familiar terms with a "right bunch." The amusement is a part of the technique of holding the group together. If interest in the merriment lags, it is stimulated in the ways suggested.

The serious side of the clubs is present, too, on all occasions. The clubs are a place where selected members of the under-structure and some members of the upper-structure of power may meet. There is a tendency for the two groups to sit at separate tables, but during the "milling period" before and after the luncheons it may help in the functioning of the social system for the under- and upper-structures to call each other by their first names. It is undoubtedly present in the minds of many of the under-structure personnel that the clubs are a place from which leaders are recruited from time to time by the top policy-makers for carrying out specific community tasks, and a few such appointees are taken in by the top leaders, if their work is satisfactory. These latter instances are rare, and there is considerable illusion among the members about how potent the clubs are in recruitment of leadership.

Big policy is not decided within the framework of the clubs. The carrying out of civic responsibilities on welfare projects and the like fall heavily to the lot of the club leaders, and the structure used is a part of the informal under-structure controlled by the policy-makers. Steiner suggests this, in discussing the manipulations of meetings, when he points out that in practice the programs of the civic clubs are frequently planned with the sole purpose of giving expression to the will of those inside the movement. The process of getting agreement is often that of having resolutions carefully prepared in advance of the meeting and of having "suitable" persons present them. Others are requested to be ready to use all the time set apart for discussion. "It is," says Steiner, "simply a prearranged attempt to get the people in attendance to endorse the plan conceived and fostered by a few interested leaders." He further suggests, "In producing this result emphasis is placed on inspirational [hammy] addresses that reiterate the point of view of the promoters until critical thought is dulled and all become suggestible to the ideas advanced." [3]

Steiner suggests the smoke-screen technique of project manipulation in a congruent statement: "The civic and social welfare issues which are always kept in the foreground [of the clubs and associations] and advocated with great earnestness and sincerity serve primarily the purpose of justifying to themselves and to the public the existence of the organization." [4] One may agree to some extent with Steiner in this, but beyond a certain point it must be said that the civic clubs and the other formal associations represent a chain of command which is necessary for the functioning of the organized community. Many projects which are of primary local importance are furthered by the interest stimulated in the clubs and associations, regardless of the methods by which this interest is aroused.

Many projects might conceivably be carried on by pushing them into the open political arena, but at the present time politics is reserved for limited objectives not always encompassing the demands for civic action which can be met through the less formally organized civic associations and clubs. The personnel which makes up the membership of the organized associations and club groups is often removed from open activity on a partisan basis, and their only recourse for satisfy-

3. *Ibid.*, p. 223.
4. *Ibid.*, p. 222.

ing public demands for civic action is through getting the endorsement of civic associations in behalf of their interests. This holds particularly true of the professional personnel of these associations. If action gets into the purely political realm, they are warned to stay out of the field or to get one of the men above them to "front" for their proposed projects.

Obviously, many of the community-wide projects have positive and significant value for the underlying population. A very worth-while undertaking being considered in Regional City today has to do with the establishment of a children's clinic. One of the top leaders in the community has an afflicted youngster. His interest in the proposed project is of long standing. He has worked with many of the professional members of clubs and associations in getting their technical advice on what would be needed to establish an adequate clinic. He has indicated a willingness to put a large sum of money into the undertaking himself, and within recent months he has interested Mr. Homer in going along with the project. He was referred by Homer to the latter's Foundation secretary with words of encouragement. The project is now in the action stage, and the associations and club groups are busy working out the details. In Regional City there is a constant stream of similar projects under way, the majority of them, to be sure, having more limited objectives.

There are other projects, however, that are really time-consuming enterprises. They may, in a way, be called diversionary projects. Each spring the community is turned upside down with activity on the part of many association leaders on a project called "Patriot's Day." Much energy goes into sponsoring this particular activity, which may serve a purpose in restating cultural values—and this is highly important in the culture of Regional City—but the time consumed on this project takes away from the more earnest considerations of problems of civic welfare that are apparent even to the casual observer in the city.

There is a host of other similar diversionary activities, such as choosing the boy of the year or the young man of the year, or organizing the school children to donate their pennies for a new animal at the zoo. Such projects are also a part of the patterned process being described. It is not suggested that there is a conscious design on the part of the leaders to get men involved in "popgun" activities when more potent approaches to community problems are indicated, but it remains true that much activity in civic affairs in the community is devoted to relatively useless projects, and such undertakings are encouraged by the power leaders.

When many of the associational leaders became interested in slum clearance a few years ago, there was a slight division between the top leaders as to the worth-whileness of an aggressive program for housing reform. The compromise arrived at by the leaders finally revolved around aiding a women's group which had as its platform, "paint up and clean up the undesirable neighborhoods." This program had all the support of the press, and a great deal of organizing activity went into the explanation and promotion of the program. Paint and brooms were not the answers to Regional City's housing problems. Bulldozers were indicated, but no one was able to get such an idea into the minds of the persons who were swept into the house-cleaning campaign. A few feeble attempts were made in the direction of developing support for a more basic program, but the tide was the other way. The ladies who were strong for the "cleaning" methods finally became discouraged. The slum dwellers showed little interest in cooperating, and the owners of the properties, when they could be located, showed the same lethargy. The publicity died out, and the ladies were off on another project which had to do with helping the girls who get into the city stockade on morals charges.

The shifting committee structure that was outlined in a previous chapter may be a device for impeding or stopping action which is deemed undesirable but on which a demand for specific steps exists within the community. The housing program is an illustration of this process, in a degree. Committee chairmen for "hot" subjects, such as housing was at one point, are carefully chosen from men who "have their feet on the ground" and who can skillfully maneuver a committee into paralysis. New committees may be formed from the nuclei of old ones, or competing committees may be set up. An aggressive committee may become labelled as controversial, a term of grave misapprobation, and interest may fall off among members who are insecure in their business positions. Worse than controversial is the current term subversive, which is used for projects which are too aggressive on issues which are considered "dynamite." Any issue in Regional City which involves fundamental changes in the power relationships between the Negro community and the larger community are so labelled. The professional personnel in the under-structure of power in the associations devoted to civic and social improvement are especially liable to such attack.

One case which came to the writer's attention in connection with the manipulation of the under-structure professional personnel was that of Joe Cratchett, a professional social worker who ran a locally sponsored neighborhood club for underprivileged boys. Joe may be described as a liberal. His training and associations for several years outside the environs of Regional City made him acutely aware of many of the problems confronting the constituency which he was hired to serve. The board of his agency was made up of second- and third-rate men in the power structure, and from the beginning of his job Joe found himself in hot water over some of the things he would say. His club put out a little bulletin which he edited, and on two or three occasions he put pieces into the bulletin that involved the larger issues which he felt confronted the community. He was warned to keep the bulletin the "safe" publication which it had been before his arrival in the city.

On one occasion Joe publicly attacked the "clean-up—paint-up" campaign as being sponsored by the power interests to shunt off any vital approach to the housing problem. One of the city politicians took exception to the published material, and quite a furor ensued in Joe's next board meeting. Joe stood his ground and some of his board members stood with him, but he was not to hear the last of the matter. George Delbert was apprised of the situation and called together a few members of the Community Chest board, the agency which underwrote the finances of the Youth Club. He asked them to "look into the matter." The Chest board passed a resolution to "make a study of the agency and to investigate Joe Cratchett's activities in connection with the agency." Joe resisted the efforts to "study" him, and this further aroused the suspicions of the leaders in the Community Chest. The Chest director was told by his board to find ways of "getting rid of Cratchett."

A sub-committee of the Chest board's investigating committee (the shifting committee structure again) was set up to make a "quiet investigation of Cratchett's previous record." This committee was headed by a "little fellow" whom Cratchett described as a hatchet man and who had at one time been the president of the association known locally as "Patriots, Inc.," a veterans' organization. As the investigation proceeded, Joe Cratchett did not cease his agitation on matters of housing. He went further and suggested in a public speech that many of the social ills which were so apparent in the neighborhood in which he worked could be traced to "low wages." This word spread quickly among the power leaders of the community. The president of Joe's board told him that he wanted to stand by him, but he (Joe) was rapidly becoming a controversial figure in the community and his actions were liable to jeopardize the whole agency program—a program in which the board president had put many years of civic work.

The president was Norman Trable, one of the men on the list of leaders but not a man in the top brackets.

The investigators sent private detectives into the cities in which Joe had worked previously to look up his record, but they evidently did not find anything which they could pin on him, and for a time the situation seemed quiescent. Things went along on a fairly normal basis for about two months until the agency was up for its budget hearings before the Chest. The committee wrangled hard and long with the representatives of Joe's agency over the proposed budget, and finally granted most of it with the exception of a scheduled increase in Joe's salary, an increase that had been agreed upon in his initial contract with the agency. Joe openly attacked George Delbert in the meeting as being the perpetrator of the troubles the agency was having. This was too much for Joe's president, and after the meeting he asked Joe to resign. Joe refused. He had a contract that did not expire for a year, and he proposed to stick to his contract. He based his contention for staying on the fact that his club program was a good one, a point on which most agreed, and that just because he had a different opinion from that of Delbert was no good reason for resignation. He felt that the board "should fight it out along this line."

Some of the members of Joe's board took the position that Joe should leave the agency, but they were lukewarm in the matter in the early stages of controversy. They recognized the program of the agency as being "re-vitalized" under Joe's direction, and they did not want to become involved in a showdown in the matter.

Joe might have won his fight if matters had remained as they have been described to this point, but he made a fatal mistake. He allowed a meeting of the Progressive party to be held in one of the meeting rooms of his club, and the fact was reported to his board president the following day. A front page story appeared in the press which headlined, "Club Executive Accused of Politics." The story which followed did not openly say that Cratchett was a part of the Progressive party movement, but the innuendoes were there and he was never able to get a straight story into the papers on the matter. He felt that the club rooms should be used for open-forum meetings, regardless of their nature, but this was too much for the power leaders who were very much set against the development of the Progressive party movement.

Eventually Joe Cratchett was fired from his job. He was first offered several months' salary in addition to the amount which he was entitled to by contract "if he would go quietly." He chose to try to carry his fight to his national professional association, but the association did not respond to his appeals until matters had reached a critical stage and it was too late to reverse the trends which had been set in motion for his release from his agency. When the professional association did get around to "looking in on the matter," their field representative "sided with the leaders of Joe's board," who by then were on record as demanding his resignation. The national group felt that Joe had gone beyond the "areas of his competence" in becoming involved in any way in partisan politics. Joe moved to another community, and an editorial in the Regional City Star breathed a sigh of relief and a warning to other men like Joe.

The forces for conformity were greater than the individual in the episode recounted. Most of the under-structure personnel around Joe were privately in sympathy with his fight but publicly they declared that his actions were foolhardy. The actions taken by the community are as described, and we are interested here in those actions rather than in the merits of Joe's cause. The point is that the power structure holds the means of coercion in Regional City, and most of the professionals are well aware of the potential force of these elements.

For those in the under-structure who are not insulated from violence the actions related to force may come into play. The police are involved in such actions, as well as private organizations devoted to police methods. The men in the upper and lower echelons of power and policy decision are linked closely with all methods of power-wielding, and any method which produces functional results will be the one chosen in a specific situation. This does not say that the men of the upper echelons of power will themselves be found engaging personally in violent action, but their sanction must be sought on most matters of public policy. Consequently the responsibility for action in the realm of power must rest ultimately with them.

The process resorted to in Joe Cratchett's case is an extreme example of community exclusion. It is the modern counterpart of Greek ostracism. But there are more subtle practices of exclusion in community life in Regional City which weld the power policy-making group into a partially closed unit. Some of these methods have already been hinted at, but they will here be treated more precisely.

In the field study each interviewee was asked to state what the best method might be of getting a project started that would ultimately be community-wide, e.g., would he call a committee meeting to initiate the project? Would he get together at a luncheon with key people? Would he make a series of personal calls? Would he merely telephone others to get informal opinions? Or would he use any of these methods in combination? Or would he use other methods than the ones mentioned?

The answers received from the top leaders answering the question indicated that getting together at an informal luncheon was by far the most satisfactory method of soliciting initial interest in a project. Thirteen men indicated that this method was the most highly successful in their experience. Five indicated that they would make a personal call upon their colleagues before going into any kind of committee meeting. Four said they would make their first contact by phone to ascertain interest and then follow up this procedure by a luncheon or dinner meeting on a more formal basis, if initial interest was expressed. Two men said they could not answer the question, since their methods would vary with the type of project. One of these said that he had in mind the problem of housing and slum clearance. There are so many groups involved in this question that he could not see getting all the groups into a single meeting since each group should be approached differently. Four of the men who chose to call upon other men personally said they would prefer not to go alone on their call but would want to go with two or three others and "wait upon" the man they were trying to interest. The latter method is used primarily in getting a top leader to take on the top position in a community venture and presupposes that much initial work has already been done.

The under-structure professional personnel in civic and social work who were asked the same questions indicated in nine cases out of thirteen that they would call a committee together with no luncheon involved. One would make a personal call by himself, and two preferred the luncheon method. Desirable meeting places for luncheons are not as readily available to the professionals as to the top leaders in Regional City, which may account for the professionals' preference in some measure. The clubs represent places open to the top leaders and are prohibitive in cost and in social sanction to the under-structure personnel. Occasionally one of the professionals may be invited to one of the clubs for a meeting on a project, and it is considered an honor which he proudly confesses to his associates. The fact that the under-structure personnel do not frequent the clubs is in itself one of the subtle exclusion devices. The "boys" of the Grandview Club are known to make policy decisions within the confines of the club dining rooms which eventually filter down to the community under-structure.

One of the members of the professional under-structure described a luncheon held recently in a private dining room of one of the corporation executives. This dining room, served by a special kitchen, is maintained in the executive office building of the corporation. It is expensively furnished and many private luncheons are held there. Several of the members of a health agency were invited to lunch in this room. They were very much flattered by the invitation. After a good meal, they were told by their host, who was on a board that controlled their agency, that several changes in administrative policy were to be put through, and he had invited them to the luncheon to inform them of the decision of the board. Several items in the board's decision radically affected some of the professional staff's working arrangements. They were astonished at the announcement, coming as it did, and some of them wanted to discuss the matter but hesitated to do so for fear of offending their host. One of them said afterward, "My right to protest had never been purchased so cheaply. The board did not want to engage in a controversy, and their strategy of flattery and food worked only too well." At least it worked momentarily.

Some of the professional workers who were to be taken in by the luncheon later protested the high-handed methods of the board, and the controversy still smoulders. One of the vigorous protestants is being singled out for attack by his erstwhile host, and a recent letter from one of his close friends states, "E. D. [the board member host] has us in a state of crisis. Jim is under heavy fire. I am calm—it's better for the ulcers!" The luncheon method of getting a consensus probably works better when there is more opportunity for discussion than was evidenced here.

The impression should not be given that members of the professional under-structure in the instance above are the only lower-structure personnel who feel the compulsive weight of conformity to the wishes of the leaders above them. The man we have been discussing, the host and board member, serves as a good example of a higher-ranking leader who was disciplined, or at least thwarted, by his superiors in the power hierarchy. This man happens to be one of the leaders who ranks in a middle position in the policy leadership pattern. He is a younger man than the very top leaders. Several months ago he resigned from a civic board in protest when he was not named on its executive committee. This particular organization has branches of its work in many communities of Old State and is well supported by the top leaders in Regional City. It solicits private donations to carry on its work. At the time of his resignation, the disgruntled leader vowed that he would break the organization, if it ever lay within his power, and he gossiped about many of the things he saw wrong with the inner workings of the policy group in control of the organization. Soon he was called to discuss the matter with one of the top policy leaders in Regional City and was told to be less critical. He has ceased being critical.

The man who has so effectively controlled the younger man is himself subordinate to one other person. The latter leader is above the former in a corporation structure. One might give examples of the relationship of obedience between these men, but it is obvious that the top man in the corporate structure would control the one below him.

Getting back to ways of starting action, one of the professionals said he would try to get the interest of one of the top leaders in a project before approaching other men on the matter—a technique which is widely practiced among this group and is known variously as the bell-wether, lead-dog or king-pin method. The sheep will follow the bell-wether, or the king-pin will knock over the other pins if struck properly. The bell-wether or the king-pin need not be physically present in a meeting of under-structure personnel, but if somone in an under-structure meeting can assure the others of the blessing of a top leader, the under-group will tend to follow the lead indicated.

The physical presence of a top leader in a meeting of lower-echelon personnel is accompanied with many gestures of flattery and mannerisms of deference on the part of the under-personnel. Such meetings are considered highly successful because assurances that action or inaction is appropriate flow from them. Persons excluded from such meetings are told of them, and the cue goes down the line on what "will go," or what "will not go," depending upon the position taken by the bell-wether.

The actions of the top leaders who may attend meetings of the lower echelons are watched with acute attention. Some top leaders may not talk much in such meetings, and their silence is often as meaningful as if they were vociferous. After a meeting in which such a leader has been unduly silent, a member of the group is liable to call the silent one and ask him the meaning of his silence, which in most instances indicates disapproval, but the leader does not want to be on record in his objections. The under-structure personnel will speculate among themselves about what Mr. So-and-so's silence could have meant. There is a general uneasiness current in the group until an official interpretation is forthcoming.

Even grunts of disapproval are carefully recorded in these meetings. One of the top leaders in Regional City has a habit of closing his eyes and softly whistling to himself as he pats his fingers together when a subject of which he disapproves is up for discussion. Such signs as these are watched for carefully by the under-structure personnel. A community agency dependent upon the good will of one of the top leaders is extremely careful not to incur his displeasure and be thereby excluded from his interest and beneficence.

The luncheons mentioned (and dinner meetings might have been included) are exclusive affairs. The membership of any policy luncheon is carefully selected. One informant on the policy group put it this way: "There is usually a lot of bickering down below—fighting for favor and position—but on the level we are talking about (the policy or power level) all that bickering fades out. When we get together, we have confidence that the man who invites us is not going to waste our time, and we are all prepared to make decisions and abide by them."

The same man illustrated the way in which the exclusion process works: "Recently some of us were invited to a rather large affair where an important matter was to be discussed. Some of us decided that we should get our lines straight before going into the meeting. We called around and arranged to get one of the private rooms at the club before the dinner for a few drinks and some discussion before going into the larger dining room. A fellow on the fringes of the group got wind of the smaller meeting and asked one of our crowd if he minded if he joined us. He was put off, and the decision was jointly made that he should not be invited to the private dining room, but we would ask him to come to our table for the dinner proper. This fellow is a pusher. He is a good man in many ways, but we did not want him in the meeting before dinner."

The exclusion process and its reverse are constantly practiced in Regional City to keep the policy-making group within manageable bounds. Most of the meetings are apparently devoted to a specific topic, but many may be general. When an outstanding personality comes to town, a hurried call may go out to some of the leaders to meet for lunch or dinner with the "visiting fireman." The visitor usually makes a few remarks at the end of such a meeting expressing his appreciation for the splendid hospitality of the city, and he may indicate why he is in the community.

In a period of crisis, such as war emergency, there may be a flood of such visitors who give the low-down on the national or international situation "straight from the horse's mouth." Men aspiring to public office or hoping to keep office are often guests at such luncheons. Their host is, of course, their sponsor. The company is select in a power sense.

The men of decision are alert to personnel appointments, too, in the realms of policy jobs within and outside government. Clearances are often made within the crowds on who should take what job. Ray Moster illustrated this by saying, "Not long ago I was called from Washington about a top job in one of the emergency programs. I was asked to name a person who could fill the position. I asked for a little time, and in about thirty minutes a man came to mind that I thought would do very well. I checked with Charles Homer, and he agreed with me. Our suggestion was taken, and the man we had in mind was approached. He accepted the position, and I do not suppose to this day he has any idea of how he was chosen."

Men who are picked up by the leaders to carry responsibilities are carefully watched and tutored by their "superiors." The process is called "subbing" for another man. A subordinate may be tried out on a community project as a substitute for one of the leaders. If he makes good, he is given further assignments. One of the top leaders in Regional City is a man who is described as having "subbed for George Delbert for years, but who is now pretty much on his own." Of course he continues to make contact and clearances with the Delbert crowd, but he also makes many independent decisions which are respected by all crowds. Not all men so chosen work out as well.

Two men who had been quite influential in Regional City affairs were pointed out as persons who had failed to live up to the expectations of the policy group or who had failed to keep business positions which would enable them to consort on an equal footing with the men of power. These men are related in their activities.

The first, Robert Vines, was the predecessor of Fargo Dunham in the Regional Gas Heat Company, one of Regional City's largest enterprises. Vines was a powerful leader in Regional City for many years and one of the most powerful men in Old State. He was very influential in the legislature, but on occasion his methods of gaining objectives had been considered crude by many of the leaders in the community. He was a rough-and-tumble fighter against organized labor, and as labor became more powerful, public-relations methods of handling labor disputes became more prominent in the community. Vines considered such methods as "panty-waist," and he continued to "bully and browbeat" his way in matters pertaining to labor. Vines was the president of the Gas Heat Company. The chairman of the board of the company died, and many assumed that Vines would succeed to the vacant position. However, this did not happen. The national firm with which the regional company is financially affiliated decided to put another man in the place, and this rankled Vines exceedingly.

Vines did not conceal his chagrin gracefully, and as events took their course he was finally maneuvered out of his job. He was too powerful a man to fire outright; so the company officials made a trade with him, retiring him with a handsome settlement. Fargo Dunham, a young attorney in the company, succeeded Vines in the presidency.

Vines still lives in Regional City and is used on some civic projects by the power leaders, but his position is not one of authority. He dropped by one of the offices at the time one of the other leaders was being interviewed in this study, interrupting the interview. His mission was a relatively unimportant one, and when he had left the leader remarked that he felt "sorry for old Vines." The writer asked if Vines's position had changed in community affairs because of his being "eased out of the Gas Heat Company," and the reply was affirmative. The position a man has within one of the leading community business enterprises helps to determine his general community influence. This observation is obvious to anyone who may have been active in community affairs.

The second, Anthony Murdock, was a young man picked

up by Robert Vines. During Vines's scramble for power and control in the company, Anthony Murdock, who was a sub or front man for Vines, began to feel insecure and changed positions. He began working as a public-relations man for one of the large mercantile establishments. Murdock was a popular young man and was looked upon by many of the community leaders as a comer.

After a relatively brief period with the mercantile company, Murdock became dissatisfied with some of the policies of the firm and persuaded some of the men of financial power in the city to finance him in an independent enterprise. The enterprise was not too successful. There were bad market breaks, and competition was keen in the commercial line which was being exploited. Murdock tried to keep up a good many civic duties, considering this a way of building public relations for his company, but these activities did not bring in customers. He was finally forced to sell his interests in the company to a larger competing concern.

The business failure had repercussions in Murdock's community leadership prestige. He failed to be re-elected to the presidency of one of the community agency boards which he had headed for several years, and which many thought he would continue to head for some time to come. He was excluded from many of the policy discussions he had previously been drawn in on as a periphery person of influence. Some of the leaders began to say that if Murdock had paid more attention to his business and less to some of the civic enterprises he might not have failed in the former. One informant suggested that Murdock had very early "tied his wagon to the wrong star," namely, Vines.

At any rate, one sees, in Murdock, a man who was on the fringes of power and policy-making but who finally did not make top billing. He is no longer considered a community leader and has recently taken a position in one of the governmental programs as an under-structure employee at a fairly good salary. Two other men were in competition with Murdock for the latter position, but he edged them out because he still has a certain following among the leaders. He owes his present position to the influence of one of the top men in the community. Murdock has always been considered "safe," but his judgments are questioned in some quarters and it is felt that he should not be in a position of policy decision.

The sons of men of power may have more secure positions than those of the two individuals just described. The position of Mark Parks, Jr., and his rapid climb to a position of community influence has already been outlined. Other leaders' sons have been indicated who stand in the same position as Parks. This area of leadership recruitment need not be discussed in detail. The social position of a son of a large business owner or operator is more secure than that of the men who achieve position. When Mark Parks, Jr., was speculatively asked if he thought he would have achieved a position of prominence as quickly as he did if his father had not cleared the way for him, he quickly replied, "No, I do not believe so. My executive assistant, Horace Taylor, in the next room, is as smart as I am on most things connected with this business, and he may be smarter on some things than I am by far, but I take the lead in community affairs and he doesn't. That's just the way it works out!"

Brief mention should be made of the role of "gossip." There is a constant stream of gossip which goes on in Regional City about the men of affairs. The gossip may be in the nature of a discussion of purely private affairs, or it may be concerned with speculation of what one of the leaders is going to do next. When an individual is being excluded from affairs the gossip may reach a low plane. Repeating some of the specific things turned up in this area would serve no good purpose. It is perhaps sufficient to indicate awareness of the process in the techniques and dynamics of power. Both the smear techniques and the build-up techniques have elements of gossip in them. When private investigation turns up evidence of moral laxity, in some manner the word gets around. In like manner the word gets around concerning the merits of a man who is on his way up.

Another technique of power manipulation is that of the control of expenditures. In any meeting in which a community project may be up for discussion, someone is bound to ask the trite but admittedly important question, "Where in the world is the money coming from?" In so many instances the answer lies in the unspoken assertion, "It has got to come from those who have it!" The persons who have the most money in Regional City are quite aware of the fact that, either through taxes or large contributions to solicitations for private funds, they will bear a substantial part of the cost of any community project. Keeping taxes down is a keen preoccupation of this group. Through contributions of one form or another, the larger interests have a major voice in the affairs of the community, although the possession of wealth, of itself, does not mean that a monied person will speak with special weight on matters of expenditure. In recent years public solicitations have reached down into the worker groups, and there is a growing tendency for some of the leaders of labor to have a voice in the management of purely civic expenditures.

Closely allied with the manipulation of expenditures are the controls exercised over credit in any community. From the largest industrial borrower to the smallest individual needing funds, credit controls are exercised. The men who control credit relationships are for the most part bankers, and in Regional City the banking interests have a large part in the informal policy-making machinery of the community. An elaborate network of credit bureaus and banking facilities keeps close watch over this important phase of American "dollar down" activity operative in the lower social scale in the city.

The larger interests have a similar network of machinery for credit controls operating in the banking houses, investment companies, and brokerage firms. The principles of control operate in similar fashion for the under-structure and the over-structure. Some get credit and some do not, and therein lies a tale of power.

The present chapter was begun by saying that the writer did not know where public politics end and private politics begin. In a sense all the activities described in power relations are politics, if one correlates policy with politics.[5] One might review at this point the many things stated in this chapter concerning both public and private politics, but it seems preferable to let one of the professionals of Regional City speak. His statement integrates many of the elements touched upon here. The fifteen-point analysis which he gives does not differentiate sharply between public and private politics; neither can the writer. Here is his analysis of the elements and dynamics of politics:

1. The networks of influence, the clubs, private wires, the right address.
2. The newspapers that print only that which is "fit to be read."
3. The newsreels that show no news, only horse races, beauty contests, train wrecks, and screwballs.
4. Mimeograph sales-and-opinion campaigns.
5. A good share of this world's goods.
6. Playing two factions of a party, or two parties, on contributions.
7. Farming out defeated candidates in sympathetic county or ward jobs until the heat's off, then back on the public payroll.
8. Building a little business on the side if you are a "public servant."

5. Rupert B. Vance, "The Place of Planning in Social Dynamics," *Social Forces*, XXIII (March 1945), 331.

9. Letting the "practical boys" "buy in."
10. Freezing out the opposition.
11. Calling that which is unacceptable "dynamite."
12. "Public relations" in a business setting, "smart politics" in a public setting.
13. Agreement, from the top down, on the "line."
14. Use of the government as a vast clerical agency, administrators as clerks, to enforce by police power if necessary a balance of power.
15. Contacts and contracts.

8 PROJECTS, ISSUES, AND POLICY

THE getting of agreement for specific actions is one of the major functions of the policy-makers in Regional City. When agreement is reached, it becomes policy on any given issue or project.

Four related topics will be discussed here: policy in general, "big" policy, "lesser" policy, and policy on specific projects and local issues, the chief concern being with the fourth topic, namely, policy as it relates to specific issues and projects.

A dictionary definition of policy will suffice to set the stage for the ensuing discussion. Policy, by definition, is "a settled or definite course... adopted and followed by a government, institution, body, or individual."

As suggested previously, long-settled policy presents no extreme challenge to community leaders. Such matters as private property, representative government, universal education, religious tolerance, and moral behavior tend to be regarded as settled policies. They are never quite settled, of course. The ideals and goals inherent in each of these concepts do not always square with reality, and in a living, moving community there is a constant examination and re-examination of the rights, duties, and privileges embodied in each concept. The more firmly fixed a policy is in the habits and customs of a community, the easier is the task of the policy-makers. In Regional City the mobility of the population, the character of the industries, and the composition of the population, along with the multiplicity of other factors found in any commercial and industrial community, keep the policy-makers relatively busy.

It has been pointed out that policy decision tends to center in the actions of a relatively few men in the community. These men are highly conscious of their position as community leaders, and they use all the propaganda media and the various devices described thus far to keep established policies settled. In the majority of cases the ordinary sanctions of social pressure, the abiding institutional rules of behavior, and relatively fixed customs among the citizenry are sufficient to ease the load of decision, but there are, nevertheless, a great many new issues which constantly clamor for attention along with the reaffirmation of the established rules of social order.

In meeting new situations the older, established rules of conduct are not always applicable, as Carroll D. Clark has suggested:

When the social organization is widened and complicated by economic and cultural differentiation that entails incompatible schemes of group behavior, issues cannot always be met by the application of uniform, traditional controls. It is at this juncture that ... public opinion commences to function.[1]

The policy-makers in Regional City always hope to be a little ahead of public opinion, and their actions tend in the direction of making it appear that they, as a policy group, have thought of any proposal before the public has demanded its adoption. They may welcome demands that something be done in a given situation, and stimulation by the policy-makers for such demands may be a constant factor in the situation; but it remains true that any project should have the appearance of having been under consideration by the policy group for some time.

1. "The Concept of the Public," *Southwestern Social Science Quarterly,* XIII (March 1933), 315.

When new policy is laid down it must be consistent with the general scheme of old policy and should not radically change basic alignments of settled policy. This does not mean that structural alignments do not undergo drastic overhauling on occasion, but consistency is a prime virtue which must not be passed over lightly, so that the basic equilibrium in the social systems of the community may undergo as little disruption as possible. Dubin gives us a thought along this line:

Within particular areas of decision there is a tendency toward consistency in policy. This consistency may be seen in two ways: (1) decisions making changes from established policy or practice are tested and generally brought into alignment with (or necessitate change in) the existing body of procedure and policy; and (2) in putting the change into practice organizational realignments may be necessary.[2]

Organizational realignments are usually made in the structures of government and selected voluntary local organizations to meet the demands of public policy. But now and then business organizations may be affected by changing community conditions, as shown in the case of Mr. Vines, the deposed president of the Regional Gas Heat Company, who did not follow the shift in community attitudes toward the handling of labor problems.

Of all the men talked to in Regional City, only one indicated that he was aggressive in "raising issues" for a realignment of policy. No doubt many of the policy-makers are involved in the same process, but the raising of issues is an activity in which the under-structure personnel are called into play. The one man who said he raised issues was the Mayor. He claimed credit for raising an issue on street improvement, which will be discussed presently, but George Delbert of Allied Utilities also mentioned that he had been actively interested in this par-

2. Robert Dubin, "Decision-Making by Management in Industrial Relations," *American Journal of Sociology*, LIV (January 1949), 294.

ticular project for more than ten years—that it had been his idea. The process, generally speaking, is for a man like Delbert to "think up" such a project, and for the Mayor to raise the issue. Obviously the men of decision do not think up all the projects in the community, but much deference is accorded them in this area.

At the time of this study the national and international situation in regard to war mobilization was uppermost in the minds of many. The men of decision were worried about international developments and expressed many points of concern. Community policies in relation to war plans were being shaped in accord with national plans. Men and materials were being shifted to meet the national needs. Such plans involve "big" policy, whereas some of the purely local decisions and projects involve "lesser" policy. Let us discuss these two concepts briefly.

The terms "big" policy and "lesser" policy are used in their correct sense of magnitude and not in any sense of importance. Policies related to community mobilization for war would be big policy, while the establishment of a children's hospital would be considered lesser policy. The scope of the activity in the first instance is clearly greater in magnitude than that in the second. The relative importance of the two projects depends upon one's point of view. Big policy may also affect a large proportion of the members of the community either directly or indirectly. Lesser policy may reach only certain segments of the population. A lesser policy might have implications for big policy in a latent sense. Using the children's hospital project as an example, one might say that the project is lesser policy in the decision-making processes of the community in relation to all things that must be considered in total community development. But the development of the children's hospital may have implications in the realm of larger policy, in that the men who are sponsors of such a project are helped to maintain their policy-making positions by being identified with so worthy a cause as the hospital represents. As a means of holding the power structure together, such a project performs a latent function in relation to big policy.

Lesser policies promulgated in communities may have a real bearing on national policy, which is in most cases big policy. If one community after another elects to carry forward projects similar to the establishment of children's hospitals and if there is a growing tendency for the national government to aid and sponsor such projects on a nation-wide basis, the policy of establishing such hospitals community by community is cumulative and becomes national or big policy.

Big policy in Regional City may have a variety of aspects. Key has outlined some of the major elements of such policy in a statement in connection with the political machine of Virginia:

The quid pro quo for support of the organization (political machine) is said to be taxation favorable to corporations, an anti-labor policy, and restraint in the expansion of services such as education, public health, and welfare. The organization pursues a negative policy on public services; if there is an apparent demand, it will grudgingly yield a bit here and there, but it dedicates its best efforts to the maintenance of low levels of public service.[3]

This is an example of the underlying implications of big policy. To the power leaders of Regional City, all other policies are lesser when compared to the areas Key has described; and, as has been pointed out, the lesser policies may be functional in relation to the big policies. A big policy which Key did not mention in relation to the Virginia situation but one which is dominant in Regional City is that of segregation of the two major racial groups.

In matters of big policy it is permissible for the larger in-

3. V. O. Key, *Southern Politics in State and Nation* (New York: Alfred A. Knopf, 1949), p. 27.

terests to speak through the newspapers and through other media, such as the lower-echelon men who speak for the policy-makers. National and international policy in its formative stages is discussed only by the representatives of the policy-making group, generally speaking, and the lower-echelon men wait for the cue from the leaders. The line in an emergency or crisis situation is usually rather quickly set by having one of the top leaders make a public pronouncement which is quickly repeated by all instruments of communication such as the newspapers, radio, and through such instruments as the pulpit and the speaker's rostrum of the luncheon clubs. If one of the lower-echelon men should speak out of turn, that is, before the line is set, he would be accused of getting into controversial matters, and appropriate sanctions would be applied. Once the line is set, he may speak in favor of it but must be cautious of anything that hints of dissatisfaction or disagreement. He must go along, or remain silent. If he has serious objections to the line and feels compelled to disagree, it is permissible for him to voice his opinions to someone near him and above him in the hierarchy of informal command. If the objections are deemed valid, they may be transmitted to those in the top power level who may in turn modify their own decisions. However, he must not voice his unorthodoxy publicly. This applies particularly to unsettled policy. Objections to settled policy are rarely voiced, nor would they be acted upon favorably if transmitted to the higher policy-determining group.

The domain of policy discussion for the men of the lower echelons of power is pretty largely centered in the lesser issues which usually pertain to local matters. World issues may be discussed privately with one's peers, but a professional person who had a compulsion to discuss world affairs publicly and too often in Regional City would be looked upon with considerable suspicion. None of the professional men in the city gave world affairs as one of the policy matters which lay before the community at the time of the study. This was not true of the top leaders, however. The line on the international situation given by one of these leaders went as follows:

"We are committed to defense and war mobilization . . . as much as I hate to see it. I hate to see it because it means inflation, unless drastic steps are taken to prevent inflation. We are going to have to take these steps, if we are to preserve our 'way of life.'

"For the next three years we are going to pinch the people—pinch them harder than they have ever been pinched before. They will not be able to buy the things they want—simple things like screw drivers, pieces of pipe and such. . . . All the while wages will be high, and industrial output will be at an all time high—but it will be mostly for war goods, not consumer goods. . . .

"Our people have never faced anything like the conditions, as I now foresee them. We have never had any huge personnel losses in any war. We have never faced a real inflationary crisis, and our cities have never had to stand up under bombing attacks. I don't know whether the morale of our people will hold. It worries me, but we've got to go through with this thing.

"After three years of top production for war, the dangers of inflation will be at a maximum, and the dissatisfaction of the people will be growing. We will be faced with two things—we can cut down on military expenditures and back down—or we will go to war. We will then do the latter, in my opinion. . . .

"During this period we must cut out all welfare spending—or at least to the bare essentials. We cannot spend both for war and for welfare. It is a hard choice but one we must make. Men should work for what they get, anyway, and not have it handed to them!"

When this man was asked what he proposed as a solution to the inflationary danger he had mentioned, he replied, "Slap on the stiffest tax program that can be mustered. Tax clear down to the little fellow."

Several other informants in the policy group expressed like sentiments, but in no case was it as clearly put as in the case above. The speaker was a man of big policy proportions.

All informants were asked the question: "What are two major issues or projects before the community today?" The answers are indicated in Table 8. When the professional under-structure were asked the same question, their answers

TABLE 8

MAJOR ISSUES OR PROJECTS REPORTED BY 26 TOP LEADERS AS
BEFORE THE COMMUNITY OF REGIONAL CITY, 1950-1951

Issue or Project	Number of Times Reported
Plan of Development	23
Traffic Control	9
Sales Tax Measure	4
Negro Question (general)	4
Voter's Plan	3
Medical Plan, Negro Housing, Morale-Building for War Emergency, General Taxation	2 (each)
Education (University project), Negro Education, Meeting Facilities for Luncheon Clubs, Increased Bonded Indebtedness	1 (each)

differed somewhat (Table 9). It will be noted that in only two instances did the power leaders in the community choose a matter related to international affairs as a major issue before the community. These men spoke of morale-building to prepare the nation for war. This is not in contradiction to the previous discussion related to the information given by the top leaders relative to big policy. Many gave an answer related to international affairs when the question was put to them, but opinions were being sought on issues that directly affected Regional City proper and each informant was so told. Even with this explanation two top leaders insisted on putting down morale-building for the war emergency. None of the professionals mentioned an issue pertaining to the threat of war, and few spoke of the international situation in interviews with them.

TABLE 9

MAJOR ISSUES OR PROJECTS REPORTED BY 14 PROFESSIONALS AS
BEFORE THE COMMUNITY OF REGIONAL CITY, 1950-1951

Issue or Project	Number of Times Reported
Plan of Development	4
Housing and Slum Clearance	4
Negro Question (general)	3
Voter's Plan, Segregation, Traffic Control, Negro Education, Political Reform	2 (each)
Rent Control, Safety (fire), Increased Welfare Grants, More Adequate Financing through Community Chest, Police Action Against Negroes	1 (each)

It can be seen that the Plan of Development has high priority both in the top leader group and among the under-professionals. A total of twenty-three out of twenty-six top leaders chose this problem and four of the fourteen professionals did likewise. Traffic control, the general Negro question, and the Voter's Plan all received consideration by both the top leaders and the professionals. The sales tax measure mentioned by several of the top leaders stands out as differentiating them from the under-group. Housing and slum clearance had considerably higher priority among the under-professional personnel than with the top leaders. Each of these projects or issues which received the largest number of choices in both groups will be discussed, leaving with only brief mention some which received single votes.

Regional City's Plan of Development is actually a plan for annexation of outlying areas not now incorporated in the city boundaries. The city is operating under a charter from the state given several decades ago in which the boundaries of the city were specified. The growth of the city has made it impossible adequately to extend municipal services to the population that has spilled over the original city boundaries, and the county in which the city is located has been called upon to provide these services. For many years there has been a growing dissatisfaction with this arrangement. The matter of tax levies on property and industry has been a problem between the overlapping units of government. Conflicting traffic regulations have had to be ironed out. Suburbs have sprung up outside Regional City's boundaries and have become incorporated, thus multiplying the problems involved.

The state legislature has been unwilling to review and revise the city charter for many years because new industries coming into the area have tended to locate in the county outside the jurisdiction of the city. Certain tax concessions were made to many of these industries because they were located in the county, and the leaders of these industries are loath to give up this economic privilege. Citizens in the suburbs have felt that incorporation into the city proper would increase property taxes, since much of the property in the central section of Regional City is "blighted" and produces far less revenue than it costs to maintain these districts. Much of the slum area is inhabited by Negro citizens.

In recent years, however, there has been a growing awareness on the part of many of the leaders and of a substantial portion of the citizenry that the situation was one that needed to be remedied. Several surveys were made by outside planning firms regarding the need for combining certain city and county services, and for coordinating others. The leaders began to see that in one way or another the rising costs of government were carried by them in a large measure, whether they were inside or outside the city limits. Also, as the Negro community became aggressive in demanding voting rights, it was seen that through their numbers they could control, in some measure, the actions of elected officials within the city. There are, perhaps, a score of other factors which have entered into the present demand for extension of the city boundaries beyond their present limits. The main fact is that there is now substantial agreement among the leaders that this improvement in governmental operation should be made.

About four years ago the Mayor of Regional City proposed a vote on the issue which was county-wide in its scope. The Mayor and certain public figures were prominent in putting the issue to the people. The top leaders were generally in agreement with the plan, but few of them actually engaged in the campaign for annexation. The problem was to convince the outlying sections to come into the city. It was promised that for a period of at least ten years taxes would not be raised on properties annexed. If an outlying area voted not to come in, they were not forced to do so.

The vote within the city was favorable to the plan by a large majority, and some of the smaller unincorporated areas favored the plan in the voting. However, the largest outlying districts voted negatively, though in some cases not overwhelmingly so. The vote gave the leaders confidence, and they went to the legislature through a citizen's committee composed of some of the top leaders and were successful in getting a "home rule" bill passed. This was a first step toward placing the revised plan on a legal footing and a maneuver which enabled the community leaders to compel outlying areas to come into the city if a majority in all areas voted favorably for the plan. The leaders strengthened the committee through inclusion of an impressive array of names of prominent sponsors. The suggestion by a public-relations man to call the idea the Plan of Development rather than an annexation plan was followed. The word annexation had nega-

tive connotations that the word development had not acquired in the community. A very lively campaign ensued, and
a favorable majority vote was taken on the issue. The plan
is now being put into effect by the responsible authorities in
the metropolitan area but not without some difficulty.

County officials have refused to be as cooperative in the
plan as it was hoped they might be. They were active in trying to defeat the plan and they had some powerful adherents
in their camp, but the power balance seems to be on the side
of the winners in the recent election. The policy in this issue
is becoming settled. It will be remembered that there is a
high degree of concerted opinion among the top leaders favoring the plan of development—twenty-three leaders out of
twenty-six answering the question are in favor of the plan.
Pressure is being put on the county officials to bring them into
line. The newspapers are carrying stories of any hint of dissatisfaction voiced by any individual county official, and particular attention is being paid to one of the political leaders
of the opposition. There is talk that this particular official
may not be re-elected in the next county election. Many
of the county politicians are, as they put it, lying low.

There would seem to be no particular merit in attempting
to analyze why each of the power leaders was vitally interested
in the improvement plan. It was evident that property rights,
bonded indebtedness, and taxes would be changed in the
process of putting the plan across. All of these elements are
closely scrutinized by the business and power leaders of the
community. They involve major policy decision.

In order to be more concrete in the discussion of the Plan
of Development, a brief analysis of some of the roles played
by various top leaders may be in order.

Both George Delbert and Peter Barner take credit for putting forward the idea of the Plan of Development. The project, at the time of this study, had been ten years in the making.
Much informal discussion preceded the present stage of de-

velopment. It seems probable that Delbert handled the problem of getting a policy decision on the matter and that Barner brought the issue to public attention.

During the policy discussions personal contact was made with at least fifteen of the top leaders in the community. These contacts varied from one or two informal conversations to a long series of discussions on the matter. Advice was sought from Mark Parks, Harry Parker, Harvey Aiken, and Charles Homer, among others, in a fairly consistent way. These top men had a hand in the whole operation, but with the exception of Parker the latter group could not be said to be out front on the project. Percy Latham was called upon to be the front man when the project reached the committee stage. He also was a go-between on any relations that were connected with interracial matters.

Luke Street drafted legislation related to the project. Elsworth Mines helped get a bill through the legislature. Others helped by testimony and in other ways, but these men led out in this phase of the work.

Fargo Dunham and Edward Stokes helped to publicize the project when the time was right. Joseph Hardy, Bert Tidwell, and Arthur Tarbell did a great deal of work in carrying the project into civic clubs and associations for discussion. Jack Williams was persuaded to take the presidency of one of the major associations for a year to see the project through. Latham, Williams, and Grover Smith were put on the official board of the project after it got out of the policy stage and into an action phase.

There were perhaps thousands of "actions" taken in getting the project under way and in bringing it to a successful conclusion. It is not possible to fully appraise all the actions taken, but the pattern of action and the roles played by the men mentioned illustrate a stability of structure in action that is worth noting. If one observes the same group of people attacking policy problems over and over, in relation to major community events, he may be fairly sure that he has touched upon a part of the power structure of the community.[4]

Traffic control is to some extent bound up with the Plan of Development. This traffic plan is concerned mainly with providing by-pass highways which will skirt the central business district and provide rapid transportation lanes for traffic going through the city without stopping in the central business district. For several years the Central Business Association blocked this plan, clinging to an outgrown idea that all traffic should go through the central business district because it was felt that many through travellers would "stop and shop." The congestion of the central business district has, however, become so great in the past few years that it has become quite generally recognized that a through traveller would have much difficulty in stopping to shop, even if he so desired. Traffic improvement in Regional City has many facets which concern the community leaders, and there is every indication that much effort is being extended in solving some of the major problems involved. Off-street parking is being discussed, and a traffic committee composed of top leaders has been formed. The physical planning agencies are being coordinated in both the central city and its satellite communities. Thus, the traffic problem appears in this study as an important issue.

The sales tax question, which was turned up in the study, deals with a proposal recently put before the state legislature which would levy a tax on all retail sales. Old State has no such tax now. Corporation taxes are relatively low, and there is much pressure to keep them low because one of the settled policies of importance is to encourage industrial movement

4. A proof of the latter statement may lie in the fact that at the time of the present study the Plan of Development had top priority in the community. The Voter's Plan had only three votes, but today this is one of the top issues in the community. The same men, in the main, are setting policy and doing work in relation to the Voter's Plan.

into Old State. It is felt that a low corporation tax rate is an inducement to any company contemplating a move to the region. Income taxes in the state do not reach down to the lower income families, and the sales tax is designed to tap this taxable source.

Many of the welfare workers, labor officials, and other professional personnel have voiced feeble opposition to the sales tax proposal, but no concerted effort to defeat the measure has been made within the recent months by any organized group. The bill seems to be sure of passage. Currently the proposal is tied to the inflation fears of the leaders, and the legislature is controlled in large part by the men described as power leaders.[5]

The Voter's Plan which has some adherents among the top leaders of Regional City deals with a proposal before the state legislature which would make all state elections follow the pattern of the national electoral college—that is, each county would be allowed so many electoral votes in determining the winner of any political race for federal and state posts. The measure would partially disfranchise many city dwellers in their federal voting rights. The scheme would give the rural areas a preponderance of power in federal elections—the same power they now hold in the elections of the governor, but not in relation to all state candidates for public office. The leaders of Regional City are somewhat divided on the Plan. Many are for it, but also many are against it. It represents an unsettled policy and augurs to be an issue until there develops more unified agreement among the top leaders.

The Negro question is a problem with which the leaders of the community are in constant contact. The position of the Negro in the community has already been described. His social and economic position, generally considered, is a precarious one. There seems to be no formula for a quick and easy

5. Since this was written, the Old State legislature has passed "one of the most comprehensive and sweeping sales taxes" yet assessed by any state.

solution to the many problems current among this group. The Negroes are restive under prevailing conditions and are aggressively asserting their rights on many issues which they bring to the attention of the leaders.

Recently they have initiated a suit in the federal courts which asks that the children of Negro citizens be allowed to have access to school facilities equal to those provided children of citizens in the larger community. The leaders of the larger community are against the suit and hope to make concessions to the Negro community in the matter. They feel that the Negroes are not serious in their suit but are bringing it forward to have a better bargaining position with the community leaders. Negro leaders say they are quite serious in their contentions and expect to "fight the issue all the way to the Supreme Court of the United States." This issue is far from settled and is causing much concern in all quarters.

In this instance policy formerly settled is being challenged by a group which is organized to a point where its voice must be heard, and the older methods of intimidation and coercion against this group are no longer effective. Many of the Negro leaders are relatively secure financially, and their own positions of leadership are threatened within their community if they remain subservient to the dominant group. The leaders in the larger community are in a quandary at the present writing, but there is indication that institutional and associational alignments are in process of change to meet the current situation in a manner that will keep the present balance of power intact.

If one looks at a listing of the issues and projects deemed to be important among the Negro leaders, he finds that the list does not correspond to that of the larger community policy leaders. It compares more closely with the list provided by the professional under-structure. The list in Table 10 was obtained from replies by twenty-two sub-community leaders. Almost all of these sub-community leaders agreed that the improvement of school facilities was a primary community issue. Almost half of the group were concerned with housing conditions. Both of these issues are found at the bottom of the listing of the top power leaders. Percentage-wise they would rate relatively higher with the under-structure professionals. The Plan of Development, which is of so great concern to the top leaders, got only one vote from the sub-community leaders.

The Voter's Plan mentioned by the top leaders and the under-structure professionals finds its counterpart in the sub-community listing of issues under the heading of "Voting Rights." The sub-community leaders view the Voter's Plan as a disfranchisement plan, and consequently they are in direct opposition to it.

TABLE 10

MAJOR ISSUES OR PROJECTS REPORTED BY 22 SUB-COMMUNITY LEADERS AS BEFORE THE COMMUNITY OF REGIONAL CITY, 1950-1951

Issue or Project	Number of Times Reported
Improvement of Schools	18
Housing and Slum Clearance	10
Voting Rights	7
Child Welfare, Liquor Licensing, Recreation Facilities, Equal Employment Rights, Control of Crime, Civil Defense, Plan of Development	1 (each)

The unformulated issue, the general Negro question, mentioned by the top leaders, becomes articulated in the demands of the sub-community leaders. There is so little overt awareness on the part of the top leaders concerning the issues that are of pressing importance to the sub-community that the situation portends increased community conflict, unless structural arrangements can be utilized to communicate these issues to the community policy-makers.

A place for the sub-community leaders in the top policy-making structure of Regional City is long overdue, but there is little evidence to indicate that they will have such a place soon. There are occasional slight departures from the old patterns, however. For example, one of the leaders pointed out that the leadership of the community had been making concessions to Negroes during recent years in allowing them to sit on some of the associational boards where their interests were involved. A new hospital which has been built for Negroes by subscriptions of capital from the total community has several Negroes on its board. They are in a minority on the board, however; so the balance of power remains essentially the same even with this concession. It was pointed out, nevertheless, that ten years ago such an interracial board could not have existed in Regional City.

The housing question has been a problem within Regional City for many years as it has been in many American communities. It has been aggravated because much of the slum area is inhabited by Negro citizens and low-cost housing for this group has not been considered a must. The passage of federal legislation to help in the matter has been long proposed by many groups in the community. The issue was not one on which the top leaders could present a united front. Some leaders stood to benefit by housing legislation, while others did not. Adherents on both sides of this question spoke up forcibly, and it was relatively safe for many of the under-structure professional personnel to choose sides in the matter. Most of them were for low-cost housing, and consequently they checked this issue as one of their major concerns in answer to the study questions. This issue represents a split in the forces of "unanimity," and is thus contrary to the general mode of community behavior. The passage of federal legislation for slum clearance and community redevelopment gave courage to the proponents of action in the housing area, but the leaders are said to have "dragged their feet." The emergency mobilization effort appears to have stopped many plans in the housing field, and the issue in Regional City remains an unsettled one.

The issues and projects that have been briefly outlined here are considered big policy matters in Regional City today. They are the major issues upon which policy is being developed and settled. Five years ago the issues would have been largely different. Some few might have been the same, but in any event policy may be said to shift with the currents of pressing issues at any given time. Lesser issues are multiple in Regional City. Some issues considered lesser today may become big issues tomorrow. The under-structure personnel play around with the lesser issues in many cases, and, through their channels of communication with the power leaders, some of their issues may be picked up for top level policy consideration. When major policy is to be decided on any issue, the top leaders will be well represented on any boards or committees devoted to the particular matter.

Each leader was asked to indicate whether he had participated on a board or committee connected with the issues or projects that he named as having top priority in the community. Fifteen of the power leaders indicated having had a place or having been represented on such bodies. Only one professional in the under-structure was on such a committee, and his place was that of technical adviser in the traffic program. None was represented on the committee.

On given issues, the under-structure professional personnel tend to be more aggressive than the top leaders in contacting others in relation to a project, although the figures given are not decisive on this question. The leaders indicated that they had been contacted on the issues they mentioned in thirty-seven instances, while they had contacted others in only twenty-eight instances. The reverse situation was true with the under-structure personnel. They had been contacted in seventeen instances, and had contacted others in twenty-three cases. These figures are intended to indicate roughly how aggressive a leader may be in relation to a given issue or project. The power leaders have action initiated for them more often than they initiate action. With the under-structure professional personnel the reverse is true. In relation to some of the issues, the leaders had not been contacted nor had they contacted others, but they recognized the existence of a particular issue or project in the community. The greatest number of contacts among the leaders were in relation to the big issues while for the under-structure people it was generally the lesser issues.

The lesser issues in the community tend to revolve around specific programs devoted to the welfare of the whole community or to specific groups, Fund appeals for various activities included educational programs, and extended health services and welfare activities on a minor scale would seem to catch most of these programs and projects. The sums of money involved are often minor in comparison with total expenditures for all services in the community, and top policy decision is usually not required to allow these activities to proceed. The associations, including the luncheon clubs, are always active in gathering funds for scholarships, to purchase medical supplies for a well baby clinic, to bring in an inspirational speaker, and the like. The top leaders contribute methodically to these minor fund appeals, and the under-associations are always figuring out ways to "interpret" their programs to the public. This activity, boiled down, often means interpreting their program to those persons of means in the community who will give financial and moral support to the association's activity. Few of the associations are in position to attack the big issues which confront the community. Many of the clubs, however, have the continuing function of being a public-relations medium.

In the pilot study, made prior to the Regional City study, a list of projects and community issues was prepared for interviewees to scan and pick out items that appeared to be of major importance in the community. This method was not considered satisfactory because of the subjective elements that are bound to creep into the initial selection of such a list of issues and projects prepared by the researcher and a panel of community judges in advance of a wider program of inter-viewing.

In the Regional City study the method of asking each inter-viewee to name projects and issues seemed much more satisfactory. By utilizing this method, a list was gathered that was current, and the issues and projects selected were those in which the men being interviewed had a primary interest. They were related to community matters upon which the men of leadership were active. It has already been shown that there was a good correlation of opinion among the top leaders as to which issues were of primary importance to them.

The isolation of policy matters and projects flowing from top policy-decision is, in the opinion of the writer, one effective way of approaching the tricky problem of action research. When action is related to specific issues or projects, structured patterns of action may be observed or reconstructed with a minimum of difficulty. Every man in Regional City could conceivably be placed in relation to his actions or lack of action concerning the Plan of Development.

The lack of action on the part of many of the citizens in the community studied, and in relation to some of the major issues and projects, was of real interest to this researcher. Why some men move in relation to policy matters and others do not may be touched upon, as a question, now.

9 THE ORGANIZED COMMUNITY AND THE INDIVIDUAL

FEAR, pessimism, and silence are three elements in the behavior of individuals with which any community organizer or social analyst must deal. These elements will be traced in relation to organized community activities with the notion that if each of these factors could be dispelled or allayed, the organized structure of the community might be able to function more adequately in the enrichment of the lives of its individual members. In a certain sense, this phase of discussion borders on an analysis of categories that have been considered latent in this study. Social philosophy and psychological motivation are such latent categories. The remarks made here in the analysis of each of the elements mentioned will be merely suggestive rather than exhaustive.

Expressions of fear in community life are prevalent among the top leaders. Pessimism is manifested among the professionals, and silence is found in the mass of the citizenry in Regional City.

The fear spoken of here is not a craven, personal cringing from the raw facts of life on the part of the top leaders, but it is an element of behavior which is obvious in the actions of the leaders. It is manifest in a cautious approach to any new issue which may arise and is apparently rooted in the feeling that any change in the existing relations of power and decision in the community would be disastrous for the leaders who now hold power.

Among some of the "economic thinkers" of the top leadership group there is the expressed desire that more goods and services be made available to more people in the community, but the fear is also expressed that there may not be enough to go around if a more equitable distribution of resources were demanded by any substantial portion of the population. There is fear that this latter idea may become a topic of open discussion. There is fear that the American way of life is in danger both from within the community and from forces abroad in the world. There is also fear that the true alignment of power may become known and that the actual distribution of goods will be criticized. I am not prepared to discuss the validity of these fears, but must point out that they are manifest, if one is to analyze adequately the community under discussion.

There may be pride among leaders in being named as leaders, but also there may be some guilt feeling attached to the informal positions they hold. It was obvious in our interviews with the leaders that they were generally pleased that their colleagues had chosen them as leaders, but many of them disclaimed any distinction. Few wished to be singled out as leaders. The American ideal of equality may be operative in the situation. Christopher Smith says:

One of the most cherished ideals that has been handed down from generation to generation in American society is the one that pictures America as the land of infinite individual opportunity. Provided a young man has the combined qualities of ability, which he invariably possesses because of the alleged fact that all men are created equal, and ambition, the supreme virtue in American civilization, there is nothing to prevent him from attaining a position of prominence and leadership in society. If he cannot rise to the position in the White House as the boy from the log cabin did, he can at least reach a position of importance and esteem in his own community.[1]

The facts of social life in American communities generally, and in Regional City particularly, have not borne out the popular conception which Smith puts forward and which he does not defend as true. There are leadership positions in Regional City, but they are limited in number. A few men attain prominence, while the vast majority do not. Those who do achieve such status are inclined to feel somewhat guilty about it. This may be less true with those persons who have "ascribed status." The goal that Smith outlines may be impossible of achievement for most citizens, and this condition as Arthur Hillman has suggested, must be recognized and not apologized for. Hillman says that participation in community activities need not be limited by the factor described:

It is necessary to counteract the tendency to hold back for fear of seeming to be out of line or to be a "reformer" or a "budding politician." Participation must become socially acceptable, not something to apologize or account for, if community life is to be strengthened by many contributions.[2]

Habits of community participation must be stimulated, says Hillman; such stimulation should come from leaders, and the process should not be feared by them. The fact that persons within the community should fear to be labelled "reformers" or "budding politicians," may strike one as not in accord with the fundamental notion of democracy.

It is apparently true that the leaders are afraid of reform and that they are afraid to have political questions raised without their consent, as we have witnessed in the actions taken to thwart the development of the Progressive party movement in Regional City. But the fear of opposition carried to the

1. "Social Selection in Community Leadership," *Social Forces*, XV (May 1937), 530-531.
2. *Community Organization and Planning* (New York: The Macmillan Company, 1950), p. 201.

extreme of violence in putting dissident factions down is, perhaps, an unhealthy excess of fear. There was some violence connected with the situation. There may be merit in the reformer's point of view. There may be a refreshing stimulation to the social alignments by allowing the political expression of differing opinion in such movements as that represented by the Progressive party. "Leadership" is not synonymous with "control," which is apparent in the fear situation described. Hillman writes as follows in discussing the concept of leadership versus control:

"Leaders," people of power and prestige, do not always have an active give-and-take relationship with followers. Theirs is influence and power, yes, but not necessarily a responsiveness to followers. They are ... control figures rather than representative men. The American practice is often to rely on such leaders to manipulate rather than to be channels of communication and sources of stimulation. This stems in part from the factor of "mass passivity...." [3]

There is fear on the part of "control" leaders that opening the channels of communication, as suggested by Hillman, may bring undesirable elements into the policy-making situation in Regional City. This fear is strongly expressed in reference to the growing political power of the Negro group. Methods to keep policy "flowing down" are consequently devised in this community, and the "trickle down theory" that Hillman describes is applicable to the situation:

Community action in a practical, democratic sense is more than a matter of selling key leaders who in turn will influence the bulk of the people. The use of "leaders" as "status bearers" of a community may be necessary on occasion, in genuine emergencies for example.

The tendency to rely on dominant figures ... is almost inevitable under urban conditions. However, the limitations of the "trickle

3. *Ibid.*, p. 181.

down" theory of community action should be recognized, and the values of participation examined.[4]

The point that Hillman implies in regard to the necessity for the use of some dominant leaders under conditions of urban society may offer some reason for the high concentration of the policy-making machinery in the hands of a few in Regional City, but it has been shown that the structure of power in the community is so narrow that many questions of policy are not examined at all for lack of time on the part of the leaders, if for no other reason.

Obviously the actions of individuals in so large a city must be structured in some orderly fashion. Responsibilities of leadership must be delegated and borne by selected individuals. The selection of leaders is a key point. As it presently stands, leaders are for the most part self-selected, in that the same leaders call upon each other in policy matters, and but rarely does the under-structure of power have a hand in the selection. Certainly, the very bottom structure has very little to do with leadership selection. The base of participation in selection would need to be widened considerably to satisfy Hillman's thesis. Through the process of self-selection, the controlling leader may develop a self image as described by R. A. Brady:

Almost without exception the big businessman is coming to think of himself as the person who guides, "educates," and "leads" the general public on behalf of the common or "community" good, with the result that, although he is typically the possessor of vast wealth and prepotent political and social authority, spokesmen for his interests yet seek to remold the businessman in the public eye as the least selfish of all. In this reduction, not profits but "service" becomes his leading aim. . . .[5]

One cannot join the chorus of acclaim for the businessman in Regional City, for there his aims seem to be as described in the

4. *Ibid.*, p. 192.
5. *Business as a System of Power*, p. 287.

first part of Brady's statement. The leaders are interested in maintaining their own positions which give them such things as wealth, power, and prestige. They are fearful that any swaying of the balance of power may destroy the positions they now hold, and of course they could be right, although it is felt that a case could be made for allaying their excessive fears.

The problem presented by the disparity of the economic conditions of men in Regional City is one that the whole economy has faced for many decades, and no attempt is made here to solve such a problem. However, this factor lies at the bottom of the power struggle and cannot be overlooked. The fears of the leaders are contingent on this very problem. One need not be a social scientist to see the miserable conditions which are so apparent in Regional City and to contrast them unfavorably with the conditions of luxury which also exist there. The social scientist, however, need not excuse or leave these conditions unnoticed through fear, and it may be assumed that if the conditions were faced squarely in a structural sense no one need fear them, including the men of power.

The power structure of Regional City has the capacity for attacking the important issue raised, but as it is now constituted it apparently does not have the desire to do so. It now represents a closed system of power or relatively so. The solution to the problem presented by the current structure would seem to be to open the policy-making machinery to more groups than are now represented. Such a simple device as this would enable more individuals to participate in solving the many problems that exist in the community and the fears of the men of power would be allayed in great measure if this step were taken. Social planning is the name that may be given to what is suggested.

Social planning means that groups and individuals who are concerned with issues, projects, and community problems may organize into *effective* bodies to discuss issues, coordinate opinion, help lay out policy to cover any specific problem, and suggest alternative ways of action to meet a given social need. John Dewey and others have expressed this idea in various ways. Dewey says:

The keynote of democracy as a way of life may be expressed . . . as the necessity for the participation of every mature human being in the formation of values that regulate the living of men together: which is necessary from the standpoint of both the general welfare and the full development of human beings as individuals.[6]

Charles R. Henderson says:

As a psychical person, one must find his own way in a knowable world, each human being must be taught what he can learn of the knowledge possessed by his community, and his power to learn must be developed.[7]

Baker Brownell tells us that a relatively complete "inner ordering" of life cannot be found in the individual as such, but must be sought in community life.[8] In other words, the individual is not self-contained. The community is, however, a "self-sufficing unit of interest" for the individual.

The community is a kind of group that has . . . self-containment and centrality of meaning. Though its structure has inner relevance and at the same time involves outer associations with other groups, the community is self-relevant. It is self-justifying morally, aesthetically, socially. . . .[9]

Through communication we confirm the basic unity of our common life and try to convert it into intelligent or at least successful

6. *Problems of Men* (New York: Philosophical Library, 1946), p. 58.
7. "Definitions of a Social Policy Relating to the Dependent Group," *American Journal of Sociology,* X (November 1904), 318.
8. *The Human Community* (New York: Harper and Brothers, 1950), p. 141.
9. *Ibid.,* p. 228.

action. By means either direct or indirect we identify our experience with another's. We try to live together in a fairly coherent world, share its values, and bring about mutual cooperation.[10]

Mary P. Follett presented this line of reasoning many years ago by stating, "Our happiness, our sense of living at all, is directly dependent on our joining with others. We are lost, exiled, imprisoned until we feel the joy of unity."[11] This joining with others seems to be the essence of democratic social planning, and it is a far different thing from being under the domination of others. It is the sense of belonging that is absent for most individuals who may be interested in policy decision in Regional City but who are so effectively excluded. This feeling of exclusion gives rise to the pessimism abroad in the professional group, which will be discussed presently.

"The individual enters into the picture," says Ludwig Freund, "only insofar as he is a publicly important figure. If he represents a large enough group his views and actions are politically relevant; otherwise they are not."[12] This state of affairs holds true where adequate machinery is lacking in the community for participation of the unimportant person or the little fellow, as he is called in Regional City, one who has been designated as belonging to the bottom structure of power. Properly structured social planning agencies and open lines of communication, unhampered by fear, would do much to relieve the tensions which exist in a highly controlled situation. It is true that even under the most democratic scheme of communication there would not be opportunity for each individual to have the ear of any particular leader on every issue, but the lines of communication need to be opened more than they are if the bottom structure of the population are to be heard at all.

10. *Ibid.*, p. 241.
11. *The New State* (New York: Longmans, Green and Company, 1918), p. 194.
12. "Power and the Democratic Process—A Definition of Politics," *Social Research*, XV (September 1948), 342.

Salter defines "democracy" as government by public discussion and says that only by such discussion can the citizen have facts upon which to act intelligently.[13]

In a city of any appreciable size, the apparent control exercised over all types of information presents a real problem that must be solved by groups devoted to keeping the channels of information and discussion open on both the big and the lesser issues. It has been indicated that the lesser issues may be discussed, but that discussion of the major issues is kept out of the organization and associations by the top leaders. The Community Council in Regional City *might* be a place where such issues could be fully discussed, but as an organization it is so hedged around with protocol maintained by the fears of the policy-making group that there is little likelihood of its being an effective community-wide instrument for community discussion and action. The political organizations are also so completely dominated by the power interests which have been identified that there is little hope of adequate expression being fostered by them at this time.

The personnel most acutely aware of the paralysis of action and the suppression of dissatisfaction with the community structural arrangements are the professional workers. Ludwig Stein writes that there has always been conflict between the individual personality and organized authority of any community. He says, "Personality resists the engulfing and leveling effect of authority...." [14] The resistance to the authority of the policy-makers in Regional City is expressed by the professionals privately, as has been indicated in earlier discussion, and shows up in the form of pessimism. The letter of Denny North, previously quoted, illustrates the point. Francis G. Wilson in an essay on politics says of pessimism:

13. J. T. Salter, "The Pattern of Politics: The Politician," *Journal of Politics*, I (May 1939), 133.
14. "The Sociology of Authority," *Publications of the American Sociological Society*, XVIII (December 1923), 118.

Pessimism is ... primarily a product of tension in the social system and insecurity in the individual.[15]

[It] is an intuition, a sense of fear of a changing relation between values, *i.e.*, traditions and institutions.[16]

The professional workers in Regional City, particularly those employed in the social agencies and in the planning agencies, are quite susceptible to moods of pessimism. They are employed by and subordinate to the upper-structure of power whose interests they are supposed to have in mind, and yet in most cases they work with and are dedicated to the improvement of social conditions of the underprivileged. The role of such a professional is thus a marginal one producing conflict within the personality involved and possibly leading to what may be termed professional schizophrenia. The professional is isolated from the upper reaches of power, and he is generally rather effectively isolated from the average citizen. The organization for which he works may call itself community-wide in scope, but the term community should mean a community totality of interests rather than merely a geographical or demographic concept.

Some of the points already made in connection with the community problems of Regional City have grown out of many discussions with the professional personnel of that city and from personal observation. One need not linger in a justification of the "facts" as presented and interpreted, but they lead to another set of facts which from observation also appear to be true. These facts revolve around the notion that no professional person employed in Regional City might be critical of many power decisions and not be overwhelmed with attack damaging to his professional career in the community, whether his facts were right or wrong. The suppression of

15. "Pessimism in American Politics," *Journal of Politics*, VII (May 1945), 143.
16. *Ibid.*, p. 127.

such facts as have been presented here is often called expediency.

Expediency may be defined as the setting aside of a principle in favor of facilitating an immediate end or purpose. Most professionals in Regional City have sets of principles related to their respected professions. These may be related to the "right" and "wrong" ways of handling problems pertaining to physical planning, social planning, fund-raising, care for the underprivileged, or a host of other professional codes that are extant in the society. If any one of these codes should come into conflict with the interests of the power group in the community, there is a tendency for the professional personnel to lay aside the principles of their profession in favor of immediate gains. Such action is considered expedient and is generally looked upon with favor. The problem need not be discussed on moral grounds, but it is a very real problem for the social scientist. Many of the issues of Regional City need to be analyzed without regard for the sensitive feelings or the interests of the men of power if solutions to some of the existent problems are to be met with any degree of adequacy. It is not meant, however, that it would be altogether possible to study and analyze the social conditions of Regional City and leave out the factor of personal feelings. It can be said that the social scientist may not be encumbered by the same impelling arguments for expediency which force the professional worker in the direction of conformity. The professional worker who is trying to get a program of action approved by the power interests must be aware of the facets of the situation which in his opinion call for cautious handling. Often, however, this activity becomes so much a part of the way of action of an individual that many of the principles of his profession are forgotten or rationalized into something entirely different from what they may have been in the beginning. The highly competent social scientist, too long inured to the practical way of action, may become an instrument for the distortion or suppression of social facts, if his bread and butter depend upon such distortion.

In order to stay close to Regional City in this discussion, it is not necessary to become involved in "value" questions, per se. However, in the realm of policy in the community under discussion, the social scientists, social workers, and other professional personnel who are in constant contact with the problems out of which issues arise, are not on a level of community operations where their voices may be heard. This is a structural weakness in the community, in much the same way that a structural weakness appears in the fact that a sub-community of the city is isolated from the main stream of policy discussion and decision.

Even though channels of communication may be provided for interaction between the policy-makers and sub-groups, they are often ineffective through the distortions that are bound to occur in transmission, as well as through the fact that the values of the two groups may be in conflict. The knowledge resident in many of the under-structure personnel is not fully utilized in the interaction processes carried on between them and the upper-structure. Morris Opler illustrates this:

Often it is the social scientist's presence and prestige, rather than his knowledge, that are wanted. There are powerful men of affairs everywhere who give lip service to a "scientific age" but who do not propose to alter their habits of mind or action one iota in response to it. Just as the advertiser does obeisance to "science" by posing a man in a white coat near the same old product, this type of executive or administrator is willing and even eager, in deference to the new age, to have a social scientist in the background of the setting he is arranging or have him put the seal of approval on what is proposed.[17]

From observation of events in Regional City, the manipulation of the social scientist and the practitioner of the social

17. "Social Science and Democratic Policy," *Applied Anthropology*, IV (Summer 1945), 13.

sciences in community life fits the pattern which Opler has described. Planning executives are hired to make plans in the physical and social areas of community life, but they are hedged around so firmly with restrictions by the policy-making groups that many of their ideas are never fully known to the average citizen or even a substantial portion of the more literate citizenry. Outside experts are suspect, if they probe too deeply for solutions to social disorders or become too "nosey" in questioning the dynamics of community processes. The files of the planning agencies in Regional City are crammed with "expert advice" on what should be done to relieve some of the tensions of the city, in spite of the distrust of the policy-making group in brain-trusters. But the fact that the bulk of the reports are filed indicates that action on many of the suggested programs has been effectively stopped. The under-structure personnel consider it expedient not to press for activity on scores of plans which may already have cost large sums of money and great expenditures of effort in their development. Planning, in Regional City, becomes a ritualistic panorama engaged in by reasonably well-paid under-structure personnel whose plans more often than not fail to reach the point of action. Action results when a plan fits the relatively narrow interests of the policy-makers, but on many issues there is community paralysis and inaction.

In crisis situations the social scientist may be brought into a given situation in Regional City. In the present critical situation in Negro-community relations, several studies are being conducted by health and welfare agencies to ease the tensions which exist. Educational experts may be seen shuttling in and out of the city. Such personnel are usually employed by some of the third- or fourth-rate men in the under-structure of power—men who head agency boards but who are removed from the center of community decision. The ideas gathered by them in the processes of study and investigation may be valuable if transmitted to the upper reaches of the power hierarchy, but there is considerable doubt that much of what they learn ever reaches very far if it is contrary to the existing pattern of the balance of power. Opler develops this point by stating:

Often the social scientist is brought to the scene too late to be instrumental in the formulation of policy. If he disagrees with what has been initiated, he must go through the embarrassment of being a naysayer, of attacking or defending a position instead of calmly carrying out designated research.... And too often, when the social scientist is brought in belatedly as an ineffective symbol of enlightenment, he is there as a troubleshooter, to locate the difficulty after a program has failed to operate according to plan.[18]

If the professional in one of the social agencies is too zealous in searching out the basic causes of disorganization and social malfunctioning, he is liable to suspicion and censure. If he does engage in fundamental social research which turns up elements pointing to social reform or change in existing community alignments and structure, his materials may be presented to a limited group of persons who profess interest and who dutifully place his report with many like it in the files of the organization. Over the years, to be specific, the Community Council has analyzed the conditions of poor relief in the community and has pointed out repeatedly that public relief recipients have for many years received bare subsistence grants. A recommendation is always appended to these reports that larger grants be given. Sometimes the story of the study is carried in the newspapers. But repeatedly the reports are filed for future reference by subsequent committees.

One of the professionals working in the largest "charity" hospital estimated that more than 50 per cent of the cases coming to the hospital presented illnesses that could be directly traced to malnutrition. Some patients of this type are taken

18. *Loc. cit.*

into the hospital for a few days, given proper diets, and released to make the same weary round within a few weeks or months. When asked if the situation had been called to the attention of the Community Council, this worker replied, "I have sat with the committees in the Community Council for the last twenty years—ever since I came to this community—and they are still discussing the adequacy of relief. I sometimes think it is time something were done about it!" Relief costs money. Public relief costs tax money. And the leaders in the community have never been sympathetic to the relatively large budget of the public welfare department. There is little understanding on the part of community leaders of the public welfare program in spite of the persistent effort of the Community Council and its subsidiary agencies to "interpret" the total welfare program to the community.

One of the leaders with whom the welfare program was discussed was a man who had been connected with a private welfare agency as a board member for many years. He expressed some dissatisfaction with the mounting public welfare expenditures and was asked what substitute he would make. He said, "I grew up on the philosophy of 'root hog or die.' My father gave me that bit of wisdom, and it has stuck with me through the years."

The individual and his community, so far as the leaders are concerned, is not a question of "bad" men consciously being cruel to helpless individuals. The leaders of Regional City are individually very pleasant persons to meet, and many of them appear to be good fathers, to attend church, and to have many of the virtues ascribed to "good" men. Few of them would publicly say that the socially helpless should "root hog or die." Some of the problems presented to the top power leaders of the community are too large in scope and too numerous for them to handle. The whole question of adequate relief is a national issue at this writing. "General assistance" to needy families in less wealthy areas such as Old State is considered to be a federal responsibility by many people. The policy on extending aid through this proposed category of social security is unsettled national policy. The men of policy decision in Regional City are overwhelmed with the notion of how much adequate relief grants would cost in taxes. They cannot face the demands that would be entailed at this time. And none feels individually responsible for the situation.

The professional worker, who comes into contact with the human distress occasioned by lack of clear-cut policy on the relief matter, tries to convince an unwilling public to do something about it. The top leaders are individually uncomfortable and try to isolate themselves from discussion of the subject, while the social workers are frustrated and disillusioned, and become pessimistic in their views.

The principle of keeping the taxes low, at the moment outweighs the principle of raising taxes to meet the real demand for better conditions for welfare recipients. Social workers feel some responsibility to bring the issue to the attention of the community leaders who are on their agency boards of directors. This is done from time to time through studies and committee reports. When these reports are filed—not acted upon—the social workers are inclined to feel that they have done their duty and are not responsible for the chronic conditions which exist among their clientele. The board members, designated as second- and third-rate power leaders, are liable to overlook the matter when they contact those of power above them, for there are usually more pressing matters to be taken up in meetings with the topside leadership. Thus, the top leaders may not be too conscious of the existence of a problem in the area under discussion. In a sense everyone is responsible —and yet no one is. The community structure is not adequate to express effectively the demands that are real enough but which reside with the silent members of the community.

Voiced demands for community services by the underlying population in any community are negligible as every community organizer knows, except in time of unusual crisis. Needs for community improvement may be apparent enough to any observer, but it is seldom that the general population becomes vocal in its demands for services. The general apathy among the mass of people is a phenomenon which is difficult to explain. The people generally accept the situation in which they find themselves with a remarkable degree of silence. When the people are organized for action, as in the case of labor unions, they may be vocal and powerful, but generally the people are not organized. The masses tolerate living conditions in Regional City that are a constant topic of conversation among the middle-class professionals and intellectuals. The professionals do not identify with the general mass of people in the community, although they are but one step removed from the general mass by birth and family connections in many cases. These professional leaders are acutely aware of the conditions of the working men and women and especially the socially distressed groups. They tend to accommodate themselves to their marginal position by having social interaction within their own professional groupings, and while they speak out for the underprivileged on occasion, they cannot in any sense be classified as the voice of the people. This fact is well known to the power leaders. The professionals have no strength of support by the people as is the case with labor union representatives, and consequently it is an easy matter to listen politely to the feeble protests of the professional group and not accede to their requests for action.

The professionals are particularly weak and vulnerable as a political group.[19] Many of them attend a semi-monthly luncheon which is called the Liberal Professional Club, but no action is taken by this group. Its program consists mainly of listening

19. See particularly C. Wright Mills, *White Collar* (New York: Oxford University Press, 1951).

to visiting speakers who may have travelled in Europe lately or some remote spot in the world. The connection between the discussions and important policy issues is often nonexistent. During heated political campaigns in the city or state, one or another of the members may be partisan for one or another of the contending candidates, and "literature" will be placed at each luncheon plate favoring the particular candidate. However, there is no open political activity among the members of this group since some are civil servants. The group itself is well known to the power leaders, who watch it for any signs of open movement, and these top leaders are somewhat skeptical of the membership. One of the members, when applying for a change of position, was asked by one of the power leaders about his connection with the Club. Membership in the Liberal group did not give the member a black eye with this employer, but the question in itself gave the Club members a sense of daring and importance.

Some of the more liberal members of the professional community attend a bi-racial luncheon group held in one of the associational buildings in the Negro community every two weeks. These meetings are attended by some of the leading citizens of the Negro community, and speakers are drawn from home talent, visiting sociology professors, and the like. No political action is taken by this group, but some of the speeches are definitely political in nature, especially when one of the local citizens is exercised over a political matter.

Since none of the members in the community at large are consulted over political choices for candidates for public office, there is general apathy over political affairs. Hoffer has said that, in a study made in a Michigan community, interest in political affairs of the town ranked eighth in a listing of twelve community interests.[20] No precise data on Regional City are available in this connection, but it is possible that the Michigan

20. C. R. Hoffer, "The Community Situation and Political Action," *American Sociological Review*, IV (October 1939), 666.

situation is comparable to that of Regional City. During an
election year, after the candidates are chosen by the respective
parties, the interest would be higher, of course. Wilson suggests that such apathy may result from the consistent failure
of the majority of people to bring about order through their
own efforts: "For the masses . . . an enduring failure to reach
a measure of order and security can bring about a complete
indifference to the long-run aspects of public action." [21] The
people decide that policy is made in "smoke-filled rooms," and
there is little they can do about it.[22]

It is not contended here that policy is determined entirely
by behind-the-scenes manipulation, although the policy-makers
tend to operate as a closed group. To the policy-makers their
activities are thought to be open and aboveboard in relation to
each other. Because of the structural hierarchy of command
and decision, policy may appear to be determined in smoke-
filled rooms and behind the scenes. This is the public impression, perhaps, and to the professional workers, who are closer
to the policy-making group and yet excluded from it, the
appearance of behind-the-scenes manipulations may seem to
be a reality. The situation, as observed in this study, is that the
policy-makers have a fairly definite set of settled policies at
their command, which have been historically functional in the
community. New problems which may arise are measured by
the standards of older policy decisions, and adjustments are
made to fit new conditions whenever the situation warrants
revision of older policy determination. Often the demands for
change in the older alignments are not strong or persistent, and
the policy-makers do not deem it necessary to go to the people
with each minor change. This pattern of manipulation becomes
fixed. It is functional, and the ordinary individual in the community is "willing" that the process continue. There is a carry-

21. Wilson, op. cit., p. 126.
22. Thurman Arnold, Bottlenecks of Business (New York: Reynal and
Hitchcock, 1940), p. 115.

over from the minor adjustments to the settlement of major issues.

Once policy has been determined, regardless of the way in which it has been reached, there must be obedience to the general framework of policy, or there would be social disorganization which would be intolerable to all in the community. One of our hypotheses was, "Power is exercised as a necessary function in social relationships." Obedience of the people to the decisions of the power command becomes habitual and routinized even in a democracy. Among all segments of the population, including the power leaders, there may be a vaguely formulated recognition that social and economic conditions might be improved, but the scheme of relationships extant at the moment is producing goods and services in sufficient quantities to satisfy the basic needs of the majority in the community. Those who are disadvantaged by the present arrangements are not an articulate group; and, while some of the professionals may speak for a portion of this group, they often do so only with half-hearted conviction. They cannot substitute for the underprivileged, in any event, for they are not actually of this group. It is quite possible, too, that when some of the professional and other under-structure personnel speak in behalf of the underprivileged groups they are making an ill defined bid for "political" support of the latter and are setting forth a veiled demand for inclusion in policy determination among the power leaders. Such disguised and scarcely conscious demands are recognized by the top leaders for what they are—a restiveness in the under-structure personnel—and they are handled accordingly.

The method of handling the relatively powerless understructure is through the pressures previously described—warnings, intimidations, threats, and in extreme cases violence. In some cases the method may include isolation from all sources of support for the individual, including his job and therefore his income. The principle of "divide and rule" is as applicable in the community as it is in larger units of political patterning, and it is as effective.

In the realm of policy the top leaders are in substantial agreement most of the time on the big issues related to the basic ideologies of the culture. There is no serious threat to the basic value systems at this time from any of the under-structure personnel, and many of the fears of the top leaders on this point appear groundless.

Regardless of ideology, power is a necessity in modern community relations. No utopia will disband all power relations. Some men will rule, others will be ruled. The crucial question perhaps is, "How can policy be determined so that it takes into account the interests of the largest number of people?" As it now stands, policy set within the power relationships of Regional City does not seem to cover all of the social structure, and some modification of existing structure seems necessary if certain problems which arise chronically in this community are to be met.

One of our postulates and two corollaries were stated as follows:

Power of the individual must be structured into associational, clique, or institutional patterns to be effective.

Corollary 1. The community provides a microcosm of organized power relationships in which individuals exercise the maximum effective influence.

Corollary 2. Representative democracy offers the greatest possibility of assuring the individual a voice in policy determination and extension.

The individual in the bulk of the population of Regional City has no voice in policy determination. These individuals are the silent group. The voice of the professional under-structure may have something to say about policy, but it usually goes unheeded. The flow of information is downward in larger volume than it is upward. The people generally may have a part in some of the institutional groupings such as the political, economic, and religious associations, but the under-bodies of these clusters are relatively mute groups so far as policy determination is concerned. There are undoubtedly cliques operative in all of these relationships, but there is no measure of this phenomenon. The strength of clique relationships in the policy-determining group has been measured here, and it was found that clique relationships were effective and strong at this level.

Any extended discussion of clique and institutional groupings will be foregone at this point, and the discussion will proceed with a brief structural analysis of associational groupings. It is here that all economic and political structures cross, and it is here that the policy-making machinery might be strengthened effectively to channel an individual's activities to aid in meeting the problems of community life that are inevitable in modern urban society.

One example may be given to indicate what is meant by strengthening associational groupings. This example involves the Community Council of Regional City in its operational aspects related to the problem of housing.

The structure of the Council is based primarily upon representation from health and welfare agencies. Two representatives of each of the health-welfare agencies in the community are selected to serve as delegates to the Council "assembly." From the assembly an executive board is chosen to conduct the normal business of the Council between delegate meetings. There is an executive staff and a research staff for the administration of Council affairs. All problems affecting the health and general welfare of the total community are supposed to be analyzed and recommendations formulated by the Council for meeting these needs. The structure is somewhat more elaborate, but this simple sketch will suffice.

The Council is supported by private contributions. It is not

a public body. It is felt that by being independent of tax support the Council will be less influenced by political considerations. Such has not been the result, however—that is to say, the
Council is not always free from political influence.

For many years the housing problem has plagued the community, and the Council executive staff has had some interest
in the matter. The members of the professional staff have been
keenly interested in making studies of housing needs, and certain members of the board have had an interest in the matter—
particularly the Negro representatives on the board who are
acutely aware of housing conditions in their sub-community.
A superficial study of the housing needs has been made by
the staff with some tolerance on the part of the Council board,
but there has been a general reluctance on the part of the
board to "go too far in the matter" because the subject has
been considered "controversial." It has been previously indicated that other associational groups have been interested in
the problem and that several of the under-structure personnel
in the community have spoken out in favor of improved housing conditions. The staff of the Council, as a community association, has had to be extremely cautious, however, in its
statements. The professionals in some of the physical planning
agencies and in the housing and health agencies have been
more vocal. The Council is supposed to be a coordinating
group, and many of the members of the governing board have
taken the position that getting into controversial matters
would alienate Council supporters—particularly among the
strongest financial supporters of the Community Chest, to
which the Council is beholden.

Thus, one of the major problems before the community has
been shunted aside by one of the associations which might have
had the most to say about housing conditions. The welfare
workers, who are in daily contact with the poor living quarters
of their clients, would normally be thought of as a group that
could speak with some authority on the subject. But not all of

the welfare workers have a voice in the affairs of the Council, and herein lies a structural problem that illustrates the point.

The delegates to the Council are only two in number from each participating agency. These delegates are ordinarily the president of the agency's lay board and its professional executive. The line workers, the social workers, of the agencies do not attend Council meetings. It is the top structure personnel of each agency that represents the agency and the interests of the clientele which the agency serves. The board presidents of agencies are usually men in the third or fourth layer of the under-structure of power in the city, and they tend to be cautious in their views of "what will go" and "what will not go." Through these men or their wives, as the case may be on any individual board, the men of real power control the expenditures for both the public and private agencies devoted to health and welfare programs in the community. Thus, obviously, no issues may be attacked directly which the men of policy decision are not ready or willing to have discussed. The problem of meeting housing needs in any large measure has been one of the issues which has not yet been slated for discussion and serious consideration.

While the Council calls itself community-wide in scope and function, it cannot in reality be so considered. It does not represent all members of the community. The top structure of power has some contact with Council board members through second- and third-rate leaders who represent the powerful interests of the community. Generally speaking, the ordinary citizen is not represented upon these boards. The Council structure is thus a part of the over-structure of leadership, and is representative of narrow interests rather than the community as a whole. There is in reality politics in the situation, but it is clearly one-sided politics.

It remains true that the Council alone could not have settled the housing question which has become a matter of public policy for the nation, but it might have been a potent factor in discussion and research on the problem if it had not been so hemmed-in by the restrictions placed upon it as a forum for public discussion.

The other associations in the community, from the luncheon clubs to the fraternal organizations, stand in about the same relation to public discussion on issues. The boards are controlled by men who use their influence in devious ways, which may be lumped under the phrase "being practical," to keep down public discussion on all issues except those that have the stamp of approval of the power group. This is the status and role of most of Regional City's associations, regardless of their brochures and pronouncements indicating that issues and problems of the whole community come under their scrutiny and discussion.

Alinsky tells us that there are two major fallacies in conventional community agency programs. "The first," he says, "is that they view each problem of the community as if it were independent of all other problems." [23] and "the second [is revealed in] a complete lack of recognition of the obvious fact that the life of each neighborhood [community] is to a major extent shaped by forces which far transcend the local scene." [24] Both of these fallacies are abroad in Regional City.

In the housing problem there was a tendency on the part of the Community Council to isolate the issue and to treat it purely in local and restricted terms. Substandard housing conditions (and a recent estimate puts one-third of the community's housing in this category) are a part of the multiplicity of causal factors untouched by the surveys conducted by the Council. There was apparently never too clear an idea on the part of the Council researchers that there were serious gaps within the community in the line of communication on the problem and that there was no way in which the needs of

23. Saul D. Alinsky, *Reveille for Radicals* (Chicago: University of Chicago Press, 1946), p. 80.
24. *Ibid.*, p. 83.

the community could be transmitted to state and national authorities with the force of public opinion behind the statements on the subject. The arguments pro and con public housing, revolved within an extremely limited circle and, in the main, those who were convinced remained so—those unconvinced remained likewise.

Alinsky, in discussing community councils in relation to youth problems, suggests the difficulties that face such groups in other areas as well. He might just as well have been speaking of housing when he said:

It is very clear that if any intelligent attack is to be made upon the problem of youth or the causes of crime the community council will have to concern itself with the basic issues of unemployment, disease, and housing, as well as the causes of crime. This the conventional community council cannot do. It is not equipped to attack basic social issues, and its very character is such that it never was meant to do that kind of job.... They will vigorously abstain from entering any controversial field.

Jobs, higher wages, economic security, housing, and health are some of the important things in life; and they are all controversial. These issues must be met squarely, courageously, and militantly.[25]

Alinsky's answer to all of this is to develop a network of "people's organizations" and theoretically the plan sounds good, but politically it is utopian. In essence, Alinsky calls for a new political party which will attack the big issues he has raised. He would create a new political structure to coerce the members of existing political and economic structures. Theoretically this might be done, but doubt may be expressed that it will be done for some time, given the existing patterns of American communities. There are already political parties that are in direct opposition to the policies of parties in power. One would wonder whether a new people's organization based in neighborhood centers would be more effective in organizing

25. *Ibid.*, pp. 81-82.

the bottom structure of community personnel than have been the older existing political groups of protest.

One may be in basic agreement with Alinsky's analysis of the impotency of existing community councils, but he might ask, "Do they need to remain impotent?" He might also ask, "Do other local associations need to remain impotent so far as the larger community issues are concerned?" The real question is whether broader participation in many of the existing organizations might not achieve some of the goals outlined by Alinsky. If the answers to these questions are in the negative, then perhaps it is futile to waste time working with such groups. Yet many of the associations have been in existence for decades. They have been functional in the community and this fact gives one pause.

In order to present fairly both sides of the question raised, let us examine one of Alinsky's criticisms of labor as an organized force in the community—a group which would normally be considered one of the strongest supporters of policy coordinate with the interests of the bottom structure of power. The quotation to follow reflects Alinsky's extreme pessimism over the ability of currently organized groups to cope with the fundamental issues confronting a community as a whole. It also seems to give rise to Alinsky's plea for a political substitute for existing power alignments. In regard to the role of organized labor, Alinsky says:

Labor thinks and acts as does big business. This alliance between organized labor and organized industry has reached the point where in essence it is a working partnership. The organized labor movement has openly extended itself into the sphere of stabilizing, reorganizing, financing, and expanding private industry. An analysis of their activities demonstrates that the leaders of labor are committed to the idea that the welfare of their organizations is contingent upon the welfare of industry or capitalism. Verification is to be found by scanning the history, the policies, and the actions of either your most militant and independent union, the

United Mine Workers of America, or your most respectable and conventionally approved union, the Amalgamated Clothing Workers of America.[26]

Observations of the labor movement in Regional City are in accord with this statement by Alinsky. Braunthal, among others, has traced the "non-partisan" attitudes of labor back to Gompers' conservative philosophy.[27] Yet, with this said, one may wonder whether a movement organized outside the labor groupings could redirect the policies of the labor leaders? Probably not. However, pressure from the rank and file workers within the movement conceivably would have considerable influence in changing the course of labor's policy direction relative to basic issues.

Working outside of functional groupings and organizations or attempting to cut across their organizational lines has proved in practice to be an unfruitful experience for many community organizers who feel the need of getting mass support for particular projects. Organizational structures usually do not allow for such fluidity. It is also a vain hope, perhaps, to expect to organize unorganized individuals on anything like a community-wide basis. Some early experiences along these lines have led to disappointing results. The Cincinnati experiment with the "social unit plan," which was in essence a plan to organize the community on a block-by-block basis for civic reform, died for lack of interest and because of political pressure.[28] Zorbaugh points out that many of the citizens most active in community affairs come from the upper power groups and from those close to them in the power structure. There is a tradition of community activity among some of the persons close to the apex of power, but there is no such tradi-

26. *Ibid.*, p. 45.
27. Alfred Braunthal, "American Labor in Politics," *Social Research*, XII (February 1945), 2-3.
28. Harvey Warren Zorbaugh, *The Gold Coast and the Slum* (Chicago: University of Chicago Press, 1929), pp. 265 ff.

tion "down below." On occasion the upper groups unsuccessfully attempt to impose community organization structures upon communities.[29] The lack of response on the part of local citizens has been well illustrated by both Zorbaugh and Alinsky in the works cited. A part of the failure of such organizing attempts lies, perhaps, in the fact that basic organizations and groupings are slighted or overlooked altogether in the process of activating citizens.

The notion that city dwellers can or will act like persons inhabiting small New England towns and accustomed to town meetings has also been a pitfall for many efforts in community organization. Urban life is organized along the lines of organized interest groupings whether the particular interest be in higher wages, higher profits, lower tax rates, or lower disease rates. Basic organizations have sprung up around a multiplicity of interests in urban communities and the possibility of the so-called "face-to-face relationship" of city dwellers is an illusion clung to by those who tend to speculate about community organization but who have not been actively engaged in organizing city groups.

What structural changes might allow for wider participation of the individual in community affairs? It has been indicated that such participation is desirable, and it was stated in the study hypotheses that the community offers a logical place where the individual may find fulfillment of his desires to participate with others. Let us see what has been said about the structure of power that may give a clue to a possible solution to the problem presented.

A policy-making group in Regional City has been isolated. It has been shown that this group in specific instances tends to act on policy matters without regard for various community groups. It has also been shown, however, that on specific projects members from associational groupings may be drawn into the area of policy decision as well as into that

29. *Ibid.*, pp. 216, 219.

of policy execution. The associations are, therefore, a part of the power structure. Labor groups, among others that have been traditionally excluded from policy decisions, are increasingly consulted. Labor participation is not anywhere near adequate or complete, but there is a trend in the direction indicated.

Structurally the Negro community is isolated from the power group through the individual Negro's inability to rise in the organizations which are community-wide in scope. The professional groups in the under-structure of power do not get into the policy-making meetings. Both of these groups represent relatively weakly organized bodies in Regional City. The Negro citizenry is becoming increasingly organized, however, and the politicians are paying more attention to the demands of this group. The key to participation in power decisions would appear to be in finding strength through perfecting social organizations along interest lines.

Most of the powerful national organizations have roots in smaller local groupings. Some of the leading national groups may reach a membership of hundreds or even thousands of individuals in a given community. The better-organized groups do have some voice in community affairs and with such a voice the individual may feel some security even if his own voice is not actually heard. The most powerful national organizations with local affiliates are related to political and economic interest groups. If the individual in Regional City is interested in policy decision, the only course that seems open to him for possible inclusion in the upper power groups is to become allied with a powerful organization in the areas indicated. There is, perhaps, no other sure road to power participation.

Participation in many of the organizations in Regional City would merely give the individual a social experience of being with his fellows. Some of the organizations are not set up to be "political" in nature. Some of them are designed to drain off any move in the direction of political action. The latter fact may be clearly seen by any individual who comes to know the inner workings of many organizations reputedly devoted to the discussion of civic and social issues but which are actually operated in the interests of the political and economic status quo. For the individual who becomes dissatisfied with organizations devoted to time-consuming projects related to the lesser issues, the course of direct political alignment is still open to many more persons than actually participate in political activities.

This is not to say, by any means, that inclusion in an interest grouping will automatically catapult an individual into the realm of policy decision. He may never get there, but the road is still open, to judge from observations of the power structure. This holds true for the Negro group and for the working group, which traditionally have been among the most neglected elements in the power picture. The gains in power participation by both of these groups have been made through bitter struggles. There is no doubt that further gains will be made and with more bitter struggle. The leaders in the policy-making realm are not going to open the doors of participation with charitable graciousness. It has been noted that they may even use police power and the power of governmental machinery to keep back criticism and threatening political elements. Such tactics eventually will not win out if dissident groups are in earnest concerning a voice in the affairs of government or economic operations.

The professional groups are the most inclined to lament their fate and the least inclined to participate in organizing activities which would allow them a voice in policy decision. They are extremely individualistic and consider it unprofessional to engage in union activities. It has been repeatedly pointed out that the "white collar" groups are in a similar position in political life. It can only be suggested that the same methods of organization are open to these groups that historically were open to labor when that segment of the community moved into more participation in policy determination.

It must be said that, wherever possible, wider participation by the bottom structure of power should be developed through civic organizations in Regional City. The writer is not naive enough to suppose that such club groupings as Rotary or Kiwanis are going to open their membership to many elements in the community, including Negro citizens, labor, women, and others. Such elements could logically contribute much to discussion of community policy on issues that each could bring to such associations. One could say realistically, however, that such organizations as the Community Council and related civic groups might enrich their membership with the elements mentioned if they were sincerely dedicated to doing so. At present they are only half-hearted in the matter.

The rise of interest groups has brought in its train a growing demand for the coordination of the many special interests. As interest groupings become more powerful, the demand is likely to increase rather than diminish. The coordination of economic interest groupings is a national matter. No community can hope to cope with the power that the larger economic interests bring to bear on local politicians and professional personnel in the operating units of government and industry. The desire to build local coordinating councils to meet the challenge of power of the larger economic interests is a dream with hardly a shred of practicality. This does not say that there cannot be comprehensive social planning on the local level. This is theoretically possible although it has never actually been tried. Social planning in the full flowering of that concept would mean the coordination of interest groups on all levels of national life with the community as the basic unit. To be effective it must have the sanction of government. Private social planning groups would be debilitated by the same forces which now control all private civic organizations.

But it has been said that politics is also controlled by the larger economic interest groups. Would they not control social planning bodies if they were a part of government? It is true that such bodies might be so controlled, but it is also true that government is the only agency big enough to coordinate social planning on a community-wide and nation-wide basis. If one is not completely compelled by pessimism, he may remember that government is still dedicated theoretically to the interests of both the bottom structure and the top structure of power. If this condition does not hold true in practice, then one must, with others, find ways of realigning theory and practice. If the ideal of democracy is to endure and to be strengthened, ways and means must be found to approach a solution to the problems raised here. The search must not be restricted by fear and pessimism. The writer believes that the search is being made by hundreds and thousands of earnest people. There are many such people in Regional City.

The task of social reconstruction may never be finished once and for all. It is a recurring task confronting each generation, which somehow manages to find the courage to meet social issues as they arise. In spite of the limitations that confront the individual in relation to community participation on the level of policy decision, there is still room for him in this area. He may not find himself at the top; but, with proper attention given to structural arrangements of power in the community, he may find ways of having a voice in determining who should be at the top. Naturally, if choice were free, the individual would want the top leaders to be sympathetic to his interests as expressed by his associational groupings. Such freedom of choice is not present in Regional City. Very few are aware of how their leaders are chosen.

If the basic issues which confront individuals and groups in the community are to be adequately met, it would seem necessary for the citizenry to be fully aware of who their real leaders are and how they are chosen. This would seem to be a first order of business for any individual who is interested in civic issues. Otherwise, responsibility cannot be properly lodged when decisions of individual leaders fail to meet the expectations of the underlying groups.

POPLAR VILLAGE, a community of about 7,000 population, was used as a community to test field schedules before attempting the more complex study of Regional City. Since the Poplar Village "dry run" has bearing on the final methods employed in the larger community, it will be referred to here.

The methods utilized in studying community power structure fall into three categories: (1) theoretical analysis prior to field investigation; (2) field investigation; and (3) an integration of field findings and social theory.

For a theoretical examination of materials on power structure a search of library documents was made. The books and periodicals listed in the bibliography were gleaned of excerpts which seemed pertinent to the problem. These excerpted materials were classified roughly according to the areas or topics to be studied in the field. Statements on power which seemed beyond the scope of the study, but which appeared fundamental to defining power in broad terms, were set aside as residual categories. For example, much discussion of power has centered around national and international ideologies. These may have real though indirect bearing on community power structure, but they were ruled out of consideration in this analysis. There were other similar categories.

Over a period of eighteen months newspapers from Regional City and Poplar Village were clipped of items bearing on the subject of power. Notes were taken of random thoughts occurring to the writer which were considered as being hypothetical. Documents in his possession relating to political activities in Regional City were classified. Personal correspondence and other documents relating to working experiences which seemed to have a bearing on the problem were likewise edited and classified.

From this preliminary analysis of materials and through an ordering of thought related to the writer's personal observations of community power relations, the frame of reference embodied in the postulates and hypotheses set down earlier was developed. A plan for field analysis was then devised.

The first problem in analyzing power relations in the field was that of determining which community leaders should be interviewed. The second problem was to work out a schedule of questions that would yield data pertinent to power alignments and dynamics within a given community. As has been suggested, Poplar Village served as a laboratory for working out methods and techniques for dealing with both of these problems.

Lists of leaders occupying positions of prominence in civic organizations, business establishments, a University bureaucracy, office holders in Village politics, and lists of persons prominent socially and of wealth status were secured. It was taken as axiomatic that community life is organized life, and that persons occupying "offices" and public positions of trust would be involved in some manner in the power relations of the community. It was felt that some leaders might not work through formally organized groups, but getting leaders from organizations would be a good start toward turning up leaders who might operate behind the scenes.

It was felt that getting to leaders in organizations was a direct method of turning up leadership. A rather extensive unpublished study of leadership had been made three years earlier in Poplar Village by a class in community organization which had utilized the door-to-door method of finding leadership by scheduled interviews conducted in every eighth house. All the leaders found belonged to at least one of several major organized groups, and would therefore serve as some check on the proposed approach in this study. Lists of organizational leaders were secured from University officials, records of the Village government, and the secretary of the local Merchants Association. Wealth leaders and socially prominent persons were listed by a University student, a mature person, who had lived in Poplar Village for some years and who knew intimately many of these persons. This informant began with one well known leader and "worked out from her," i.e., she took the names provided by her first informant and by a series of interviews with the persons subsequently named got from these people a consensus of opinion about others listed. None of the informants were provided with lists of names previously mentioned, but as the investigation proceeded there was a growing uniformity of opinion on who were the wealth and social leaders.

Since the list of business leaders provided by the Merchants Association was some two hundred in length, a self-rating of top leaders was made by businessmen to cut the list down for later interviewing purposes. It was, incidentally, a surprising thing to members of a team from a community organization class working on the current study to find so many business establishments in so small a village. Each businessman in a top listing of fifty chosen by the secretary of the Merchants Association was asked to select ten men from the total list who were, in his opinion, leaders of major business establishments in the community. This provided a listing of fifty-four names receiving the highest rating.

The four lists of names—civic, governmental, business, and status leaders—were then typed separately. Six "judges," persons who had lived in the community for some years and who had a knowledge of community affairs, were provided with these lists and asked to select from each one, in rank order of importance, ten persons of influence. The instructions were:

Place in rank order, one through ten, ten persons from each list of personnel—who in your opinion are the most influential persons in the field designated—influential from the point of view of ability to lead others.

If there are persons . . . you feel should be included in the ranking order of ten rather than the ones given, please include them.

The judges were also asked to choose from a list of fifty organizations the top ten in influence. In all cases assurance was given that replies would be treated confidentially. It should be said here, that immunity from having data sources revealed was promised to all informants throughout the study in both communities. It was always stated that the researcher was interested in "process" of power or influence activities rather than in identifying persons. It was necessary to use actual names to get data, but all names are disguised in this exposition of the findings.

There was a high degree of agreement among the judges as to who the top leaders were in the four fields. Among business leaders there was unanimous opinion on six out of ten leaders. Other business leaders received four votes in two cases, and three votes in two cases. Among governmental personnel there was unanimous opinion on four out of ten persons, with four persons receiving five votes, and the remaining two tied with four votes each. There was more division of opinion concerning leaders in the University personnel; yet out of 77 choices, one person received six votes, four received five votes, and the remaining five persons garnered four votes each. None received a unanimous vote in the civic personnel list. One person received five votes, five received four votes, and the remainder tied with three votes each. Only five names were added to the lists by the judges, and each of these received but one vote, that of the person naming him.

Since the schedule of questions to be asked community leaders would allow for additional leaders to be named, and because of the high degree of correlation between the choices of the judges, it was decided to carry the judging process no further in Poplar Village. The decisions of the judges had given a basic list of forty persons to interview in the community. A schedule of questions was then prepared.

The design of the schedule was arranged as follows: Identifying information was asked concerning age, sex, birthplace, occupation, kinds of property owned, number of employees supervised or directed, education, place of residence, and length of residence in Poplar Village. Questions were also asked to ascertain whether the informant's interests were local, state, or national in scope. Each informant was asked to select five top leaders from the list of 40 names provided on the schedule, and to add names, if the ones provided were not top leaders in his opinion. Each was asked why he made the choices he did.

Three questions were designed to get the degree of interaction of each person with others on the list. These questions were: Do you belong to any organization of which the others are members? Have you worked with any of the others on committees and approximately how many? Specify other contacts with others on the list, e.g., intimate business relationship, might call for advice, etc.

A scale was constructed to determine how well each person knew the others. Each interviewee was asked to indicate about each of the others whether he knew him socially, knew him, knew him slightly, heard of him, or not known to him.

Each interviewee was asked to identify persons of wealth among the community leaders and to identify persons of "society" status. A question was also asked to ascertain whether or not individuals on the list of leaders tend to act in cliques in relation to community projects. Committee groupings were also examined in relation to local, state, and national problems.

Methods of clearing with others on projects were inquired about, and the way in which an individual cleared with others was ascertained, in some degree, by the question, "In your opinion how do the men on the list operate in relation to community projects: in the forefront of affairs, behind the scenes, or in other ways?"

A final set of questions was related to two decisions which recently had been made in the community in an effort to reveal each individual's relation to these decisions.

A graduate class in community organization aided the writer in carrying the schedules into the interviewing stage of the study in Poplar Village. (Field work in Regional City was carried out exclusively by the writer.) Each member of the class carried two or three schedules to the field with written instructions. A group of periphery leaders were also interviewed—nine in number—to see whether they as a group would compare in any way with the listed leaders. The periphery leaders were persons who had been on the lists scrutinized by the judges, and had received one or more votes by the judges but who had not received enough votes to make the master list of community leaders.

A total of thirty-three of the forty persons on the master list of leaders were interviewed on the schedules provided. Three refused to answer the questions. One claimed that she did not know enough about the subject to answer intelligently. One considered the subject impertinent. The third told the interviewer that he did not consider himself a local leader since his interests were in affairs beyond the bounds of the Village. Seven people were not seen by interviewers either because they were unavailable through being out of the city or for other reasons. Most interviewees were extremely cooperative. Of the nine periphery leaders, three refused to be interviewed.

The experience of running schedules in Poplar Village brought out several things concerning methodology. First of all, and negatively, the schedule was too lengthy. In some cases one and one-half hours were required in filling out the form. It was clear that the schedule would need revision for further use in Regional City. Secondly, the interviewers were not clear on certain aspects of administering the schedule. Some let the interviewee fill out his own schedule. Others filled out the schedule for the person interviewed. This lack of clarity in instructions had value in that it was thereby learned that having the field worker fill in the schedule was a more satisfactory process than having the interviewee do it. It was decided that the field worker should hold the schedule in his hands during interviews in Regional City.

Time-consuming questions such as, "Name the organizations of which you are member with other leaders on the list," and, "Approximately how many committees have you served on with other individual leaders within the past five years?" were eliminated from the schedule of interviewing in Regional City, following the test run in Poplar Village. The schedules were streamlined to "check mark" proportions wherever possible. It was recognized that some of the leaders in Regional City carried heavy responsibilities, greater in the majority than did leaders in Poplar Village. They could not have spent even an hour being interviewed in some cases.

The methods of getting basic lists of power personnel, and of using judges to cut the list to manageable interviewing proportions, were used in Regional City much as in Poplar Village. The details varied, of course, but the methods remained basically the same. The Community Council in Regional City, a council of civic organizations, provided preliminary lists of leaders in community affairs. The Chamber of Commerce provided business leaders of establishments employing more than 500 employees and of financial houses doing the largest volume of clearances. The League of Women Voters provided lists of local political leaders who had at least major governmental committee chairmanship status. Newspaper editors and other civic leaders provided lists of society leaders and leaders of wealth.

In Regional City fourteen judges were used to give their opinions on who were top leaders on each of the lists thus provided. These judges revealed a high degree of correlation in their choices. The judges represented three religions, were male and female, young and mature people, business executives and professional people, and Negro and white. It was felt that the number of judges should be larger in Regional City than in Poplar Village because of the size of the community and because elements of bias were highly possible in so large and complex a community.

Of the leaders chosen in civic affairs, by the fourteen judges with fifty persons to choose from, the correlation was as follows: one received eleven votes, one received ten votes, one received eight votes, four received six votes, one received five votes, one received four votes, and the last received but three votes. Others receiving votes did not exceed two in any case, and the other votes were singles scattered among twenty-one persons on the list. Fourteen persons received no votes at all. The same clustering of votes held with selections from the lists of governmental officials and business leaders, with the clustering of votes more sharply defined among the latter. The widest range of opinion occurred when the judges were asked to name social prestige leaders. Some judges were unable to give replies to this question. There was apparently little consensus on "status-society" leaders among our judges. In a sense, therefore, names given in this area of possible leadership were arbitrarily included.

Negro names were included on the list of personnel submitted to the judges, but in only three instances did the judges vote for them, and they were Negro judges with one exception. The Negro community of Regional City has a population almost one-third of the total number of inhabitants. Consequently a separate and similar study was projected for this group. The same techniques of using status-rating judges was used by a panel of Negro judges, and the correlations in relation to Negro leadership were similar in pattern to the white community.

The structural pattern of the form used for studying leadership in the Negro community paralleled that used for the whites, except the names listed were Negro leaders chosen by Negro judges. The need to study the Negro community in Regional City grew out of field experience. This community was found to represent a sub-power grouping of considerable significance which could not be overlooked, particularly since many of the issues suggested to the field investigator by white power personnel revolved around Negro-white relations.

In order to ascertain whether or not there was the same degree of interaction between the top leaders in Regional City and some group with whom they might be compared, a group of fourteen professional persons were interviewed using the same interview schedule as that used with the top power leaders. All professional persons interviewed were earning more than $5,000 a year, with none earning more than $10,000 annually. The rates of interaction between these professionals fell far below those in the top leadership brackets and there were other basic differences which have been pointed out in an analysis of our field materials. As a method of checking to see how near center we were with the top leadership group, we found this method a useful tool.

The method of interviewing in Regional City consisted of going through the schedule of questions with each interviewee and noting any remarks that he made as each question was asked. If the interviewee wished to discuss any phase of a particular question more fully than the schedule allowed, the worker maintained an attentive role, asking such questions as would clarify the interviewee's statements. Early in the study in Regional City a question was added to the interview form: "Who is the top leader in the community?" This question was asked following the question related to the "top ten" leaders. It usually elicited discussion. Certain information given by individual interviewees was sometimes verified with other informants, if such verification did not violate the confidential nature of the total interviewing situation.

BIBLIOGRAPHY

BIBLIOGRAPHY

A. BOOKS AND DOCUMENTS

Adamic, Louis. *Dynamite.* New York: Viking Press, 1934.
——. *From Many Lands.* New York: Harper & Bros., 1940.
Alinsky, Saul D. *Reveille for Radicals.* Chicago: University of Chicago Press, 1946.
Arnold, Thurman. *Bottlenecks of Business.* New York: Reynal & Hitchcock, 1940.
——. *Cartels or Free Enterprise?* New York: Public Affairs Committee, 1945.
——. *Folklore of Capitalism.* New Haven: Yale University Press, 1937.
Barnard, C. I. *The Functions of the Executive.* Cambridge, Mass.: Harvard University Press, 1938.
Barnes, Harry Elmer. *Social Institutions.* New York: Prentice-Hall, Inc., 1942.
Berle, A. A. and G. C. Means. *The Modern Corporation and Private Property.* New York: Commerce Clearing House, Inc., 1932.
Brady, R. A. *Business as a System of Power.* New York: Columbia University Press, 1938.
Brownwell, Baker. *The Human Community.* New York: Harper and Bros., 1950.
Burnham, J. *The Managerial Revolution.* New York: John Day Co., 1941.
Carnegie, Andrew. *The Empire of Business.* New York: Doubleday, Page and Co., 1902.

Carr-Saunders, A. M. and P. A. Wilson. *The Professions*. Oxford: Clarendon Press, 1933.

Chapin, F. Stuart. *Contemporary American Institutions*. New York: Harper and Bros., 1935.

Cox, Oliver Cromwell. *Caste, Class, and Race*. New York: Doubleday and Co., 1948.

De Grazia, Sebastian. *The Political Community*. Chicago: University of Chicago Press, 1949.

Dewey, John. *Problems of Men*. New York: Philosophical Library, 1946.

Follett, M. P. *The New State*. New York: Longmans, Green and Co., 1918.

Gerth, H. H. and C. Wright Mills. *Max Weber: Essays in Sociology*. New York: Oxford University Press, 1946.

Gouldner, Alvin W., editor. *Studies in Leadership*. New York: Harper and Bros., 1950.

Gregg, Richard Bartlett. *The Power of Non-Violence*. Philadelphia, London: J. B. Lippincott Co., 1935.

Haldane, J. B. S. *Heredity and Politics*. New York: W. W. Norton and Co., 1938.

Haynes, Frederick E. *Social Policies in the United States*. Boston, New York: Houghton Mifflin Co., 1924.

Henderson, A. M. and Talcott Parsons. *Max Weber: Theory of Social and Economic Organization*. New York: Oxford University Press, 1947.

Hillman, Arthur. *Community Organization and Planning*. New York: The Macmillan Co., 1950.

Hollingshead, A. B. *Elmtown's Youth*. New York: John Wiley and Sons, 1949.

Homans, George C. *The Human Group*. New York: Harcourt, Brace and Co., 1950.

Hull, Clark L., Carl I. Hovland, Robert T. Ross, Marshall Hall, Frederic B. Fitch. *Mathematico-Deductive Theory of Rote Learning*. New Haven: Yale University Press, 1940.

Kesselman, Louis Coleridge. *The Social Politics of F.E.P.C.* Chapel Hill: University of North Carolina Press, 1948.

Key, V. O., Jr. *Politics, Parties and Pressure Groups*. New York: Thomas Y. Crowell Co., 1945.

————. *Southern Politics in State and Nation.* New York: Alfred A. Knopf, 1949.

Landis, Paul Henry. *Social Policies in the Making.* Boston: D. C. Heath and Co., 1947.

Laski, Harold Joseph. *Authority in the Modern State.* New Haven: Yale University Press, 1919.

————. *Foundations of Sovereignty.* New York: Harcourt, Brace and Co., 1921.

————. *Reflections on the Revolution of Our Time.* New York: Viking Press, 1943.

Lasswell, Harold D. *Politics: Who Gets What, When, and How.* New York: McGraw-Hill Book Co., 1936.

————. *Power and Personality.* W. W. Norton and Co., 1948.

Lazarsfeld, Paul and Frank N. Stanton, editors. *Communications Research.* New York: Harper and Bros., 1949.

Lenin, Vladimir Ilich. *Collected Works.* New York: International Publishers, 1927.

Lundberg, Ferdinand. *Imperial Hearst.* New York: Modern Library, 1936.

————. *America's 60 Families.* New York: Halcyon House, 1939.

Lundberg, George A. *Social Research.* New York: Longmans, Green and Co., 1942.

Lynd, Robert S. and Helen M. *Middletown in Transition.* New York: Harcourt, Brace and Co., 1937.

McConaughty, John. *Who Rules America?* New York: Longmans, Green and Co., 1934.

MacIver, R. M. *Web of Government.* New York: The Macmillan Co., 1947.

Mack, Raymond W. Housing as an Index of Social Class. Unpublished Master's Thesis. University of North Carolina, 1951.

Merriam, Charles. *Political Power.* New York: McGraw-Hill Book Co., 1934.

Michels, Robert. *Political Parties.* New York: Hearst International Library Co., 1915.

Mills, C. W. "Small Business and Civic Welfare," *Report of Special Committee on Small Business,* U. S. Senate Document 135. Washington: Government Printing Office, 1946.

————. *White Collar*. New York: Oxford University Press, 1951.

Morgenthau, Hans J. *Scientific Man vs. Power Politics*. Chicago: University of Chicago Press, 1946.

Mosca, G. *The Ruling Class*. New York: McGraw-Hill Co., 1939.

Mumford, Lewis. *The Culture of Cities*. New York: Harcourt, Brace and Co., 1938.

Myrdal, Gunnar. *Population, A Problem for Democracy*. Cambridge, Mass.: Harvard University Press, 1940.

Odum, Howard W. *Understanding Society*. New York: The Macmillan Co., 1947.

Panunzio, Constantine. *Major Social Institutions*. New York: The Macmillan Company, 1939.

Pareto, Vilfredo. *Mind and Society*. 4 vols. New York: Harcourt, Brace and Co., 1935.

Parsons, Talcott. *Structure of Social Action*. New York: McGraw-Hill Book Co., 1937.

Phillips, Wilbur Carey. *Adventuring for Democracy*. New York: Social Unit Press, 1940.

Polloch, James Kerr. *Money and Politics Abroad*. New York: Alfred A. Knopf, 1932.

Porterfield, Austin L. *Creative Factors in Scientific Research*. Durham: Duke University Press, 1941.

Russell, Bertrand. *Power: A New Social Analysis*. New York: W. W. Norton and Co., 1938.

Salter, John Thomas. *The Pattern of Politics: The Folkways of A Democratic People*. New York: The Macmillan Co., 1940.

Schram, Wilbur, editor. *Mass Communications*. Urbana: University of Illinois Press, 1949.

Simon, Yves. *Nature and Function of Authority*. Milwaukee: Marquette University Press, 1940.

Steffens, Lincoln. *Autobiography*. New York: Harcourt, Brace and Co., 1931.

Taeusch, Carl Frederick. *Policy and Ethics in Business*. New York: McGraw-Hill Book Co., 1940.

U. S. Natural Resources Committee. *The Structure of the American Economy*. Washington: Government Printing Office, 1939-40.

Veblen, Thorstein. *The Use of Loan Credit in Modern Business*. Chicago: University of Chicago Press, 1903.

———. *The Vested Interests and the State of the Industrial Arts*. New York: B. W. Huebsch Co., 1920.

———. *The Theory of the Leisure Class*. New York: B. W. Huebsch Co., 1922.

Wallace, Henry A. *Sixty Million Jobs*. New York: Simon and Schuster, 1945.

Warner, W. L. and Associates. *Democracy in Jonesville*. New York: Harper and Bros., 1949.

———. *Social Life of a Modern Community*. New Haven: Yale University Press, 1941.

Webb, Sidney and Beatrice. *Soviet Communism: A New Civilization*. New York: Charles Scribner's Sons, 1936.

West, J. *Plainville, U.S.A.* New York: Columbia University Press, 1945.

Winslow, E. M. *The Pattern of Imperialism: A Study in the Theories of Power*. New York: Columbia University Press, 1938.

Wolfbein, Seymour Lewis. *The Decline of a Cotton Textile City*. New York: Columbia University Press, 1944.

Wootton, Barbara. *Freedom Under Planning*. Chapel Hill: University of North Carolina Press, 1945.

Zorbaugh, Harvey W. *The Gold Coast and the Slum*. Chicago: University of Chicago Press, 1929.

B. PERIODICALS

Anderson, C. Arnold. "Sociological Elements in Economic Restrictionism," *American Sociological Review*, IX (August 1944), 345-58.

Angell, Robert C. "The Social Integration of American Cities of More than 100,000 Population," *American Sociological Review*, XII (June 1947), 335-42.

Ascoli, Max. "On Political Parties," *Social Science*, II (May 1935), 195-209.

Barnes, Harry E. "Durkheim's Contribution to the Reconstruction of Political Theory," *Political Science Quarterly*, XXXV (March 1920), 236-54.

Baur, E. Jackson. "The Functions of Ceremony in the Advertising Business," *Social Forces*, XXVII (May 1949), 358-65.

Bell, E. H. "Social Stratification," *Scientific Monthly*, XXXVIII (February 1934), 157-64.

Bendix, Reinhard. "Bureaucracy and the Problem of Power," *Public Administration Review*, V (1945), 194-209.

Benton, E. Maxwell. "The War Debts Policy of the United States," *Social Science*, IX (January 1934), 41-48.

Bierstedt, Robert. "An Analysis of Social Power," *American Sociological Review*, XV (December 1950), 730-38.

Born, Lester K. "Erasmus on Political Ethics," *Political Science Quarterly*, XLIII (December 1928), 520-43.

Bowman, Leroy E. "Community Organization," *American Journal of Sociology*, XXXVII (March 1932), 924-29.

Bradley, Phillips. "Barriers to Common Action," *Social Forces*, II (January 1924), 187-93.

Braunthal, Alfred. "American Labor in Politics," *Social Research*, XII (February 1945), 1-21.

Brodey, Jesse W. "Racketeering, An American Institution," *Social Science*, XII (January 1937), 46-53.

Brooks, Maxwell R. "American Class and Caste: An Appraisal," *Social Forces*, XXV (December 1946), 207-211.

Chaffee, Grace E. "Control in an Integrated Social Group," *Social Forces*, VIII (September 1929), 91-95.

Chapin, F. Stuart. "The Relation of Sociometry to Planning in an Expanding Social Universe," *Sociometry*, VI (August 1943), 234-40.

———. "Sociometric Star Isolates," *American Journal of Sociology*, LVI (November 1950), 263-67.

Clark, Carroll D. "The Concept of the Public," *Southwestern Social Science Quarterly*, XIII (March 1933), 311-20.

Coil, E. J. "The Illusion of Final Authority," *Plan Age*, IV (January 1938), 19-21.

Colm, Gerhard. "Full Employment Through Tax Policy?" *Social Research*, VII (November 1940), 447-67.

Cook, Morris L. "Power and Its Social Control," *Plan Age*, II (May 1936), 1-17.

Cooke, Thomas I. "Politics, Sociology, and Values," *Journal of Social Philosophy*, VI (October 1940), 35-46.

Cooper, Weldon. "State Police Movements in the South," *Journal of Politics*, I (November 1939), 414-33.

Coyle, Grace L. "The Limitations of Social Work in Relation to Social Reorganization," *Social Forces*, XIV (October 1935), 94-102.

Crowder, Walter F. "A Platform in Search of A Party," *Social Science*, XII (January 1937), 15-29.

Davis, Kingsley. "A Conceptual Analysis of Stratification," *American Sociological Review*, VII (June 1942), 309-21.

Daykin, Walter L. "Economics and Social Work," *Social Science*, XV (January 1940), 48-51.

DeMarche, David F. "The Superimposed Leader," *Sociology and Social Research*, XXXI (July-August 1947), 454-57.

Deuschberger, Paul. "Interaction Patterns in Changing Neighborhoods: New York and Pittsburgh," *Sociometry*, IX (November 1946), 305-15.

Dimock, Marshall E. "The Study of Administration," *American Political Science Review*, XXXI (February 1937), 28-40.

Dubin, Robert. "Decision-Making by Management in Industrial Relations," *American Journal of Sociology*, LIV (January 1949), 292-97.

Dunbar, Willis F. "Let's Appoint a Committee," *Social Education*, VII (March 1943), 121-23.

Durham, G. Homer. "Administrative Organization of the Mormon Church," *Political Science Quarterly*, LVII (Summer 1945), 51-71.

Dwight, Charles A. S. "Man as a Ceremonialist," *Social Science*, XI (April 1936), 126-30.

Dykstra, Clarence A. "The Quest for Responsibility," *American Political Science Review*, XXXIII (February 1939), 1-25.

Earle, Edward Mead. "American Military Policy and National Security," *Political Science Quarterly*, LIII (March 1938), 1-13.

Edwards, James Edwin. "Patriotism, Inc.," *Social Science*, XI (October 1936), 332-34.

Einstein, Albert. "On the Generalized Theory of Gravitation," *Scientific American*, CLXXXII (April 1950), 13-17.

Elmer, M. C. "The Evaluation and Scoring of Community Activities," *American Journal of Sociology*, XXX (September 1924), 172-76.

Embree, John F. "Japanese Administration at the Local Level," *Applied Anthropology*, III (September 1944), 11-18.

Ferris, John P. "A Question of Policy," *Plan Age*, II (April 1936), 12-14.

Field, Oliver P. "Property and Authority," *Journal of Politics*, III (August 1941), 253-75.

Flanders, Dwight P. "Geopolitics and American Post-War Policy," *Political Science Quarterly*, LX (December 1946), 578-85.

Freund, Ludwig. "Power and the Democratic Process—A Definition of Politics," *Social Research*, XV (September 1948), 327-44.

Freyd, Bernard. "Gierke and the Corporate Myth," *Journal of Social Philosophy*, IV (January 1939), 138-43.

Geiger, George R. "Science and Values in a Changing World," *American Journal of Economics and Sociology*, I (October 1941), 1-11.

Giddings, Franklin H. "The Relation of Social Theory and Policy," *American Journal of Sociology*, XVI (March 1912), 577-92.

Goldhammer, H. and E. A. Shils. "Types of Power and Status," *American Journal of Sociology*, XLV (September 1939), 171-82.

Goldman, F. J. "The Power of Congress to Regulate Commerce," *Political Science Quarterly*, XXV (June 1910), 220-56.

Gray, John H. "The State Abdicates: The Utilities Govern Themselves," *Proceedings of the Academy of Political Science*, XIV (May 1930), 52-70.

Hall, Everett W. "An Ethics for Today," *American Journal of Economics and Sociology*, II (July 1943), 433-52.

Hallowell, John H. "Politics and Ethics," *American Political Science Review*, XXXVIII (August 1944), 639-55.

Hamilton, James H. "A Neglected Principle of Civic Reform," *American Journal of Sociology*, V (May 1900), 746-60.

Handman, Max. "The Bureaucratic Culture Pattern and Political Revolutions," *American Journal of Sociology*, XXXIX (November 1933), 301-13.

Harding, T. Swann. "The Myth of Constitutional Absolutism," *Journal of Social Philosophy*, II (October 1936), 69-84.

Hayner, Norman S. "The Prison as a Community," *American Sociological Review*, V (August 1940), 577-83.

Heiman, Eduard. "Planning and the Market System," *Social Research*, I (November 1934), 486-504.

―――. "Types and Potentialities of Economic Planning," *Social Research*, II (May 1935), 176-94.

Heinz, H. F. Eulau. "The Depersonalization of the Concept of Sovereignty," *Journal of Politics*, II (February 1942), 3-19.

Henderson, Charles R. "Definition of Social Policy Relating to the Dependent Group," *American Journal of Sociology*, X (November 1904), 315-34.

Henry, William E. "The Business Executive: The Psycho-Dynamics of a Social Role," *American Journal of Sociology*, LIV (January 1949), 286-91.

Hiller, E. T. "The Community as a Social Group," *American Sociological Review*, VI (April 1941), 191-92.

Hoffer, C. R. "The Community Situation and Political Action," *American Sociological Review*, IV (October 1939), 663-69.

―――. "Understanding the Community," *American Journal of Sociology*, XXXVI (January 1931), 616-24.

Hollingshead, August B. "Selected Characteristics of Classes in a Midwestern Community," *American Sociological Review*, XII (August 1947), 386-88.

Howenstine, E. Jay. "Public Works Policy in the Twenties," *Social Research*, XIII (December 1946), 479-500.

Hughes, Everett C. "Ecological Aspects of Institutions," *American Sociological Review*, I (April 1936), 180-92.

Hyde, D. Clark. "National Economic Policy: The American Tradition," *The Southern Economic Journal*, III (October 1936), 148-60.

Hyneman, Charles S. "Who Makes Our Laws?" *Political Science Quarterly*, LV (December 1940), 556-81.

Jaszi, Oscar. "The Stream of Political Murder," *American Journal of Economics and Sociology*, III (April 1944), 335-55.

Jennings, H. H. "Quantitative Aspects of Tele Relationships in a Community," *Sociometry*, II (October 1939), 93-100.

Jennings, H. S. "Biology and Social Reform," *Journal of Social Philosophy*, II (January 1937), 155-66.

Kahler, Alfred. "The Public Debt in the Financial Structure," *Social Science*, XI (February 1944), 11-26.

Karpinos, Bernard D. "The Length of Time Required for the Stabilization of a Population," *American Journal of Sociology*, XLI (January 1936), 504-13.

Kaufman, Harold F. "Members of a Rural Community as Judges of Prestige Rank," *Sociometry*, IX (February 1946), 71-85.

Kelso, Robert W. "Banker Control of Community Chests," *Survey Graphic*, LXVIII (May 1932), 117-119.

Klein, D. B. "Colored Shirts and Politics," *Journal of Social Philosophy*, V (July 1940), 326-37.

Komarovsky, Mirra. "The Voluntary Associations of Urban Dwellers," *American Sociological Review*, XI (December 1946), 686-98.

Lauck, W. Jett. "Mineral Policy," *Plan Age*, I (March 1935), 13-18.

Lederer, Emil. "Social Control vs. Economic Law," *Social Research*, I (February 1934), 3-21.

Levi, Nino. "Internal Structure and International Order," *Social Science*, VIII (September 1941), 350-60.

Lewisohn, Sam A. "Wage Policies and National Productivity," *Political Science Quarterly*, XXXIX (March 1924), 97-105.

Lippett, Ronald. "Administrator Perception and Administrative Approval: A Communication Problem," *International Journal of Opinion and Attitude Research*, I (June 1947), 209-19.

Lippmann, Walter. "The Press and Public Opinion," *Political Science Quarterly*, XLVI (March 1941), 161-70.

Long, Norton E. "Public Relations Policies of the Bell System," *International Journal of Opinion and Attitude Research*, I (October 1937), 5-22.

Lumley, Frederick E. "Slogans as a Means of Social Control," *Publications of the American Sociological Society*, XVI (1921), 121-34.

Lundberg, George A. and Margaret Lawsing. "The Sociography of Some Community Relations," *American Sociological Review*, II (June 1937), 318-35.

McBain, Howard L. "Delegation of Legislative Power to Cities," *Political Science Quarterly*, XXXII (June 1917), 121-34.

McClenahan, Bessie Averne. "Interrelated Patterns of Community and Personality," *Sociology and Social Research*, XXXI (January-February 1947), 205-12.

Mace, C. A. "Hierarchical Organization," *Sociological Review*, XXVI (October 1934), 373-92.

MacIver, R. M. "The Historical Pattern of Social Change," *Journal of Social Philosophy*, II (October 1936), 35-54.

McKenzie, R. D. "The Concept of Dominance in World Organization," *Publications of the American Sociological Society*, XXI (1927), 138.

MacVeagh, Franklin. "A Program of Municipal Reform," *American Journal of Sociology*, I (March 1896), 551-63.

Maddox, William P. "Advisory Policy Committees for Political Parties," *Political Science Quarterly*, XLIX (June 1934), 253-67.

Martin, Charles E. "Traditional American Policy in the Atlantic," *Social Forces*, XXII (March 1944), 262-69.

Marx, Fritz Morstein. "Policy Formulation and Administrative Process," *Political Science Review*, XXXIII (February 1939), 55-60.

Mayer, Kurt. "Small Business as a Social Institution," *Social Science*, XIV (September 1947), 332-49.

Meadows, Paul. "Some Sociological Aspects of Land Use Policy," *Social Forces*, XXIV (December 1945), 231-36.

Merton, Robert K. "Bureaucratic Structure and Personality," *Social Forces*, XVIII (May 1940), 560-68.

Moore, B., Jr. "The Relation Between Social Stratification and Social Control," *Sociometry*, V (August 1942), 230-51.

Moreno, J. L. "Organization of the Social Atom," *Sociometry*, X (August 1947), 287-93.

Mukerjee, Radhakamal. "Population Theory and Politics," *American Sociological Review*, VI (December 1941), 784-93.

Murphey, Albert J. "A Study of the Leadership Process," *American Sociological Review*, VI (October 1941), 674-87.

Neeley, Twila E. "The Sources of Political Power: A Contribution to the Sociology of Leadership," *American Journal of Sociology*, XXXIII (March 1928), 769-83.

Nickle, Clarence F. "Community Control," *Social Forces*, IV (December 1925), 345-55.

Northrop, F. S. C. "The Scientific Method for Determining the Correct Ends of Social Action," *Social Science*, XXII (July 1947), 218-27.

Ogburn, William F. "Technology and National Policy," *Plan Age*, III (September 1937), 165-67.

Opler, Morris Edward. "Social Science and Democratic Policy," *Applied Anthropology*, IV (Summer 1945), 11-15.

Pape, Leslie M. "Sources and Limits of Political Power," *Social Forces*, XVIII (March 1940), 424-28.

Parsons, Talcott. "An Analytical Approach to the Theory of Stratification," *American Journal of Sociology*, XLV (May 1940), 841-62.

———. "The Place of the Ultimate Values in Sociological Theory," *International Journal of Ethics*, XLV (April 1935), 282-316.

———. "The Professions and Social Structure," *Social Forces*, XVII (May 1939), 457-67.

Pate, James E. "Federal-State Relations in Planning," *Social Forces*, XIV (December 1936), 187-95.

Pinney, Harvey. "Administocracy, Inc.," *Social Forces*, XIX (March 1941), 402-09.

Queen, C. N. and S. A. "Some Obstacles to Community Organization," *Journal of Applied Sociology*, VIII (May-June 1924), 283-88.

Ratchford, B. U. "Certain Bases of Political Power Politics," *Southern Economic Journal*, XI (July 1944), 20-33.

Reckless, Walter C. "The Distribution of Commercialized Vice in the City," *Publications of the American Sociological Society*, XX (December 1925), 164-76.

Rice, A. K. "The Role of the Specialist in the Community," *Human Relations*, II (1949), 177-84.

Richberg, Donald. "A National Labor Policy," *Proceedings of the Academy of Political Science*, XXII (May 1946), 86-93.

Riezler, Kurt. "Will to Power," *Social Science*, IX (February 1942), 123-40.

Robey, Ralph. "Fiscal Policy and Credit Control," *Proceedings of the Academy of Political Science*, XVII (1936-1938), 10-16.

Roucek, Joseph S. "Political Behavior as a Struggle for Power," *Journal of Social Philosophy*, VI (July 1941), 341-51.

———. "The Sociology of the Diplomat," *Social Science*, XIV (October 1939), 370-74.

Salter, John Thomas. "The Pattern of Politics: The Politician," *Journal of Politics*, I (May 1939), 129-45.

———. "The Pattern of Politics: The Politicians and the People," *Journal of Politics*, I (August 1939), 258-77.

———. "Personal Attention in Politics," *American Political Science Review*, XXXIV (February 1940), 54-66.

Salter, Leonard A. "Do We Need A New Land Policy?" *Journal of Land and Public Utility Economics*, XXII (November 1946), 309-20.

Scholz, Karl. "Transitions in the Exercise of Power," *Social Science*, XVIII (July 1943), 135-40.

Shotwell, James T. "Democracy and Political Morality," *Political Science Quarterly*, XXXVI (March 1921), 1-8.

Simmel, Georg. "Superiority and Subordination," *American Journal of Sociology*, II (September 1896), 394-415.

Slichter, Sumner H. "Wage Policies," *Proceedings of the Academy of Political Science*, XXII (May 1946), 3-15.

Smith, Christopher. "Social Selection in Community Leadership," *Social Forces*, XV (May 1937), 530-35.

Sorokin, Pitirim A. "Is Accurate Social Planning Possible?" *American Sociological Review*, I (February 1936), 12-28.

——— and Robert K. Merton. "Social Time: A Methodological and Functional Analysis," *American Journal of Sociology*, XLIII (March 1937), 615-29.

Soule, George. "Planning for Abundance," *Plan Age*, I (February 1935), 1-2.

Spaulding, Charles B. "Cliques, Gangs, and Networks," *Sociology and Social Research*, XXXII (July-August 1948), 928-37.

Speier, Hans. "Social Stratification in the Urban Community," *American Sociological Review*, I (April 1936), 193-202.

Staudinger, Hans. "Planning in Electricity," *Social Research*, IV (November 1937), 417-39.

Stein, Ludwig. "The Sociology of Authority," *Publications of the American Sociological Society*, XVIII (December 1923), 116-20.

Steiner, Jesse F. "Community Disorganization," *Social Forces*, II (January 1924), 177-87.

———. "Community Organization and the Crowd Spirit," *Social Forces*, I (March 1923), 221-26.

———. "Community Organization in Relation to Social Change," *Social Forces*, I (January 1923), 102-08.

Tannenbaum, Frank. "The Balance of Power in Society," *Political Science Quarterly*, LXI (December 1946), 481-504.

Timasheff, N. S. "Business and the Professions in Liberal, Fascist, and Communist Society," *American Journal of Sociology*, XLV (May 1940), 863-69.

Timmons, John F. "Land Tenure Policy Goals," *Journal of Land and Public Utility Economics*, XIX (May 1943), 165-79.

Tugwell, R. G. "The Super-Political," *Journal of Social Philosophy*, V (January 1940), 97-114.

Ullman, Edward. "A Theory for the Location of Cities," *American Journal of Sociology*, XLVI (May 1941), 853-64.

Useem, John, Ruth Useem, and Pierre Tangent. "Stratification in a Prairie Town," *American Sociological Review*, VII (June 1942), 331-42.

Vance, Rupert B. "The Place of Planning in Social Dynamics," *Social Forces*, XXIII (March 1945), 331-34.

von Beckerath, Herbert. "Economics and Politics," *Social Forces*, XIV (October 1935), 42-53.

Warburton, Clark. "Monetary Policy in the United States in World War II," *American Journal of Economics and Sociology*, IV (April 1945), 375-83.

Weidenhammer, Robert M. "A National Fuel Policy," *Journal of Land and Public Utility Economics*, XIX (May 1943), 127-40.

Wilson, Francis G. "Human Nature and Politics," *Journal of Politics*, VIII (November 1946), 478-98.

———. "Pessimism in American Politics," *Journal of Politics*, VII (May 1945), 125-44.

———. "Prelude to Authority," *American Political Science Review*, XXXI (February 1937), 12-28.

Wirth, Louis. "Ideological Aspects of Social Disorganization," *American Sociological Review*, V (August 1940), 472-82.

———. "The Urban Society and Civilization," *American Journal of Sociology*, XLV (March 1940), 743-55.

Wood, Arthur Lewis. "Social Organization and Crime in Small Wisconsin Communities," *American Sociological Review*, VII (February 1942), 40-46.

———. "The Structure of Social Planning," *Social Forces*, XXII (May 1944), 388-98.

Woolston, Howard B. "The Urban Habit of Mind," *American Journal of Sociology*, XVII (March 1912), 602-14.

Wray, Donald E. "Marginal Men of Industry: The Foreman," *American Journal of Sociology*, LIV (January 1949), 298-301.

Zimmerman, Carle C. "Centralism versus Localism in the Community," *American Sociological Review*, III (April 1938), 155-66.

INDEX

INDEX

Publicity, avoidance of by power leaders, 37, 87; adverse, 183

Public opinion, 208. *See also* Propaganda; Silence

Pyramid, control, 182

Pyramids, power, 62 ff.; business enterprises, 79; sub-community, 148

Regional City, physical structure of, 8-9, 23-25; location of power in, 8 ff.; and the county, 22-23; pessimism in, 55, 286; businessmen community leaders in, 81; and the state, 100; channels of interaction in, 107-8; clubs of, 125; interest of in politics, 126 ff.; and the larger community, 128; in state politics, 151 ff.; structure of power in, 160 ff.; projects, issues, and policy in, 207 ff.; fear in, 228 ff.; structural weakness in power-wielding in, 239; power relationships in do not cover whole social structure, 248

Residential areas, 18 ff., 120-21, 123

Residual categories. *See* Categories, residual

Roles, 87-88, 110-11

Roucek, Joseph, cited, 158

Salter, J. T., on democracy, 236

Segregation, 131, 144 ff., 190, 211, 295

Silence, 244 ff. *See also* Democracy

Slums. *See* Housing reform

Smith, Christopher, on community leadership, 229

Social planning, 233 ff.; coordination in, 259-60

Social scientists, 239, 240

Social workers, 239, 243

Society leaders, 38; prestige not essential to leadership, 80

State, the, and Regional City, 100, 151 ff. *See also* Institutions

Status, achieved, 29, 33; ascribed, 29; and power, 88

Stein, Ludwig, on personality versus authority, 236

Steiner, Jesse F., on luncheon clubs, 184-87 *passim*

Sub-community. *See* Negro subcommunity; Suburban development

Suburban development, 48-49, 148

Taxation, concessions, 216; sales, 220, 221

Traffic control, 214, 215, 220

"Trickle down" theory, 231-32

Unanimity, forces of, 224

Under-structure professionals. *See* Professionals in civic and social work

Union leaders. *See* Labor leaders

Values, moral and ethical, a residual category, 4-5, 239

Vance, Rupert B., cited, 205

Violence, 146-47, 179, 193-94

von Beckerath, Herbert, on connection between political and economic structures, 103; on force, 106

Voting, pocket, 50

Washington, Booker T., 143

Wilson, Francis G., on pessimism, 236; on political indifference, 246

Wolfbein, Seymour Louis, cited, 72

Woolston, Howard B., on the urban habit of mind, 156

Zorbaugh, Harvey W., cited, 255, 256